TALKING SIXTIES DRIVE-IN MOVIES

TOM LISANTI

This book is dedicated to my friends
Gail Gerber and Aron Kincaid.
I still miss them to this day.

Published in the USA by:
BearManor Media
P O Box 71426
Albany, Georgia 31708
www.bearmanormedia.com

Printed in the United States of America
ISBN   978-1-59393-997-7 (paperback)

Book & cover design by Darlene Swanson • www.van-garde.com

TABLE OF CONTENTS

ACKNOWLEDGMENTS

MY DEEP APPRECIATION TO THE following people who allowed me to recently interview them and to share their anecdotes and memories about working in sixties Hollywood—Diane Bond, Arlene Charles, Nancy Czar, Lada Edmund, Jr. Mimsy Farmer, Gail Gerber aka Gail Gilmore, Lara Lindsay, Nicoletta Machiavelli, Christopher Riordan, Richard Rogers aka Steven Rogers, Bobbi Chance aka Bobbi Shaw, Valerie Starrett, Maggie Thrett, Irene Tsu, Jan Watson, and Stephen Yafa.

A special thank you to my dear friend Shaun Chang for his great detective skills and his loyal support; and to writer and Italian film historian Roberto Curti for allowing me to include his reflections on the career of Nicoletta Machiavelli. Also my deep appreciation goes to Carmen Rogers for facilitating my interview with her husband Richard Rogers.

Thank you to Diane Bond, Arlene Charles, Lada Edmund, Jr., Christopher Riordan, Bobbi Chance, Stephen Yafa, Joel Gibson, and Lee Pfeiffer of *Cinema Retro* magazine for sharing photos from their collections. I truly appreciate it, as they help enhance the book greatly.

Thanks to my family, friends, and fans of my web site *SixtiesCinema.com* and my Facebook page *Sixties Cinema Books* for their continued support. A special shout out, as always, to Jim McGann my friend and web master. I will forever be your servant.

This book was greatly enhanced by the vast collections at the Margaret Herrick Library in Beverly Hills; the General Research Division at The New York Public Library, and the Billy Rose Theatre Division at The New York Public Library for the Performing Arts, with a special thanks to librarian Jeremy Megraw and photographer Peter Riesett.

Finally, a special thank you to Ernie DeLia, even though I know he does not like these interview books, for putting up with my sixties drive-in movie and starlet obsessions these many years. He even let me drag him recently to an art house to see *Hatari* on the big screen, not for John Wayne, but for Elsa Martinelli!

PREFACE

TALKING SIXTIES DRIVE-IN MOVIES IS a collection of profiles, interviews, and tributes about actors and films popular with the drive-in movie crowd during the sixties. Genres covered include beach party films, Elvis Presley musicals, spy spoofs, spaghetti westerns, biker films, and alienated youth exploitation movies. Some of the chapters center on one movie or a genre, while others are career profiles with a main focus on one or two drive-in movies.

The book is arranged in somewhat chronological order based on the release of the genre or the particular movie the interview with the actor focuses on. It begins with Elvis Presley's three-time co-star Shelley Fabares and supporting players Arlene Charles, Nancy Czar, Gail Gerber, and Christopher Riordan talking about working with him during his MGM days from 1964-1967 in such films as *Viva Las Vegas*, *Girl Happy*, *Spinout*, and *Clambake*.

Bobbi Shaw remembers making her AIP Beach Party films, including *Pajama Party*, *Beach Blanket Bingo, Ski Party*, and *The Ghost in the Invisible Bikini*.

Perpetual bikini girl Arlene Charles recalls her fun times in Hollywood working in teenage movies and her adventures in Hawaii shooting *I Sailed to Tahiti with an All Girl Crew*.

Rediscover drive-in heartthrob Steven Rogers from *The Girls on the Beach*, *Ski Party*, *Wild, Wild Winter*, and *Angels from Hell* with brief observations from the actor.

Jan Watson remembers what was like being a decorative Slaygirl opposite Dean Martin in the Matt Helm spy spoofs *The Silencers*, *Murderers' Row*, and *The Ambushers*.

Irene Tsu recounts her time in Hawaii with Elvis Presley filming Paramount's *Paradise, Hawaiian Style*.

Mimsy Farmer talks about how she went from being the Queen of the Drive-In starring in such movies as *Hot Rods to Hell*, *Riot on Sunset Strip*, and *Devil's Angels* to working in Europe.

Diane Bond shares memories of going from beach parties and Elvis movies to becoming a Flint Girl opposite James Coburn in the spy spoof *In Like Flint*.

Italian actress Nicoletta Machiavelli talks about all her spaghetti westerns, including *Navajo Joe* with Burt Reynolds, and her experience being under contract to producer Dino De Laurentiis.

Lara Lindsay recalls her days as a 20th Century-Fox contract player attending their talent school and the making of the last sixties Hollywood surf movie, *The Sweet Ride*.

Stephen Yafa explains how he came to write the screenplay for *Three in the Attic* and offers a behind-the-scenes look at the making of this drive-in hit, while co-star Maggie Thrett also shares her stories about the movie and her singing and acting career.

Valerie Starrett relives her time making one of the most popular biker films of the sixties *Run, Angel, Run* where she was not only the female lead but the screenwriter as well.

One of the busiest young dancing actors in Hollywood during the sixties, the outspoken Christopher Riordan dishes on Elvis, beach and teenage movies and his memorable role in the cult comedy *The Gay Deceivers*.

Lada Edmund, Jr, reflects on her career as a dancer on TV's *Hullaballoo*; actress—particularly her role opposite Jon Voight in the teenage coming-of-age film *Out of It*; and stunt woman.

A salute to Edy Williams for giving a wonderfully over-the-top performance in *Beyond the Valley of the Dolls,* with comments from fellow Fox contract player Lara Lindsay and co-star Christopher Riordan.

A few of the interviews are in the Q&A format while others are strictly narrative. This was decided because—though some of the interviewees only had minor roles in some movies—they had a lot to say about them or the people they worked with. Rather than try to fit within the text, a Q&A approach seemed a better choice and an easier read.

1. TALKING ELVIS PRESLEY AND HIS MGM MUSICALS 1964-1967

WITH ARLENE CHARLES, NANCY CZAR, SHELLEY FABARES, GAIL GERBER, AND CHRISTOPHER RIORDAN

BY THE TIME THE KING of Rock 'n' Roll co-starred with popular teen idol Shelley Fabares of TV's *The Donna Reed Show* for the first time in 1965's *Girl Happy*, the budgets and quality of his movies had declined. He had signed a contract with MGM previously and appeared in two slick well-received medium budgeted hits, *It Happened at the World's Fair* and *Viva Las Vegas*. But once the studio realized they could produce low-budget quickie musicals surrounding Elvis Presley with pretty girls and scenery and still make a boatload of money, beginning with *Kissin' Cousins* (1964), the standard was set for the rest of his tenure with MGM.

Elvis Presley was a national singing sensation with a number of hit records under his belt including "Hound Dog," "Don't Be Cruel," and "Heartbreak Hotel" before making his film debut in the Civil War western *Love Me Tender* in 1956 co-starring Richard Egan and Debra Paget for 20th Century-Fox, who signed the singer to a picture deal. The film was originally titled *The Reno Brothers* but when it was announced that there were advanced sales of almost a million copies for the song "Love Me Tender" to be warbled by Presley in the film, the title was changed to capitalize on it. Elvis was then upped to equal star billing with his more experienced co-stars. When *Love Me Tender* was released the movie and the title song (which was nominated for an Academy Award) were phenomenal hits.

Seeing the grosses mount for *Love Me Tender*, everybody wanted a piece of the King.

Elvis signed a contract with independent producer Hal B. Wallis who had a distribution deal with Paramount Pictures. Elvis quickly starred in *Loving You* (1957) and *King Creole* (1958) for Wallis and made *Jailhouse Rock* (1957) for MGM. Playing the singing rebel in all three dramatic movies, critics gushed that Elvis was the new James Dean and proved that he really was the King of Rock 'n' Roll. However, in 1958 he was drafted into the army and when he returned to Hollywood a more genteel persona emerged on the screen.

Elvis began the decade after his return from military service with *G.I. Blues* (1960), his first musical-comedy, produced by Hal B. Wallis and directed by Norman Taurog. As Tulsa McLean, a tail gunner on duty in Germany, he reluctantly accepts a wager that he can "spend the night" with a frosty nightclub performer named Lili (Juliet Prowse). Tulsa only agrees to the bet because he is trying to save money to open a nightclub with some buddies back in the states. Complications arise when Tulsa begins to fall in love with Lili and her icy veneer begins to melt.

G.I. Blues features picturesque locales (though all of Elvis and the cast's scenes were filmed on soundstages in Hollywood) and pretty European starlets Leticia Roman and Sigrid Maier decorating the background. Juliet Prowse was one of Elvis' more formidable leading ladies and is quite good. The movie was not much of an acting stretch for Elvis as Hollywood toned down his rock 'n' roll persona for a more clean-cut, All-American image befitting a returning serviceman (hence the missing trademark sideburns and hip-swiveling). Though fans noticed, it seemed to suit most just fine, as the movie grossed $4.3 million dollars and was the 15th highest grossing film of 1960.

Elvis still owed 20th Century Fox two more pictures, so they cast him again in a dramatic role in another western hoping to copy the financial success of *Love Me Tender*. *Flaming Star* (1960), directed by Don Siegel, was "the story of racial intolerance towards Native Americans in the Old West." Elvis was Pacer Burton the son of a white father (John McIntire) and Kiowa Mother (Dolores Del Rio) whose loyalties are torn when members of the Indian tribe massacre some nearby white neighbors starting a war between the two. Elvis was filmed singing four tunes due to the insistence of his manager Colonel Tom Parker but two were cut from the final print. Despite the critical raves Elvis received for his sensitive performance, it did not draw the crowds like *G.I. Blues* did.

Audiences also were indifferent to Fox's *Wild in the Country* (1961) a turgid soap opera ala *Peyton Place* directed by Philip Dunne with a screenplay by Clifford Odets, no less.

Elvis was Glenn Tyler, a poor Southern juvenile delinquent with writing aspirations who gets involved with three women: Older court-appointed psychiatrist Irene (Hope Lange); drunken, trashy country cousin and unwed mother Noreen (Tuesday Weld), and dull-as-dishwater good girl Betty Lee (Millie Perkins). By the fade out, he surprisingly opts for college, leaving them all behind though Betty Lee "threatens" to wait for him. *Wild in the Country* was another box office disappointment, proving to Col. Parker that Elvis' fan base preferred their idol in more lightweight fare.

Seeing the slumping returns at the box office, all hopes were pinned on Elvis' next movie, *Blue Hawaii* (1961) from producer Hal Wallis and director Norman Taurog for Paramount. In the movie, Elvis portrayed Chad Gates, a returning G.I. who rebels against his wealthy parents (Angela Lansbury and Roland Winters) because they want him to work in the family pineapple plantation. Instead, he hides out in a shack on the beach surfing with his Hawaiian buddies and rendezvousing with his half Hawaiian girlfriend Maile (Joan Blackman replacing Juliet Prowse who was let go by Hal Wallis for her diva demands and then suspended by her studio 20th Century-Fox that had loaned her out to Wallis) who works as a travel agent. Needing to make some money, Chad takes a job as a tour guide chaperoning sexy school teacher Abigail Prentice (Nancy Walters) and her jailbait charges (Jenny Maxwell, Pamela Austin, Darlene Tompkins, and Christian Kay) around the islands to the chagrin of Maile, causing typical romantic complications before the happy ending. The film has one oh-no-they-didn't moment when Chad tired of being pursued by the immature snobbish Ellie (Maxwell) takes the underage girl over his knee and gives her a good old-fashioned spanking! No one expected that in an Elvis musical.

To everyone's surprise and delight, *Blue Hawaii* was a box office smash grossing $4.7 million and making it the second highest grossing film of Elvis' sixties career. The soundtrack was also a hit selling over $6 million worth of LPs. On the downside, it helped pigeon-hole Elvis into appearing in musical comedies and began what was to become known as—the Elvis Film, a genre all its own that really took hold beginning with *Girls! Girls! Girls!* in 1962 through his movies with Shelley Fabares. During this period, the Elvis Film could be counted on to feature a picturesque locale; romantic complications; lots of songs; a fistfight or two with a romantic rival; and an abundance of pretty girls.

Elvis did have a respite before the formulaic scripts came rolling in and that was because his next two films (produced by David Weisbart for United Artists) were already in pre-production before *Blue Hawaii* was released. *Follow That Dream* (1962) was more a straightforward comedy about a family of squatters in the Florida panhandle, while *Kid Galahad* was a boxing drama and a remake of the 1945 movie with Barbara Stanwyck. Neither featured many songs or a gaggle of bikini-clad girls going gaga over the King, so perhaps that is why they did not perform as well as *Blue Hawaii* at the box office.

Publicity photo of Elvis Presley with Pamela Austin, Darlene Tompkins, Joan Blackman, Jenny Maxwell, and Christian Kay in *Blue Hawaii* (Paramount, 1961).

Trying to capitalize on the success of two of Elvis' biggest sixties hits, *G. I. Blues* and *Blue Hawaii*, Hal Wallis recruited their director Norman Taurog and sent Elvis back to Hawaii for the musical comedy, *Girls! Girls! Girls!* (1962). Ensuring that Elvis would sing thirteen songs at a drop of a hat (including the hit single "Return to Sender"), he played Ross Carpenter, a tuna fisherman who moonlights as a nightclub singer to earn extra money to buy his own boat. There he works with his former lover and vocalist Robin (Stella Stevens), who stills carries a torch for him, but he is now drawn to Laurel Dodge (Laurel Goodwin taking the role after it was turned down by Dolores Hart and Pamela Tiffin), a nice wholesome rich girl hiding her wealth because she knows Ross is too macho and proud to take help from a woman.

Girls! Girls! Girls! is quite colorful and entertaining. Though reviews were mixed, it surprisingly scored a Golden Globe Award nomination for "Best Musical Picture." Its box office take was an impressive $3.6 million making it the fourth highest grossing Elvis film in the sixties basically cementing the pattern for the typical Elvis' films to come.

Keeping Elvis in colorful locales, his next movie (and first for MGM in the sixties) *It Happened at the World's Fair* (1963) was a glossy musical comedy shot on location at the Seattle World's Fair. Presley played Mike Edwards, a pilot-for-hire, who after jilting a luscious small town girl (Yvonne Craig, whose father chases him off with a shotgun), heads to the Fair with his gambling-loving partner Danny Edwards (Gary Lockwood) to get work so they can earn enough money to re-claim their airplane that has been repossessed. There Mike becomes involved with a precocious seven-year-old Chinese girl Sue-Lin (Vicky Tiu) left in the boys' care by her farmer father and a pretty nurse named Diane Warren (Joan O'Brien) who he'd rather spend time with, though she plays hard to get.

After coming on the heels of *Girls! Girls! Girls!*, *It Happened at the World's Fair*'s box office returns were not as good though it still turned a profit. It was at this point when the producers and studio bosses began to realize that perhaps they did not have to spend the money to send Elvis on location and could get away with using second unit footage to fool the public as they previously did with *G.I. Blues*. Hal Wallis was the first to attempt this again with *Fun in Acapulco* (1963). Elvis was cast as a troubled trapeze artist working as a lifeguard in Acapulco. Now suffering from a fear of heights due to a fatal accident, he needs to overcome his phobia to win a cliff diving competition while juggling two women—Ursula Andress ridiculously cast as a virginal co-worker (what were they thinking?) and Elsa Cardenas as a worldly bullfighter.

The year 1964 began the next phase of Elvis Presley's film career. He appeared in a string of musicals for MGM with a side movie or two for other studios. Except for *Viva Las Vegas*, the films Elvis appeared in for MGM during this time are usually dismissed by the mainstream critics as nothing more than forgettable frothy lightweight entertainment. They all stick to the standard Elvis Film formula as his prior movies such as *Blue Hawaii* and *Girls! Girls! Girls!* The difference though was they were now done on the cheap. For some fans though this period contain some of their favorite films. Of course most of this is due to the King, but a lot has to do with the casting of some of the most beautiful and popular sixties starlets of the day particularly his movies with Shelley Fabares arguably his favorite leading lady.

Elvis' first MGM musical released in 1964 was the lower budgeted *Kissin' Cousins* (1964) produced by Sam Katzman and directed by dancer/actor Gene Nelson. They had just teamed on the country musical film *Hootenanny Hoot* also for MGM. *Kissin' Cousins* was actually shot after *Viva Las Vegas* but was so rushed that it beat it into theaters. It is very entertaining in a *Li'l Abner* sort of way and featured a hit title song for the King who played the dual roles of Josh and Jodie Tatum. Josh is a dark-haired G.I. who is recruited by Col. Jack Albertson to travel to the mountains of Tennessee to persuade his blonde look-a-like cousin Jodie, who likes to wrestle country-style, and his hillbilly kin Arthur O'Connell and Glenda Farrell as ornery Pappy and Ma Tatum, to vacate their home so a missile silo can be built on it.

The starlets in the movie help raise the enjoyment level immensely. Pamela Austin (also from *Hootenanny Hoot*) and Yvonne Craig are Pappy Tatum's daughters, Selena and Azalea, sexy, scantily-clad, bare-footin' Daisy Mae-types who go gaga over their distant cousin and compete for his attentions. It reaches a kinky climax as Josh sings "One Boy, Two Little Girls" expressing his frustration about being torn between the two sisters though enjoying the pursuit. In 1964, a three-way was out of the question. When he plants a peck on the lips of Selena, the disappointed blonde demands, "mountain style honey" and aggressively makes out with the G.I. tongue and all. Not surprisingly, a put-off Josh chooses the more demure Azalea (perhaps to make up for Yvonne Craig losing Elvis to Joan O'Brien previously in *It Happened At the World's Fair*).

Also in the cast are Beverly Powers, a former exotic dancer sometimes billed under her stage name of Miss Beverly Hills, as the leader of the Kitty Hawks—man-hungry, bare-footin' vixens who roam the hills looking for men who they drag off sort of caveman-style. And pretty Cynthia Pepper, best known as the star of the TV series *Margie*, is a perky WAC who enchants blonde Jodie. When she easily manhandles the amorous boy, he instantly knows it's love. Pepper (a last minute replacement for Shelley Fabares per the *Los Angeles Times*) got the role in part due to Elvis who saw her on TV and recommended her, and because she was able to stuff her behind (with help from studio seamstresses) into the already designed costume.

Elvis does well playing opposite himself though in some of the shots the features of the actor doubling for him are carelessly noticeable. When his dark-haired Josh first meets blonde cousin Jody they do not get along, culminating with a wrestling match with Selena and Azelea rooting for their new kissin' cousin. It is quite amusing seeing Elvis tussle with himself.

Cynthia Pepper and a blonde Elvis Presley in *Kissin' Cousins* (MGM, 1964).

Writing in her memoir *From Ballet to the Batcave and Beyond*, Yvonne Craig described Elvis as "having that indefinable *something* that makes a camera love you." She admitted while shooting scenes with him she didn't notice. It wasn't until she eyed the dailies that she was wowed by his on-screen presence. Recalling a scene they did together, she said, "Elvis not only had a great self-deprecating sense of humor...but was absolutely aware of what was expected of the 'Elvis Presley' persona. I remember one instance when we were shooting...by a tree and he was (yes again) singing ["Catchin' on Fast"] to me. For some reason he felt I was standing too far away from him. He asked if I could move closer because his fans expected it. And I'm sure he was right."

Craig also revealed that Elvis was embarrassed having to wear a blond wig and hid in his dressing room. Gene Nelson had to assure him that no one was going to laugh and coax him out. Craig had only praise for the director. "He was terrific," she wrote in her book. "He always yelled, 'Cut!' followed by something encouraging even if he wanted to do the scene again. This resulted in everyone wanting to show his or her very best." According to the book *Katzman, Nicholson, Corman* by Mark Thomas McGee, Nelson did reveal that since this was only his second film as director that he would get "uptight" over the short shooting schedule. This distressed Elvis, who offered to slow things down to help him out by feigning an illness or showing up late. Nelson thanked him for his support, but said he would cope. He did and they finished the movie on time.

Kissin' Cousins was produced by Sam Katzman, nicknamed "King of the B's." The film had a lower budget and shorter shooting schedule compared to Presley's previous movies, which meant most of it was shot on the MGM studio's soundstages with a few days on location, not in Tennessee where the movie was set, but at nearby Big Bear Mountains. Katzman was known for his cost-cutting ways and for delivering his movies on budget and on time. Recalling the producer, Craig wrote in her memoir, "[This] may have been the most expensive film *he'd* produced but by the nature of his *being* the producer, considered both fast and cheap."

Dancer Christopher Riordan, who would go on to work in six Elvis movies beginning with *Viva Las Vegas,* had just worked for Sam Katzman on *Get Yourself a College Girl* (1964) and would work with him again. He expounded on the producer's work ethic and demeanor stating, "No matter what the movie, Katzman was on the set everyday. He was absolutely insane when it came to money matters and it was just awful working with him. The only thing worse than working for Sam Katzman was doing a film at Universal-International, which was like a factory. Sam was under the gun to come in on time and under budget but I think it was more for personal reasons. I am sure the studios gave him a budget and he was told whatever you don't spend you can keep. He overpowered everybody on the set including the director. It could have been directed by William Wyler and Sam would have run roughshod over him. I felt that he had no respect for anybody, especially the talent. But he always made sure his dear little rotund wife, Hortense Petra, had great footage and terrific close-ups. There was a dreadful feeling working on his sets where you didn't feel special in any shape or form. With that said, I couldn't turn down work with a child to support, so I do appreciate the opportunities he offered me."

Being the producer's wife seemed to have gone to stout Hortense's head. Craig and Austin had a bit of trouble with the scene bully. Here Petra played a nosy reporter investigating why the military would pay for a shopping spree for the Tatum sisters. Petra's reporter is standing between Selena and Azalea as she questions Presley's Jody. After the first take, the actresses realized that Petra was trying to elbow them out of the frame. Craig recalled, "She was short but strong. We decided to treat this as a challenge and each of us braced and wouldn't budge. She finally gave up."

Mainstream critics were very dismissive of *Kissin' Cousins*. *Variety* described as being a "dreary effort," but found that Elvis "does as well as possible under the circumstances." Howard Thompson of the *New York Times* thought it to be a "broad meandering rehash of *Li'l Abner*" and that "Sam Katzman's production is "tired, strained, and familiar." Margaret Harford in the *Boston Globe* was a bit more generous to director Gene Nelson and remarked that he "keeps it lively as a hoedown."

Surprisingly, its screenwriters Gerald Drayson Adams and Nelson received a Writers Guild Award nomination for Best Written American Musical of 1964. It lost to *Mary Poppins*. The soundtrack had more of a country feel to it since it was set in Tennessee, but critics felt the songs sounded nothing like real country music of the time. Even so, the soundtrack album peaked at #6 on Billboard's Top LP's chart and the title tune hit #12 on Billboard's Hot 100. However, what was released as a single was not the song played over the opening credits. Elvis re-recorded the song and it was much better with a faster beat.

Kissin' Cousins is nicely photographed on location and moves at a brisk pace. Some of the country humor is funny but some of the jokes fall flat. Surprisingly, Elvis does not put forth much effort playing either role, but he is fine and receives strong support from Pamela Austin and especially Yvonne Craig one of his most fetching leading ladies. Songs are passable except for one cringe-inducing ballad called "Pappy, Won't You Please Come Home" that Ma croaks out (Glenda Farrell lip-synching to an unidentified female vocalist) after Pappy goes missing. If he would have heard her sing, he would never have come back. Despite its flaws, the movie is breezy entertainment and what you expect from an Elvis mid-sixties movie.

Even with the cost-cutting imposed by MGM, the fans came anyway to see *Kissin'*
Cousins and it turned a nice profit. The film raked in $2.8 million at the box office. Col. Tom
Parker decided this was to be the norm on Elvis' subsequent movies such as *Girl Happy,*
Harum Scarum, Tickle Me, Spinout, Clambake, etc. which were all quickie productions ala
Kissin' Cousins. It showed that Elvis' non-discriminating fans would accept cheaper pro-
ductions as long as Elvis was front and center singing lots of songs and the pretty girls
were still surrounding him.

Elvis did get a respite from the low-budget fare with the already filmed *Viva Las*
Vegas (1964) directed by George Sidney and shot on location. Here he is a racecar driver in
Las Vegas for the Grand Prix and is paired with the fiery Ann-Margret as a hotel lifeguard.
She is his first co-star to get above the title billing with him.

Pretty blonde actress and former champion figure skater Nancy Czar was a special
friend with Elvis and just knew this duo would work together as early as 1962. She met
the King due to her idolization of singer/actor Ricky Nelson. A friend took her to a touch
football game he was playing in and the opposing team was Elvis and his friends. For
Nancy it was quickly goodbye Ricky and hello Elvis! They met and began casually dating.

"I had a whole different relationship with Elvis, who was about eight or nine years
older than me, than probably nine tenths of the people who walked into this man's life,"
opined Nancy Czar. "We dated for about a year off and on. I was fascinated with Elvis and
his lifestyle was interesting to me as I think it would have been for any teenage girl. I was
still growing up when I met Elvis. It matured me very fast. We clashed on a lot of areas
because even at my young age I could see the stupidity surrounding him. You are a grown
man—are you going to let an eighteen year old girl tell you what to do? I don't think
so—definitely not Elvis. As I entered the next phase of my life I already had figured out
that there was something not quite right with Elvis, but I was too young to know exactly
what it was.

"I predicted the pairing [with Ann-Margret] after I went to a screening of the movie
State Fair in 1962," continued Czar. "The big stars of it were Pat Boone and Bobby Darin,
but this unknown redhead blew me away in this wild dance scene. She was totally un-

believable. I was at Elvis' house for dinner and all the boys were sitting around the table. I said, 'You know E, I got a girl that I saw the other night at a screening who could be the female Elvis. Her name is Ann-Margret. She should be your next leading lady.' And sure enough a few films later it happened. Up to that point I had never seen anyone like her."

Nancy Czar in *Wild Guitar* (Fairway International Pictures, 1962)

Viva Las Vegas features some outstanding choreography by David Winters. Among the dancers hired were Lori Williams, who also shimmied with Elvis in *Kissin' Cousins*, *Roustabout*, and *Girl Happy* before finding cult notoriety as one of the stars of Russ Meyer's *Faster, Pussycat! Kill! Kill!*, and Christopher Riordan who was working with choreographer Hermes Pan on *My Fair Lady*. Knowing Riordan had a child on the way and needed extra money, the choreographer recommended him to Winters when there was a break in filming *My Fair Lady*.

"Elvis was delightful—right from the very beginning," Riordan exclaimed. "He was the kind of man that if he saw that you had some kind of talent or had dedication or what have you, he'd zero in on that immediately. He asked Pam Freeman [another dancer] about me. On the next film [*Roustabout*] he found out my son Sean had been born and I was a single father. He then made sure I had a job in his movies. They'd call me every time to see if I was available. If I was, they told me when and where to report. I found out years later from another dancer named Suzanne Covington, who was very friendly with Elvis, that he evidently had a list of dancers he especially wanted to work with all the time. There were only a few guys on it and I was one of them."

Riordan danced with Lori Williams during Elvis and Ann-Margret's big roulette wheel number. "Lori Williams was like horse shit in the street scene of a western," said Christopher with a laugh. "She was just all over the place in those days and we did many films together dancing in the background particularly beach movies. Lori had a lot more talent than what she was given credit for."

In *Viva Las Vegas*, Elvis played Lucky Jackson, a racecar driver in town to compete in the Vegas Grand Prix. Lucky is immediately attracted to Rusty Martin (Ann-Margret) a red-headed stunner who wiggles her way into his garage with car trouble. Lucky's racing rival Count Elmo Mancini (Cesare Danova) also flips for her charms. With his racecar needing major repairs, Lucky moonlights as a hotel waiter where Rusty coincidentally works as the swimming pool manager. At first Rusty rejects Lucky due to the dangers of his profession, but as expected in an Elvis movie she relents. After her daddy-dearest (William Demarest) purchases a new motor for the racer, father and daughter help Lucky get his car in shape. He goes on to win the big race and the girl—what a surprise!—in a too abrupt ending that closes with a quick shot of their wedding before a reprise of the title tune sung by Elvis with a split screen of Ann-Margret shaking that mane.

This slick MGM production was considered by some to be Elvis' best of the sixties and a lot of the credit went to sex kitten Ann-Margret who more than held her own singing and dancing opposite him. Their chemistry lit up the screen and continued once the cameras stopped rolling as Elvis famously romanced the redhead throughout the entire shoot only to fade out once production wrapped. The gossip columnists of the time had a field day reporting on their affair. It reached frenzied proportions after the London press erroneously announced their engagement forcing the pretty redhead to set the record straight. She confessed to syndicated columnist Sheila Graham, "It was such fun. Elvis and I were going steady but were never engaged."

As with Elvis, Christopher Riordan too found the actress just as wonderful but not in a romantic way. "Ann-Margret is shy, but a sweet, sweet lady and not at all pretentious," commented the actor. "She was having a grand time on *Viva Las Vegas* even though she worked really hard on this. I wound up working with Ann-Margret two more times."

Most critics felt the combination of Elvis and Ann-Margret (who is treated like an equal co-star here unlike all his other leading ladies) raised *Viva Las Vegas* above the usual Elvis Film fare even though the story was less than passable. The critic in *Variety* perfectly nailed the movie remarking, "The sizzling combination of Elvis Presley and Ann-Margret is enough to carry *Viva Las Vegas* over the top, The picture is fortunate in having two such commodities for bait, because the production is a pretty trite and heavy-handed affair, puny in story development..."

Today, the film doesn't hold up as well due to its weak script by Sally Benson. There are no funny bits like there are in *Kissin' Cousins* and *Girl Happy*. Even so Ann-Margret rocks the house in the musical dance numbers and her swinging duets with the King. However, Elvis has the best musical moment with the tender jazzy ballad "I Need Somebody to Lean On" sung by a forlorn Lucky in an after hours casino after he thinks he has lost the girl and his chance to race.

Due to the popularity of the two leads, *Viva Las Vegas* turned out to be Elvis' biggest hit of the sixties. It brought in $4,675,000 at the box office and, per *Variety*, was the 11th highest grossing movie for 1964. The pairing of the King and Ann-Margret proved so popular they won the Photoplay Gold Medal Award for Favorite Actor and Actress of 1964 and they each placed third in the Laurel Awards poll for Best Musical Performance, Male and Female.

Surprisingly, box office dollars did not translate over to big record sales. The title track was a modest hit reaching #29 on Billboard's Hot 100 and a soundtrack EP consisting of four songs only reached #92 on Billboard's Hot LP's chart. It was the King's poorest showing on the album charts since the start of his career. One of the key reasons the EP was not a hit had to do with the dawn of Beatlemania.

Per Nancy Czar, not everybody was ecstatic over the critical and box office success of *Viva Las Vegas*. She revealed, "I do know that Col. Parker was not happy with *Viva Las Vegas*. Director George Sidney was in love with Ann-Margret. He had directed her previously in *Bye Bye Birdie* that made her a star. Parker felt that Sidney favored Ann-Margret in the shots she and Elvis were in together and gave her more close-ups.

"I never liked Col. Parker, who to me just used Elvis as his meal ticket," continued the outspoken blonde. "A lot of people would say that Elvis did exactly what he wanted to do. Yes, he did probably later on in his life but when I was around him if Col. Parker said, 'Jump' Elvis would say, 'How high?' Elvis would defy the Colonel on certain issues but when it came to bigger decisions he deferred to the Colonel. Elvis hated doing those movies because they were the same old travelogues with different pretty girls. As long as Elvis got his quote and his 10% of the box office receipts that is all the Colonel gave a damn about. He never read a script."

Going forward, Col. Parker made sure Elvis never had as strong a leading lady as Ann-Margret in the areas of singing and dancing, though a few wandered in such as Nancy Sinatra in *Speedway* and Marlyn Mason in *The Trouble with Girls*.

Elvis was next able to sneak in a film for producer Hal Wallis. Paramount's Studios' *Roustabout* was Elvis' last musical to be released in 1964 and one of his best, perhaps even better than *Viva Las Vegas*. It was manna from heaven for girl watchers as it was chock full of curvaceous starlets from leading ladies Joan Freeman, Sue Ane Langdon, and Joan Staley to bit players Raquel Welch, Marianna Hill, Beverly Adams, and Lori Williams. Also featured was tough-talking Barbara Stanwyck as the owner of the carnival, who out butched even the King. He played Charlie Rogers a motorcycle-riding drifter who gets fired from his job as a singer at a club after getting into a brawl with some loud-mouthed frat boys and joins the carnival as a roustabout where he falls for her niece (Freeman) to the chagrin of the girl's lush of a daddy (Leif Erickson).

Seeing the success of the Frankie and Annette beach movies during 1963 and 1964, MGM decided to go back to the well that started it all for Elvis Presley's first movie of 1965. Produced by Joe Pasternak and directed by Boris Sagal, *Girl Happy* was a combination of the studio's *Where the Boys Are* and AIP's *Beach Party*. Elvis now needed his Annette. MGM was so thrilled with the Elvis and Ann-Margret pairing that they wanted her to co-star. However, Col. Parker was not going to let that happen again and nixed the reteaming. Enter Shelley Fabares.

Publicity photo of Shelley Fabares in *Girl Happy* (MGM, 1965).

The niece of comedienne Nanette Fabray, Shelley followed her aunt into a very successful career in show business. She began taking tap dance lessons at age three. At four years old, Shelley began modeling and at age nine Frank Sinatra sang to her on one of his TV specials. Appearances on such early TV shows such as *Matinee Theatre*, *Captain Midnight*, and *Annie Oakley* followed. She made her film debut in 1956 playing Rock Hudson's daughter in the weeper *Never Say Goodbye,* where she said, "I was awful." Nevertheless, she was good enough to land the role of John Saxon's younger sister Twinky in one of the earliest rock 'n' roll films *Rock, Pretty Baby* (1956) and its sequel *Summer Love* (1958).

Shelley's big break came at age fourteen when she was cast as Donna Reed's teenage daughter Mary in the sitcom *The Donna Reed Show* co-starring Carl Betz and Paul Petersen. The show was an immediate hit and ran for eight seasons. During the run of the show, the producers asked Shelley to cut a record to try to draw more of a younger audience. Despite her limited singing ability, Shelley agreed and the Colpix release "Johnny Angel" hit #1 on the Billboard charts on April 7, 1962 after she warbled it on the show. Shelley attributes its popularity not to her singing but to the "great production of the song by Tony Owen and Stu Phillips." Her success catapulted her to the highest echelon of teen idols. In the early sixties, numerous fan magazines ran cover stories on her with such titles as "Teens Are Looking at Shelley" and "The Many Sides of Shelley Fabares."

She left the series in 1963. "Leaving was one of the most difficult decisions I ever made in my life," confessed Fabares. "We really were like a family on the show. It took me a year to make up my mind because I was so happy there. But I decided to leave the show mainly because I had been working all of my life. I was nineteen and I was about to get married in real life to Lou Adler. I felt I needed some time to be sort of myself. It was incredibly painful but I felt it was the right thing to do at that time."

A new platinum blonde Shelley Fabares scored the film lead opposite Fabian in the hit beach movie *Ride the Wild Surf* (1964) for Columbia Pictures. MGM then swooped in and signed the popular actress to a three-picture deal. Because she could sing, Fabares was cast as Elvis leading lady in *Girl Happy*.

"I was a fan of his but I was not a rabid fan," said Fabares. "I remember—and always will remember—the first day that I met him on the set. We were getting ready to rehearse our first scene and all of a sudden he was walking across the soundstage and I suddenly thought, '*Oh my God. It's Elvis Presley!*' You're always nervous when starting a film but until I saw him that's when I *really* got nervous. It wasn't because he was beautiful—though he looked great on film he was much more gorgeous in person—but he was like a God walking across that stage. It really sort of took my breath away, but happily we clicked right away. It was like we had known each other for a long time. Thankfully I quickly got over the nervousness because you can't act with someone if he awes you."

Though Fabares eased up about working with Elvis, she was dreading the fact that she had to sing. She explained, "Recording 'Johnny Angel' was a devastatingly difficult experience because I'm not a singer and don't like singing. But I am very proud of the song and how it has brought joy to many people. When I got this role and they said I would be singing I said, 'I don't think I could do this.' And they said, 'Sure you can.' Of course by that time I had cut two albums so I didn't have much of a leg to stand on. In the scene Chris Noel, Lyn Edgington, and I are bopping along singing the song "Spring Fever" and it's inter cut with Elvis and the guys singing as we're all driving down to Fort Lauderdale. I sound like Minnie Mouse my voice is so high! I think they had to do that so Elvis could sing in his key and I guess I could sing in that higher key, such as it was."

Since this was a film about the college crowd, MGM surrounded Elvis and Fabares with a talented bunch of good looking young people including former Miss America Mary Ann Mobley, Joby Baker, Gary Crosby, Chris Noel, Fabrizio Mioni, Jimmy Hawkins, Peter Brooks, Lyn Edgington, Gail Gerber, and Nancy Czar. Credit goes to producer Joe Pasternak as his supporting cast truly gives wonderful support to Elvis.

Pasternak was a reportedly hands-on producer but it wasn't only the film he wanted to get his hands on. Boris Sagal informed the late Gail Gerber (whose stage name was Gail Gilmore) that the producer was extending an invitation to his home that weekend. Gail was a former ballet dancer from Canada who also worked in summer stock and on Canadian television. When she landed in Hollywood in 1963, she quickly scored an agent and began working almost immediately in television. *Girl Happy* was her second movie after copping a co-starring role in *The Girls on the Beach* (1965). Knowing that Pasternak discovered some huge stars such as Elizabeth Taylor and Deanna Durbin and feeling flattered that he noticed her, the naïve actress quickly accepted. Recounting in her memoir *Trippin' with Terry Southern*, Gerber revealed that later on the set, "He [Pasternak] walked by me and asked hopefully, 'You're coming to lunch?' When I replied yes, he whispered, 'Wear black underwear.' I smiled politely but I was thinking to myself, 'Fat chance, you old letch.'"

Gail did show up ("in full body armor") but to the producer's chagrin one of his teenage sons was home and spent the whole time talking with the young starlet. Gail was also approached by Elvis' guys bearing invitations to Presley's home. But she was starring at night in the stage production of *Under the Yum Yum Tree* at the Ivar Theatre and had to pass.

Gary Crosby ogles bathing beauty Nancy Czar in
Girl Happy (MGM, 1965).

Girl Happy would be the first appearance in an Elvis movie for his friend Nancy Czar though her bit did not enable her to work directly with the King. She was "the blonde on the beach." Wearing a leopard skin-spotted bikini, Czar is a knockout as she lies on her blanket in the sand distracting guitar player Gary Crosby from keeping an eye out for Shelley Fabares whom they are secretly chaperoning. When Fabares slips away, Crosby makes a run after her but first stops to give the startled Czar a kiss. When asked why she didn't use her connections to Elvis to get a bigger part here and later in *Spinout*, especially after playing leading roles in *Wild Guitar* (1962) and *Winter a-Go-Go* (1965), she replied, "Those were the parts I was up for and those are the ones I got. I never asked him for larger roles because I wasn't using my friendship with Elvis to push my movie career—not my MO. Although, I'm sure if I asked, he would have helped."

During the course of the shoot Shelley Fabares was dreading the scene where her character gets drunk and jumps on stage at a nightclub and begins singing while stripping her clothes off. She revealed, "It was one of the times that I was going to get out of the business. I was terrified and just thought there was no way I could sing, dance and act drunk and hopefully be funny all at the same time. But I remembered a story Donna Reed told me when I was nervous about doing a tap dance routine on her show. She said to me, 'Early in my career I had to do three things in this movie—sing, dance the jitterbug, and fall over backwards into a pool. I really thought about bowing out of the film because those three things scared me so much. But I had to do it. One of the things you'll find in life is that the things that scare us the most are the things we should go forward and do.' The movie she was talking about was *It's a Wonderful Life*. It was a great pep talk and has stayed with me all of my life."

Though Gail Gerber got to know Elvis, she didn't have much interaction with him on screen. She recalled, "I worked mostly with Jimmy Hawkins, Pamela Curran and Rusty Allen who played the girlfriends of Joby Baker and Gary Crosby who I thought was a really talented guy. Pamela, who was a blonde Julie Newmar-type, and I worked together previously on *The Loved One*. I was one of the cosmetologists at the funeral home and she was one of the hostesses. The other gals on [that] film thought Pamela was haughty. I just thought she was stoned because we shared a trailer and she was always popping some sort of pills. During the seventies when I was living with writer Terry Southern on a farm, we spent a lovely day with Joby Baker and his wife Dory Previn who lived nearby. By that time Joby was concentrating on his art and I was teaching ballet. We reminisced a bit about working on *Girl Happy*."

"I actually never even met Shelley Fabares," continued Gerber. "The only time we worked together was at the end of the movie in the nightclub scene. I was at a table on the side when Elvis walks over to her and brings her on stage for the finale. They were so cute together. Their chemistry is why I think the movie is really good. You could just tell they adored each other. I am not surprised she was his leading lady two more times."

After filming was completed, Gerber, Allen, and Curran had to take various cheesecake photos to promote the movie. Per Gail, "Neither one seemed comfortable in front of the camera and posed so awkwardly. I think they ruined the photos. One turns up a lot on the Internet. I hated it so much I decided not to use it in my memoir."

Gail Gerber's hated publicity photo of Pamela Curran, Rusty Allen,
and Gail in *Girl Happy* (MGM, 1965).

In *Girl Happy*, Elvis played Rusty Wells, lead singer of a successful combo (consisting of Gary Crosby, Joby Baker, and Jimmy Hawkins) drawing sell-out crowds at a night spot owned by tough-talking Mr. Frank (Harold J. Stone) in snowy Chicago. He renews their contract for another six weeks, scuttling their plans to head to balmy Florida. Overhearing their boss arguing with his daughter Valerie (Fabares) about going on spring break with her college friends (Chris Noel and Lyn Edgington) to Fort Lauderdale, Rusty offers to be her secret chaperone. Soon he and the boys are off to the Sunshine State. Thinking Valerie has hooked up with a bookworm named Brentwood (Peter Brooks) Rusty concentrates on sexy Deena (Mary Ann Mobley) while the guys find their own bikini babes (Pamela Curran, Gail Gerber and Rusty Allen). But Valerie rejects Brentwood and is attracted to Italian playboy Romano (Fabrizio Mioni) so every time Rusty and his boys get cozy with their gals, Valerie winds up in some sort of predicament and they have to rush to her rescue. Rusty then decides to romance her to keep her away from Romano and in the interim falls for the coed. However, she discovers he is being paid to watch over her. Hurt, she winds up drunk performing a striptease in a nightclub. After being broken out of jail by a contrite Rusty, she forgives him and they wind up happily ever after...maybe.

Girl Happy is extremely pleasant fare and one of Elvis' biggest post-*Viva Las Vegas* hits at the box office proving that Joe Pasternak played it smart by aping the Frankie and Annette beach party films. Timing is everything. Though filmed mainly on the back lot with a few beach scenes shot on location, the colorful production is first rate, the action never lets up, and the film has that glossy vibrant MGM sheen to it. Credit goes to director Boris Sagal who keeps the action moving at a brisk pace. Elvis is in top form and, unlike with *Kissin' Cousins*, seems to be enjoying himself more making this and it shows on screen. He is helped by arguably one of the strongest supporting casts he ever had with Shelley Fabares, Gary Crosby, Mary Ann Mobley, Chris Noel, and Fabrizio Mioni standing out.

Critics of the time seemed to agree. Margaret Harford of the *Los Angeles Times* remarked, "Another 'beach musical' that looks livelier and fresher than most." James Powers of the *Hollywood Reporter* found *Girl Happy* to be "a picture with a sharp trim and bright decoration, lively action, and some good jokes, as well as the usual blend of song and romance." Elvis himself was singled out by William R. Weaver of the *Motion Picture Herald* who raved, "Presley...never seemed freer or happier in any picture than here."

With a budget estimated to be a bit less than *Viva Las Vegas*, *Girl Happy* grossed $3.1 million at the box office. The popular soundtrack is one of the King's most varied and best from this time period. It catapulted all the way up to #8 on Billboard's Top LP chart. From the touching "Puppet on a String" (#14 on Billboard's Top 100), to the swinging "Do the

Clam" (#12 on Billboard's Top 100), to the romantic "Do Not Disturb" the songs help buoy the movie and propelled Elvis' fans to purchase the album.

Elvis Presley serenades a disinterested Shelley Fabares
in *Girl Happy* (MGM, 1965).

Authors and historians have been writing about Elvis movies since the seventies and *Girl Happy* is considered one of his sixties' standouts. Paul Lichter in *Elvis in Hollywood* called it "quite entertaining." Marshall Crenshaw in *Hollywood Rock* opined, "The pacing is fast, the '60s color palette is often glorious. . .and many of the musical numbers are engaging."

Shelley Fabares agrees with the film's good notices and remarked about *Girl Happy*, "I think it was the best movie Elvis and I made together. It is also my favorite because it is a good movie—maybe one of Elvis' best films too. It had a strong, wonderful director in Boris Sagal, a good script, tuneful songs, and a talented cast. All those ingredients that went into an Elvis film worked particularly well in *Girl Happy*."

Before Shelley Fabares could work with Elvis again, he had four pictures to do. He saved the ailing studio Allied Artists by starring in the very low-budget, not well-received though profitable *Tickle Me* (1965). He played a singing rodeo cowboy moonlighting as a handyman at a health spa for nubile actresses and models, but falls for fitness trainer Jocelyn Lane.

Back at work on the MGM back lot, Elvis' next movie was not much of an improvement over *Tickle Me*. To this day, fans are split on *Harum Scarum*—some love it for trying to give Elvis something different with this parody on Valentino and old-time desert musicals, while others detest its cheapness, ridiculous plot, and absurd casting. As with *Kissin' Cousins*, it was produced by Sam Katzman and directed by Gene Nelson ("Who surprisingly wasn't gay," quipped Gail Gerber with a laugh). The movie went through various title changes during shooting and post-production. It started off as being called *In My Harem* and *Harem-Scarum* before it was announced that the final title was *Harem Holiday*. Just before it was released, the name was changed to *Harum Scarum* though for the rest of the world it remained *Harem Holiday* because the slang phrase had no meaning outside the U.S.

Produced on the cheap, some of the sets were used in Cecil B. DeMille's *King of Kings*; the extras' costumes were leftovers from *Kismet*; and some of the props were previously used in *Lady of the Tropics*. Sam Katzman bemoaned in the *Los Angeles Times*, "It cost DeMille $6,000 to build his entire set. Just to refurbish and renovate it, I spent $40,000." The musical was shot in twenty-eight days, per Mary Ann Mobley, making it one of the more lavish Katzman productions and one where he could thankfully not find a role for his wife Hortense Petra.

On the advice of her agent, Gail Gerber usually hid the fact that she was a ballet dancer so she would be hired for her acting talent and not her dancing skills. She had previously worked with Elvis in *Girl Happy* and so wanted this role of a gypsy that she announced to producer and director alike of her ballet background. Despite being a fair-skinned blonde from Canada, she got the part of an Arab gypsy (they just put a black wig on her to fool the American filmgoer) and had the time of her life making this. Remembering Sam Katzman, Gail Gerber said, "He was a little friendly guy and always on the soundstage making sure we stayed on schedule—delays meant budget over runs and we couldn't have that! But what really impressed me was that he brought Billie Burke, the Good Witch from *The Wizard of Oz,* to visit the set one day. I was surprised that she still had that high-pitched voice that she had some twenty-five years prior."

Mary Ann Mobley liked Katzman as well, despite that fact that when he learned that she could ride a horse, he cancelled hiring a stunt double for her to save money. When time came to shoot this scene, the stunt coordinator was baffled that the leading lady was going to do her own riding. After putting her on the horse, he asked not to be blamed if something went wrong. The horse then took off like a rocket with Mobley hanging on for dear life.

The only dangers Gail Gerber encountered making this movie was tripping over her two feet. It allowed her to show off her dancing prowess in two big production numbers. She does an exotic dance in the town square while Elvis croons "Shake That Tambourine." And the finale finds Gail, and fellow gypsies Brenda Benet and Wilda Taylor, in Las Vegas as part of Elvis' revue as he sings "Harem Holiday," the film's working title. She remembered fondly, "I had so much fun working with Elvis on this movie. I got to dance with him and play tambourine. I even showed Elvis how to do Chaînès Finger Turns for the film's last number. I had a picture of us going off stage. He was not planted right but we did it and nobody broke their neck but it was cut from the final print.

"I recall another scene where Mary Ann Mobley had to enter the town square standing in a cart being pulled by a donkey while a band of thieves are trying to scale the prison walls where Elvis is being held captive," continued Gerber. "I was part of that ragtag bunch that included little Billy Barty and a really tall actor whose name escapes me. Gene Nelson instructed Mary Ann to act shocked and after glancing our way, she replied, 'How can I not?' I cracked up laughing. Mary Ann was very sweet and I liked her a lot."

Another funny incident, as reported by the *Los Angeles Times*, had to do with upstaging peacocks. Some of these colorful birds were used to decorate a garden where Elvis was to serenade some harem girls. One of the peacocks could not help but squawk away along with Elvis, whom it was reported dubbed him "a ham." Time is money on the set so the bird was given the boot and replaced with a potted palm tree.

In the musical, Presley is matinee idol and pop singer Johnny Tyrone who is kidnapped by gang of assassins while on tour in the fictional Middle Eastern country of Lunarkand. While in captivity, Johnny learns that his kidnappers are in cahoots with Prince Dragna (Michael Ansara) and his girlfriend Aishah (Fran Jeffries) to kill the prince's brother, King Toranshah (Philip Reed). Johnny escapes with the help of Sinan (Theo Marcuse) and joins up with his band of petty thieves including three beautiful dancing gypsies named

Sapphire (Gerber), Amethyst (Benet), and Emerald (Taylor).During the course of his adventure, Johnny falls for the King's daughter Princess Shalimar (Mobley) and of course thwarts the bad guys and gets the girl come fade out.

Elvis Presley performs "Harem Holiday" while Gail Gerber and the other girls dance around him in *Harum Scarum* (MGM, 1965).

Harum Scarum was trounced by the critics who called it "absurd" (*Boston Globe*), "not much fun" (Margaret Harford, *Los Angeles Times*), and "asinine and third-rate" (Tom Gray, *The Atlanta Constitution*). The musical played in New York City on a double bill with *Gidrah, the Three Headed Monster* prompting Vincent Canby of the *New York Times* to quip, "'Something terrible is about to happen,' muttered an inscrutable, English-dubbed Japanese actor early in *Gidrah*. . . and during the next three hours his prophecy comes only too true."

To be fair, *Harum Scarum* at least tried to be an atypical Elvis film. Instead of racing cars and chasing bikini babes, here he gets to ride a horse and romance harem girls. The film featured a pleasant score and better than usual dance numbers thanks to choreographer Earl Barton. Elvis really tries here probably do the change of pace plot, and looks great in his Rudolph Valentino-like garb, but is hampered by a cliché-filled script though there are a few very funny moments supplied by the supporting cast of characters. Still at least it was a good try and for some fans it remains one of their favorites because of that.

Not surprisingly, *Harum Scarum* was one of Elvis' lesser earning mid-sixties movies taking in an estimated $2.0 million at the box office per *Variety*. Though the movie was not up to Elvis' box office standard, the soundtrack album still sold and peaked at #8 on Billboard's Top LP's chart. However, no song was released as a single.

Asked to muse about Presley, Gail Gerber remarked, "Elvis was intelligent, quiet, and very sweet. But at that time, he seemed like a young man in turmoil—sort of like a '*Who do I have to fuck to get off this picture*' kind of thing. Elvis was a tortured guy who obviously hoped for something better."

Elvis' next two films were not from MGM. *Frankie and Johnny* (1966), directed by Frederick de Cordova for United Artists, was loosely based on the popular folk song. It was another film that that tried to offer Presley a change of pace role and its merits divided his loyal fans. Here he is Johnny, a riverboat performer and gambler in 1865, torn between his love for sweet singing partner Frankie (Donna Douglas from TV's *The Beverly Hillbillies* but sans her critters) and sultry Nellie Bly (Nancy Kovack). When Elvis next returned to the fold of Hal Wallis, the producer decided to send the singer back to Hawaii like he did with *Blue Hawaii* and *Girls! Girls! Girls!* two of Presley's biggest hits. *Paradise, Hawaiian Style* (1966) featured not one, not two, but five leading female roles as Elvis played a pilot who woos the ladies to send tourists to his newly formed helicopter charter service.

When Shelley Fabares finally got to co-star with Elvis a second time in their next MGM musical, she had to share him with Diane McBain (a former Warner Bros. contract player whose films included *Parrish* and *Claudelle Inglish*) and Deborah Walley (star of *Gidget Goes Hawaiian*, *Beach Blanket Bingo*, and *Ski Party*, amongst others). *Spinout*

(1966), who's working title was *Never Say Yes*, had Elvis back in the comfortable hands of director Norman Taurog who surrounded him with friendly faces from his past movies including Jimmy Hawkins, Jack Mullaney, Nancy Czar, Arlene Charles, and Christopher Riordan. New faces in this Elvis film were Carl Betz, Warren Berlinger, Will Hutchins, Dodie Marshall, and Thordis Brandt, amongst others.

Writing in her autobiography *Famous Enough: A Hollywood Memoir*, Diane McBain revealed that Tippi Hedren was the first choice for her role but her asking price was too high. Diane took the part "for five times less than what Tippi would have considered acceptable." After being dropped by Warner Bros. in 1964, McBain had not made a motion picture since and went on to opine that since she was not financially compensated weekly by a studio any longer, "I didn't know what to ask. My agent didn't seem to know either."

Publicity photo of Shelley Fabares
in *Spinout* (1966, MGM).

By all accounts, *Spinout* was a fairly pleasurable shoot for all involved. Diane McBain wrote in her memoir, "The cast and crew were terrific, supportive, and great fun. Elvis was a huge help, too. He was slim and gorgeous, at the top of his form. I hadn't been a big fan, so I didn't know what to expect...He behaved like a complete gentleman. He was relaxed and accessible...Elvis had a spiritual side that surprised me. We incessantly talked on the set about our favorite books and what we were currently reading."

Shelley Fabares recounted, "One of the funniest experiences I ever had happened during *Spinout*. In this particular movie I wore a red pageboy wig. I was sitting on this chair, very prim and prissy, and Elvis was singing this very sweet love song to me. It was our second movie together and we had a lot of laughs behind us. Every time he said the word 'please' it sort of popped and flipped up the ends of my hair just a bit. It was all we needed to burst out laughing. As he kept trying to redo it, he'd see my eyes start to twitch from trying to hold back the laughter, and he'd crack up. It was just awful as we constantly kept making each other laugh. On the set, time is money."

Presley was once again cast as a singing racecar driver ala *Viva Las Vegas*. Here he is Mike McCoy who is pursued by three marriage-minded cuties—spoiled rich girl Cynthia (Fabares) whose daddy Howard Foxhugh (Carl Betz her TV pop from *The Donna Reed Show*) wants Mike to drive his sports car in an upcoming race; sophisticated glamorous author Diana St. Clair (McBain) who declares Mike "The Perfect American Male;" and tomboyish drummer Les (Deborah Walley saddled with a very unflattering short hair style) who tries to impress Mike with her gourmet cooking skills. Conniving Cynthia with help from her father's assistant Phillip Short (Warren Berlinger) gets Mike and his combo (Jack Mullaney and Jimmy Hawkins) ensconced in the house next door to keep them close by to make Mike change his mind about entering the race. He does and wins. The playboy then marries all three girls—Cynthia to Phillip, Diana to Howard, and Les to police officer Tracy Richards (Will Hutchins) while he, still single, romances his new band member Susan (Dodie Marshall) who boasts that she has no intentions of marrying until she is "fifty, fifty-five—maybe."

In one of the film's big production numbers "Beach Shack" sung around an outdoor pool, Elvis is closely surrounded by nubile bikini-clad babes and one shirtless hunk Christopher Riordan. The King liked having dancers he could trust in eyesight and Riordan was one of the very few males he would specifically request. Remembering the shoot, Christopher remarked, "It was a fun picture and lasted longer work-wise for me. Shelley Fabares was a doll and I had known Deborah Walley from doing the AIP beach movies. Deborah and I got along very well and in fact she moved into my old house after I relocated to Oregon. I enjoyed working and spending time with Diane McBain who I found to be very intelligent. She was a very good actress—a lot better than what she was given credit for. Will Hutchins was a really nice guy unlike that Jimmy Hawkins who was just horrible. I could never understand how an actor (especially someone who was in show business as long as he was) could stand around in a musical number with all those young male dancers knowing full well that most were gay and to spout off these nasty hurtful comments. I thought somebody should just slug him and one day I thought Deborah Walley was going to. She was losing her patience with him and it was beginning to show."

Diane McBain (*far left*) and Shelley Fabares (*far right*) close in on Elvis Presley who sings while Dodie Marshall (*center*) dances in *Spinout* (MGM, 1966). *Billy Rose Theatre Collection, The New York Public Library for the Performing Arts*

Another background player in *Spinout* was Arlene Charles getting her second chance to work with Elvis after doing a very brief bit in *Paradise, Hawaiian Style*. Here, she was one of a myriad of beauties (six of them, including her and Thordis Brandt, were touted by MGM as "the most beautiful girls in the world") that could be seen dancing or fawning over the King. Though Arlene had no lines, she gets lots of close-ups with the King especially at the indoor mansion party where she stands out wiggling up a storm in her pink and orange outfit as Elvis rocks out to the title tune. She was very excited to be working with the King a second time:

"Though it was only doing background, I jumped at the chance," exclaimed Charles. "My agent got mad at me and said I would never be taken seriously as an actress if I kept excepting this type of work. There was a big production number on the patio of a mansion. In the scene Elvis was supposed to come over to me while singing [the title track]. The first take he tripped and said, 'See, I'm falling for you.' I started laughing. That was the kind of guy Elvis was. I never dated him because I knew he would break my heart and would rather be friends, which we were. He was interested in horses and a lot of time between takes that's what we would talk about and a lot of other things. It worked out perfectly.

"At that time I was sort of going out with Sonny West who was one of Elvis' boys," continued Arlene. "We became real close. I really didn't get to know any of the other dancers on *Spinout*, except Thordis Brandt, and basically hung around with Elvis and his entourage. I was sort of a loner I guess you can say."

Unlike in *Girl Happy*, here Nancy Czar not only has a scene with Elvis, she gets to kiss him on screen as well. Asked what she thought of Elvis' friends who were on the set with him, the actress remarked, "Joe Esposito, Charlie Hodge, Lamar Fike, Red and Sonny West were just great guys and were like brothers to me. Lamar to me resembled Elvis' mother Gladys. George Klein was a disc jockey who knew Elvis since high school. He hung around and coined the phrase, 'Nancy Czar the skating star in her Cadillac car starring in *Wild Guitar*.' Elvis got the biggest kick out of this and would always sing it when I came over.

"The reason they were with him on the movie sets was to keep Elvis from getting bored," continued Nancy. "Elvis needed to do something between takes because he could not sit still. He had to constantly move but looking back that is probably from the uppers and downers he was prescribed. When I did *Girl Happy* he was into playing football with the crew. By the time we did *Spinout* a year later, he was into karate. Elvis was so terribly polite all the time but he had a temper that you could not believe. I was with him a few times when he would throw something at the TV and walk out of the room in a huff."

It was at this point where Nancy Czar's friendship with Elvis began to wane. Her last movie was the obscure exploitation film, *The Wild Scene* (1970). She played Clarette a rich girl who hated her parents so she married a much older man (Barry Kroeger) who owns a trucking company. Her analyst (Alberta Nelson) helps her come to terms with her Lesbianism. "I went after this role because I thought I could really show my range," revealed Nancy. "The day we shot the scene I left the house feeling that I had an acting challenge ahead of me. When I revealed to my husband that I am a Lesbian, I was standing by a fireplace mantel with a mirror behind me and Barry in front of me. I was directed to pick up this pointy object off the fireplace and I almost killed Barry with it. I sliced all the buttons off his shirt. I was so in the moment and into the part I realized why actors go so crazy. The crew gave me a standing ovation. I thought, 'Maybe I can really act.'" However, she was distracted after investing her savings in a South Korean clothing company. It was such a success any urge to act again was squashed.

Elvis too was getting restless and wanted a change. He seemed not to keep his boredom or dissatisfaction with the movies being offered him hidden from his co-stars anymore though he still acted the consummate professional. One person who detected based on his demeanor on the set was Christopher Riordan. "I noticed Elvis was getting bored with these movies and I was getting bored too. I finally did tell him after *Clambake* that I wasn't going to be doing any more of these musicals. It's terrible to say because I appreciated the work very much and had fun but I thought, 'Why do I keep doing these films? I am just shaking my ass and not doing much.' I did get a nice bit here in *Spinout* but it was not what I wanted to do. I did not desire to be just a dancer—that kind of dancer especially. I really loved dancing with Barrie Chase and working with Fred Astaire but all this gyrating on the beach or a clambake party was just froth and nonsense."

Spinout received typical notices for an Elvis film from this period and a particular rave from Kevin Thomas of the *Los Angeles Times*. He gushed that *Spinout* was "perhaps his best picture yet—with none of the past detriments and some new pluses. Lots of freewheeling fun..." It is but perhaps not on the level of *Girl Happy*. It is pleasant standard Elvis film fare though the quotient of stunning starlets surrounding the King was higher than usual and the dialog sharper than in previous movies. It was exactly what his fans wanted and brought in $3 million at the box office making it Elvis' third highest grossing movie after *Viva Las Vegas* and *Girl Happy* during this period. Soundtrack-wise, the film featured three standout songs, the title tune, "Beach Shack," and "Never Say Yes." The album reached #18 on Billboard's Top Pop Albums though the title song barely cracked the Top 40 peaking at #40.

Trying to keep up with the times and be socially relevant, producer Hal Wallis' *Easy Come, Easy Go* (1966) for Paramount Pictures, had Elvis encountering beatniks, the counterculture, and yoga (with Elsa Lancaster as his instructor!) as a navy frogman who discovers a treasure chest in a sunken ship on his last military assignment. He joins forces with the late skipper's yoga loving granddaughter Dodie Marshall to reach the gold before villainous playboy Skip Ward and his girlfriend Pat Priest. This lighthearted movie featuring only six songs was Elvis' second film with director John Rich who purportedly was not a favorite of the King's. It was also his last for Wallis who passed on renewing his contract with the popular singer. The producer remarked, "It's not so much that Elvis is changing, but that the times are changing. There's just not the market for no-plot musicals that there once was."

Continuing to try to keep Elvis "with it," MGM's *Double Trouble* (1967), originally titled *You're Killing Me*, tried to cash in on swinging mod London and the popularity of spy movies of the time. Despite being set in Europe, this was another quickie production with the entire movie shot on the studio's massive soundstages. Elvis played an international pop star, not much of an acting stretch for him, and his leading lady was eighteen year old Annette Day, a non-actress discovered specifically for this movie, playing an heiress with a greedy guardian. It was produced by Judd Bernard and Irwin Winkler, and directed by, once again, Norman Taurog. Supporting players included John Williams, Yvonne Romain, Christopher Riordan, and statuesque blonde Mary Hughes from the *Beach Party* movies.

Though Riordan didn't appear dancing in the same scenes as Mary Hughes in *Double Trouble*, he knew her very well from working at American International Pictures. "I was very close with Mary and we always had a great time," recalled Christopher. "She was a sweetheart and was always asking me to go out with the cast at night. I'd reply, 'Thanks Mary but I can't—I'm a single mother.' Bewildered, she'd look at me and say, 'huh?'"

Leading lady Annette Day was literally plucked from a market stall on Portobello Road in London where she had met producer Judd Bernard months before. Remembering Annette's fresh-faced innocence, he contacted her to arrange a screen test. Impressing the MGM brass who must have been trippin' on LSD at the time, Day became Elvis' newest leading lady despite no prior acting experience or any screen presence. Very protective of the novice actress, Elvis went out of his way to make her feel comfortable during the shoot knowing she could take him down with her if he didn't help.

An appreciative Annette Day, who never acted again after *Double Trouble* (no surprise there after you see her less than stellar performance) told the BBC News in 2003, ""I thought 'My goodness, what have I let myself in for here', but he (Elvis) had tremendous patience with me. He very kindly took me through it. He said 'It's no problem, just take it easy.'"When learning that the girl didn't even own a car, Elvis gifted her with a white Mustang!

According to Christopher Riordan, Elvis not only helped Annette Day but others as well. "When he started out in films he didn't know left from right either and people were very helpful to him. And he repaid that in-kind after he had become a big star. You could tell this little girl who looked like some librarian was nervous and didn't know what she was doing or where she was going. I remember the director was having a lot of trouble with Day. Elvis was very sweet and patient. He'd whisper in her ear, 'We're going to turn here and then look for your mark.' Despite his kindness, I felt here was no chemistry between them. I kept thinking to myself, 'Why do they keep doing this to Elvis—saddling him with weak leading ladies.' Elvis was very sensual and had a lot of chemistry going for him. There were several actresses that he played opposite where I thought he did very well such as Marlyn Mason in *The Trouble with Girls*. They are wonderful together and just sizzle."

In *Double Trouble*, Presley is worldwide singing sensation Guy Lambert who meets mysterious teenage heiress Jill Conway (Annette Day) while performing in a London discothèque surrounded by hip swaying go-go girls. Underage Jill becomes infatuated with the singer much to the chagrin of her uncle and guardian Gerald Waverly (John Williams) who sends her away to Belgium to keep the pair apart but to also stop Guy from discovering that he was trying to steal his niece's inheritance. While searching for her, Guy gets involved with spies, jewel thieves, and foreign intrigue. Inexplicably Guy chooses the teenage twit over sophisticated playgirl Claire Dunham (Yvonne Romain) by fade-out, which ends with the pair's wedding a rarity for an Elvis movie.

Double Trouble had critics scratching their heads. The reviewer in *Variety* sums it up for all by commenting, "*Double Trouble* has the sketchiest of story lines, which leaves the spectator wondering what's it all about." The movie had an interesting premise but was sunk by a confusing script and the inexperienced Annette Day. When an Elvis film is not populated with a strong young supporting cast as here, he needs a strong leading lady. Ann-Margret in *Viva Las Vegas* is a perfect example. Her talent and chemistry with Elvis elevated that movie despite the missing cadre of friends surrounding them and a very weak story. *Double Trouble* needed an "Ann-Margret" as well. You would have thought with all the talented young British actresses around at the time including Hayley Mills, Suzy Kendall, and Judy Geeson they could have found someone who at least knew their way around a soundstage. Obviously, they were doing the movie on the cheap and hoped the novice would deliver. Alas, Day did not. Not to lay all the blame on the newcomer for the film's failure, Elvis' lazy performance didn't help matters much. Perhaps this was due to the fact that he was distracted trying to help his clueless leading lady and couldn't concentrate fully on his role. This is by far Elvis' worst MGM movie from this period.

The movie grossed $1.6 million, per *Variety*, making it one of Presley's poorest showings at the box office. The soundtrack was one of Elvis' lesser efforts too reaching #47 on Billboard's Top LP chart. "Long Legged Girl (with the Short Dress On)" was the only song released as a single and it did not make the Top 40 peaking at #63.

Elvis returned to the racing milieu, this time though with speedboats rather than cars, in *Clambake* (1967) his third and last movie opposite Shelley Fabares. It was released through United Artists and directed by Arthur H. Nadel. Though set in Florida, the movie was shot entirely in Hollywood. Elvis veterans Will Hutchins, Arlene Charles, and Christopher Riordan were back, along with first timers Bill Bixby, Suzie Kaye, and Angelique Pettyjohn, amongst others.

In *Clambake*, Presley's Scott Heyward is fleeing his controlling oil baron father Duster Heyward (James Gregory) and switches identities with poor water ski instructor Tom Wilson (Will Hutchins) whom he has just met in a roadside diner. They both head on to the Shores Hotel in Miami Beach where Tom is the new water ski instructor. Scott becomes "Tom" and starts work there, while Tom becomes "Scott" and lives it up as a rich guy only out to have fun. The resort is populated by rich husband hunting gold diggers, including Dianne Carter (Fabares), Sally (Suzie Kaye), Gloria (Angelique Pettyjohn), and Olive (Charles). Dianne is looking for a rich husband and keeps rejecting "Tom," thinking he is not wealthy. All of them desire suave rich playboy James J. Jamison III (Bill Bixby) who becomes "Tom's" rival in and out of the water as he is the three-time champion of the upcoming Power Boat Regatta. Flighty Sally though hooks up with "Scott" while Dianne, drawn to "Tom," is attracted to money more and keeps choosing to spend time with Jamison instead. Deciding to knock Jamison off his pedestal, "Tom" teams up with local boat designer Sam Burton (Gary Merrill) and enters the race. Of course, he wins the regatta and Dianne.

"Elvis and I had the most fun on this," exclaimed Fabares. "We just literally laughed from beginning to end. I think Elvis was very happy at that time because he and Priscilla were planning to get married as soon as the film was finished. Nobody knew this then. Also it was our third film together, so I knew him and his guys really well. The man who directed this was a sweet, sweet man by the name of Arthur Nadel. It was one of those magical times the cast and crew just jelled."

This was the first film Elvis did with director Arthur Nadel. When asked if she noticed any working difference with Elvis and Nadel versus the other directors whose films she worked on, Arlene Charles replied, "No, Elvis was a true professional and very, very easy to work with. When he walked onto the set he knew his dialog and everything he was supposed to do. He was having fun and would kid around. Elvis just enjoyed being on the set, but I think he eventually got tired of it."

Elvis took "kidding around" to a whole new level on *Clambake*. He was unhappy about doing another nonsensical musical comedy that he gained weight and the studio demanded he lose the extra pounds. On the first day of filming, he slipped in his bathroom and hit his head. Diagnosed with a concussion, the picture was shut down for two weeks. When he finally returned to the shoot, he and his entourage acted up mightily to keep Elvis from being bored. Their antics here were sometimes out of control.

Arlene Charles finally graduated from background work to a supporting role as Olive in *Clambake*. She is one of the many beautiful gold diggers who descend on the resort looking to trap themselves a rich husband. Clad in a low-cut lime blouse and yellow slacks, the full-lipped Charles with the big blonde bouffant hairdo (no doubt hair sprayed to the max) is first introduced when Bill Bixby's rich playboy James Jamison accidentally flips an olive into her cleavage while enthralling a bevy of beauties with his stories about speed boat racing. After scoring a second bull's-eye straight down her blouse, he asks the gals if one of them would like to "squeeze in" with him while he tests out his new boat. Just as he is about to pick Shelley Fabares' salivating Dianne, Olive pipes up and coos, "Mr. Jamison, I just *love* to squeeze." He chooses the busty gal and they go off. On the lake, to Olive's dismay, Jamison is distracted by the skillful water skiing antics of Dianne who has purposely followed them.

Charles remembered filming the water skiing scene vividly. "This was so much fun. In one of his books, Sonny West wrote about a water fight that happened when we were doing process shots on the set. That was true. Bill Bixby (who was a super guy and very, very nice) and I are in a boat and Elvis is supposedly chasing us with Shelley Fabares water skiing. The crew would throw some water on us to make it look real. But then it got to be a little more water and then even more water. It ended up with Sonny, Elvis, Red West, and I chasing each other with water all over the sound stage. A klieg light blew up. My wardrobe and hair got soaked. I chased Elvis into his trailer and he locked himself in his bathroom. I yelled, 'Elvis, I am going to kill you! Get out here!' Then someone yelled, 'Charlie, here comes the Colonel. Cool it!' Everybody then scattered. Funny, but I never got to meet the Colonel, but I knew they were all scared of him.

"Elvis' guys trusted me so much that one day they allowed me to bring a Polaroid camera onto the set to take pictures," continued Arlene. "That was definitely a no-no. The Colonel would never allow it. But they asked me if I did would I promise not to publish them. I agreed. I have photos of Shelley Fabares and Sonny West together. Two are of Elvis and me, and many more. I was able to get photos that no one was ever allowed to do. That is how trusting they were of me. I felt really honored by that. It wasn't until Elvis passed away before I ever shared one of the photos of Elvis and me together."

Though of course Elvis' entourage would favor the starlets working on his pictures, they treated the male actors and dancers just as well. Recalling his interaction with Elvis' friends, Christopher Riordan remarked, "Joe Esposito, Red West, and Lance LeGault were all really nice guys. They were not sophisticated by any means and at first I think they probably looked at me and thought, 'Good God, who is this elegant creature?' I was rather elegant back then. And of course I thought, '*Who are these boys!?!*' But they were there to protect Elvis. My friend came to the *Clambake* set and watched a scene being filmed.

Elvis stepped out of the shot as he was supposed to and stood next to my friend standing on the side. Within three seconds, Elvis was surrounded by all his guys pushing my friend aside. That is what his guys were paid to do.

Publicity photo of Suzie Kaye, Elvis Presley, and Angelique Pettyjohn in *Clambake* (United Artist, 1967).

"It would get weird though when Col. Parker would show up because you could see it had an affect on Elvis, " continued Riordan. "I don't think he enjoyed having the Colonel around because the atmosphere on the set would change from easy going to stiff and business-like. Especially around this time, I think Elvis was aware that the Colonel was making decisions that he was really not in accordance with. But Elvis had a tremendous loyalty so he continued to let the Colonel manage him. It's a shame."

Riordan also reveals that it wasn't only Elvis and his entourage who were getting out of hand on *Clambake*. "Angelique Pettyjohn was very sweet but that girl would fuck a snake," quipped Christopher. "Seriously, Angelique just wanted to have sex with everybody. She came on to me and I said, 'Look, relax and find somebody else. I'm doing two movies at the same time *and I'm tired*!' I didn't think much of her but I was saddened when I learned that she past away relatively young from cancer."

For Shelley Fabares the movie has one gape that though minor embarrasses the actress to this day. She explained, "In those days almost all the actresses wore pantyhose with our bathing suits for two reasons—your legs look better and you didn't have to wear body make-up. Everybody always hated getting body make-up. It was so awful. You did it at five o'clock in the morning and you'd be freezing. Anyway, if you look closely at those movies most of the girls have very shiny legs because we all wore pantyhose.

"There is this one scene where my character hires Elvis to give her water ski lessons as a way to snag rich Bill Bixby," continued Fabares. "While we'll out on the water, Bill goes by in his boat and I try doing some very fancy moves to impress him. Well, we filmed this in a tank on a soundstage at Universal Studios. They had this big screen in back of us with wind and water machines. Elvis and I are on this barrel that is rolling back and forth in the water while people are holding on to our ski ropes. When Bill goes by on the screen, I put the rope underneath my foot like they do at Cypress Gardens and wave to him. When *Clambake* was released I went to see this with my sister and I said, 'Oh, my God!' In that scene as my foot comes up in front of the screen you can see the reinforced toe of my pantyhose. I couldn't believe it that they kept it in the film. For years I thought maybe I imagined it. A few years ago a friend gave me a copy for my birthday. Well, I wasn't imagining it. It's there—so much for my slim shiny legs."

Christopher Riordan thought this would be his last movie with Presley but he was personally asked to appear in his concert movie, *Elvis* (1968). He admitted, "I didn't want to do this since by that time I was getting some nice film roles. Elvis was very nervous about doing this because he'd been away [from live performing] for a little while. I think it just made him feel better to have some familiar people around him. I was talked too and felt it was the least I could do in return, but I really did try to hide myself on that one."

Arlene Charles would go on to work with Elvis one more time in *Speedway* (1968) but you would be hard pressed to find her. "Again I was just hired for the background," she stated. "My agent threw another fit about me doing this. And again he warned me and said, 'I will never be able to get you acting jobs if you keep this up.' You don't really even see me in this. I wish I had a really good speaking part in one of Elvis' movies. But I was up against actresses that had years of training like Ann-Margret who had the talent to also sing and dance. I was lucky and happy for what I was given."

Clambake, by the way, ends on both an intentional and unintentional funny note. While driving down the highway, "Tom" reveals his true identify and Dianne, realizing she snagged a multi-millionaire, faints dead away, while in the distance you can see "Florida's" beautiful snow covered mountain peaks.

Clambake was a big improvement over *Double Trouble* though the mainstream critics (the few that reviewed it), for the most part were not overly impressed, with comments such as "more of the same" (*Boston Globe*) and "unconvincing" (John Allen, *The Christian Science Monitor*). Even Kevin Thomas, of the *Los Angeles Times*, was not overly impressed and rightly remarked that the movie was "pleasant and unpretentious yet has a synthetic appearance. The starlets look lacquered, the sets plasticized and there's much reliance on process work."

Despite Thomas' spot-on criticisms, *Clambake* is a breezy, mindless entertaining affair that his undiscerning fans expected from the King. Director Arthur Nadel seemed to inject new life into the production numbers, though except for the title tune there are no standout songs. Once again Elvis and Shelley Fabares interact quite well with each other and buoy the film. They have an easy going banter and nice chemistry. Elvis is quite good as the unhappy rich boy and Fabares convincingly goes from an upfront money grubber to realizing that a man's character is more important than the size of his bank account. That is what makes the film's ending quite amusing when Dianne learns the truth. The *Boston Globe* thought she did a good job too and described Shelley as being "dark and graceful." *Clambake* was not a big moneymaker and its soundtrack peaked at #40 on the Billboard 200 chart.

The times they were a-changin', but the Elvis film remained the same. Even Hal Wallis knew the Elvis film had become passé by 1968. Perhaps, because of the negative reviews received for *Clambake* and declining box office take, Col. Parker finally relented and let Elvis stretch his acting muscles but not too much. He would go on to play a Native American again in the slapstick comedy *Stay Away, Joe* (1968); return to form as a singing racecar drive in the musical comedy *Speedway* (1968) opposite Nancy Sinatra as an IRS agent; a nudie photographer in the mod *Live a Little, Love a Little* (1968); a reformed gunslinger in the spaghetti western wannabe *Charro!* (1969); the manager of a traveling Chautauqua in the period musical *The Trouble with Girls* (1969); and finally a ghetto doctor in the drama *Change of Habit* (1969) before calling it quits on his movie career.

Reflecting on her feelings about working with Elvis, Shelley Fabares opined, "He was a wonderful person—kind, sweet, and funny. Doing those pictures with him were some of the happiest experiences I ever had, professionally or personally. Even if the movies weren't great—they were okay and perfect for what they were, at that time—the experience of doing them was extraordinary. And I feel blessed and lucky that I was able to work with him."

Nancy Czar last saw Elvis during his triumphant run in Las Vegas, but she felt that was his death sentence. She explained, "Even though I knew this man for years and worked with him on two movies, the first time I saw him perform live in concert was at the International Hotel in Vegas. My socks were blown off. He was phenomenal and looked incredible. For Elvis to get up to put on a show like that not once but sometimes twice a night must have been exhausting. Keeping up that pace coupled with his horrible eating habits took at toll on him. Nobody really monitored him. The Colonel was raking in the money so all he cared about was getting that check every week and a cut of the house to pay his gambling debts."

Nancy never saw Elvis after that so she was shielded from his decline. She echoes Shelley Fabares' sentiment about Elvis and will have the last word. "One of the great things about Elvis was that he would always say, 'When I die I wonder if people will remember me?' That is a direct quote from him and has to be the understatement of the century. I just sat there and looked at him and said, 'You have got to be kidding.'

"I have been living in Bangladesh and despite of all my accomplishments here I am known more for dating and working with Elvis Presley. Even in this poor rural country, Elvis lives. You don't know how many people want to meet me just because I knew him. I still can't get that through my head. When I am introduced to ambassadors of other countries, they say, 'She was not only our Consul-General but she was Elvis' girlfriend.' It amazes me the interest Elvis is still generating. He is still bigger than life and probably the most famous person who ever lived."

2. YAH! YAH! IT'S BEACH MOVIE STAR BOBBI SHAW

BLONDE BOMBSHELL BOBBI SHAW WAS known for her trademark saying, "Yah! Yah!" clad in her trademark fur bikini in a series of American International Pictures' beach party movies beginning with *Pajama Party* (1964) where she was the sexy foil to comedian Buster Keaton. She made such a huge impression and became an instant fan favorite that AIP paired her again with Keaton in *Beach Blanket Bingo* (1965) and *How to Stuff a Wild Bikini* (1965). The studio let her stretch her acting chops to great amusement in bigger roles in *Ski Party* (1965) as an amorous Swedish ski instructor and *The Ghost in the Invisible Bikini* (1966) as a conniving carnival worker. Once the tide rolled out for the beach movies, Shaw began doing improvisation and then teaching.

Bobbi Shaw was born Barbara Shaw in New York City but grew up outside of Philadelphia. She attended the University of Miami in Florida studying psychology. While there she entered and won the Miss Miami beauty pageant. It has also been reported that she made her film debut in a bit role, as Miss Miami Rendezvous, in *Passion Holiday* (1963) about four young women fleeing broken relationships who run into each other in Miami and decide to vacation together. Or did she? Bobbi insists she did not make this movie. She has absolutely no recollection of it "unless I was sleeping when I did it." Perhaps because the character is a beauty queen, Shaw was mistakenly credited or the producers used a clip of her from another source.

Newly married, Bobbi Shaw left Florida and, with her husband in tow, headed to California where she settled in Malibu. She met a producer named Monty Proscia. Shaw recalled, "He wanted me to come to Las Vegas to appear in his show [*High Button Shoes*]. I said, 'I don't sing or dance.' He replied, 'You are so beautiful you don't have to do either.'" Standing 5'5" with measurements of 38-23-35, it is no surprise the blue-eyed blonde awed the producer. "That was nice so I ended up going to Vegas," continued the actress. "It was a lot of fun. Dick Shawn was the star and he was just amazing." Bobbi stayed in Vegas for a second show *Anything Goes*.

Publicity photo of Bobbi Shaw in *Pajama Party* (AIP, 1964). *Courtesy of Bobbi Chance*

When she returned to Los Angeles, a family friend told her to look up agent Jack Gilardi (who would soon wed Annette Funicello). "I went to see Jack and he said there was an audition for a Swedish girl in this movie at American International Pictures," said Bobbi. "He sent me over. I didn't even know what an audition was. I met with the director Don Weis who asked me if I could do a Swedish accent. I answered, 'Of course I can.' And I just winged it and did a ten minute monologue with a Swedish accent. I didn't know how to end so I just walked out of his office and left. They couldn't find me. I got in my car and drove home. The next day Jack called me and told me that I got the role."

The role was that of Helga and the movie was *Pajama Party* (1964). It was the third AIP beach movie after the studio scored a box office bulls eye with *Beach Party* in 1963 starring Frankie Avalon and Annette Funicello. It was also the first of their movies not to pair the duo. Tommy Kirk was Annette's leading man instead, though Avalon does make a cameo appearance as a Martian. The regular cast of beach boys and girls are here (including Jody McCrea, Donna Loren, Candy Johnson, Mike Nader, Patti Chandler, Mary Hughes, Ed Garner, etc.) but they are joined by a cadre of young dancers (Toni Basil, Lori Williams, and Teri Garr, amongst them) brought in by first time beach party choreographer David Winters.

In this science fiction/beach party movie hybrid, Tommy Kirk plays a Martian named Go-Go who comes to Earth to set in motion an invasion, but gets mixed up with wealthy kindly shop owner Aunt Wendy (Elsa Lanchester), her not-too-bright beach volleyball-playing nephew Big Lunk (Jody McCrea), his long-suffering girlfriend Connie (Annette Funicello), and accident-prone biker gang leader Eric Von Zipper (Harvey Lembeck). Shaw's fur bikini-clad Helga is a Swedish knockout who, along with Buster Keaton as Chief Rotten Eagle, are recruited by con man Jesse White to help fleece Aunt Wendy. The Chief's job is to make sure that Helga is able to entice information from Big Lunk regarding the location of his aunt's safe. Problem is Helga doesn't speak English and answers every question with "Yah! Yah!" And then she actually falls for the big lunk.

Arriving at the studio, Bobbi Shaw was sent to wardrobe and was told to don this fur-trimmed gold lame bikini. A true knockout when she put it on, it not surprisingly became her signature look and she wore it in two movies to follow. Bobbi quipped laughing, "I burned it in effigy when I left AIP. I wish I hadn't. It is probably worth a lot of money now!"

Bobbi Shaw met on-screen love interest Jody McCrea on the set just before they were to film a kissing scene. She remembered, "It was in a car that was bouncing up and down. I was sitting on Jody's lap. It was so embarrassing because he was getting hard. I had to move down his thigh a bit and asked, 'Does this car have to bounce like that?'" That's really putting the wood in Hollywood.

"Jody McCrea was like a big teddy bear to me.," continued Shaw "Everybody came on to me, It was part of the territory. I was very blessed to be born voluptuous and beautiful. Jody would look at me though with hungry eyes but knew he hadn't a chance. That was the end of it. He really was a sweet guy."

When asked if she was nervous to work with actors with a lot more comedy experience such as Jesse White and Buster Keaton, Shaw replied, "Being nervous or jealous are two emotions I am proud to say that I don't possess. I don't remember much about Jesse White. I was never in conversation with him at all."

Buster Keaton was a whole other story. Of the entire cast, it was he that the newcomer truly bonded with. The pair immediately hit it off and became fast friends. "Buster Keaton to me was a really cool old man," said Bobbi. "He was fabulous. I didn't know at the time that he was a comic genius and known for his comedic brilliance even greater than Charlie Chaplin. I was only about eighteen at the time. To me he was just a sweet darling old man. We would sit in his dressing room and he would teach me comedy timing. I think it was magic between us. They were grooming me to be his dumb blonde foil but I had a natural gift for comedy. I think Buster really appreciated that. He showed me double entendres and how to look at each other without saying anything. I think he liked that I was so willing to learn from him.

"His wife would come by for lunch with his food on a tray and we would eat together every day," continued Bobbi fondly. "One day I asked Buster why his wife called him sir. She'd say, 'Sir, here's your lunch.' He was so funny and replied, 'I trained her very well.' He never ever smiled—not on camera and not even in his dressing room. I couldn't handle it any more and said to him, 'Buster, how come you don't smile?' He smiled and he was missing two teeth. We laughed our heads off. I don't think anybody ever knew that about him. I remember that was such a joyful day with him."

According to one of the film's press releases Shaw had "to be provocative while being funny and had to perfect the Keaton deadpan style in order to blend in with his brand of comedy." And blend they did. They provide the film's comedic high points.

Bungling duo Bobbi Shaw and Buster Keaton in *Pajama Party* (AIP, 1964). *Courtesy of Bobbi Chance*

Bobbi Shaw first appears on screen in *Pajama Party* as an exhausted Helga, wearing a tight white low-cut dress, lugs her heavy suitcases to meet with Chief Rotten Eagle. Noticing she needs a bath to cool off, the Chief mistakenly takes her into Aunt Wendy's house thinking it is J. Sinister Hulk's. One scene in particular is very funny with Helga taking a bubble bath and interrupted by Tommy Kirk's swim trunk clad Go-Go. Grabbing a red towel and draping it around her, she runs screaming from the bathroom and down the stairs. Chief Rotten Eagle is standing at the bottom of the staircase and he gets a face full of Helga's cleavage as she continues to yell. Both go running out of the house chased by Go-Go trying to return Helga's wash brush.

Hulk next sends the inept duo to Aunt Wendy's dress shop to buy Helga new clothes and for her to meet Big Lunk who wears a "goofy broad red baseball cap." While Helga is fitted for a new wardrobe, Rotten Eagle gets into a perfume fight with Luree Holme's counter girl. They are interrupted when Connie (Annette Funicello) and Go-Go wearing Big Lunk's cap enter. Rotten Eagle sees them and says, "goofy broad and red baseball cap." He immediately finds Helga wearing a mink-trimmed gold lame bikini and tells her red baseball cap guy is out front. She begins planting kisses on Eric Von Zipper (Harvey Lembeck) who put the cap on and then lets him fall to the ground when Rotten Eagle tells her wrong Paleface. She begins kissing Go-Go and drops him when Big Lunk (Jody McCrea) arrives, grabs his cap, and leaves. Helga and Rotten Eagle jump into his convertible and drive off with Von Zipper's motorcycle gang in pursuit. Lots of process shots of Helga kissing Big Lunk as he tries to drive the bouncing car with Rotten Eagle in the backseat. These were Bobbi Shaw's first scenes with an excited Jody McCrea.

Later, wearing a beautiful blue tight cocktail dress, Helga and Big Lunk are on an official date. Hulk has taught the Swedish bombshell some English and when she and Big Lunk are necking in his car, Helga asks very slowly, "Tell me do you know where your Aunt keeps her money?" Then pointing to a broach hiding a tape recorder pinned to her cleavage, she says, "Speak in here slowly." Big Lunk obeys, but he has no idea only that it is somewhere in her house. Later Hulk throws a pajama party for the teens with Aunt Wendy as chaperone at his abode so he can search her empty house for the hidden money. After a pool fight melee started by Eric Von Zipper and his gang invited by Hulk's inept flunky Fleegle (Ben Lessy), Go-Go telepathically reads Helga's mind and she reveals what J. Sinister Hulk, Fleegle, and Chief Rotten Eagle are up to. At Aunt Wendy's house, Go-Go sends the scheming trio to planet Mars. The movie ends with Helga and Big Lunk united as a couple as is Go-Go and Connie.

Tommy Kirk, Annette Funicello, Bobbi Shaw, and
Jody McCrea in *Pajama Party* (AIP, 1964). *Courtesy of Bobbi Chance*

Bobbi Shaw succeeded admirably as the busty newcomer was an immediate hit with the fans and the critics. *Variety* raved, "Bobbi Shaw as a non-English-speaking Swede but who knows all the holds is a standout as the sexy lure…" Though she won over the public and her male co-stars, she did not hit it off with Annette Funicello. She explained, "I had no rapport with Annette. She was always kind of standoffish. I was always friendly towards her and I felt she was jealous of me. It was like a '*Who's this*?' type of deal. Earl Wilson came to the set to report on the movie and paid more attention to me than her. After that there was always a bit of an edge. I still tried to be friendly because we had to work together."

There was one female co-star, however, that took a particular shine to the naïve girl. "Elsa Lanchester was *overly* friendly to me," she said laughing. "Buster protected me like an uncle and said something to her. She was then just very polite." Though married to Charles Laughton for years, Lanchester was rumored to be a Lesbian though she never publicly admitted it.

Bobbi Shaw and Susan Hart, who also made her AIP debut performance in *Pajama*

Party, were the first two signed by studio heads James H. Nicholson and Samuel Z. Arkoff for their Starburst of Youth program. Shaw said, "I was put under contract and they were actually grooming me to literally be the next Marilyn Monroe. They wanted me to keep working with Buster Keaton, which was an amazing experience. They built me up to be special and not like the other beach girls. They really were aiming for me to be the next teenage movie star. I was very grateful for that and thought it was really terrific."

Regarding her bosses with whom she had much contact, Bobbi opined, "James Nicholson was very soft-spoken and well-mannered. Arkoff always had a cigar in his mouth and was very gruff. I got along fine with both of them."

Impressed with the laughs that they brought to *Pajama Party*, AIP paired Keaton and Shaw again in *Beach Blanket Bingo* (1965). But this time they were only used as a running gag as Keaton's dirty old man could be seen chasing the nubile bikini-clad bombshell (Yah! Yah!) around the beach and the airport where the beach gang takes up skydiving or dancing together at the local teen club. The duo also turns up during the film's end credits where they are dancing once again.

Earl Wilson played himself in *Beach Blanket Bingo* and bemoaned in one of his columns how the movie was shot in December 1964 on the beach in damp, chilly weather. Shaw told the columnist how much she adored working with Buster Keaton. Per Wilson, the comedian responded, "'I played an Indian in the other picture, *Pajama Party*. She played my squab.' That's what he said, 'squab.'"

Though most *Beach Party* movie fans feel *Beach Blanket Bingo* is the best of the genre, Bobbi was disappointed. "Buster and I were part of *Beach Blanket Bingo* from the beginning but I really feel that they did not use us the way they should have. Look at his genius talent and they just had us running around."

On this movie, she also began to see more clearly the division between the cast once the director yelled cut. Bobbi echoes what a number of her co-stars have said in the past. "It is true that Harvey Lembeck and his guys stuck together and all the beach girls and boys stuck together. Annette was always on her own and I hung out with either Buster or by myself. There was a little tension between the beach girls and me because I was given more attention. They were treating me like a star the same way as Annette. The beach girls were there for the past three or four movies and it was sort of like, 'Who is this girl and who does she think she is?' That is the way it felt to me. But it was okay. I had that all my life and it didn't matter. I was always friendly and walked away."

Sans Buster Keaton, Bobbi Shaw was given another big co-starring role as a Swedish ski instructor enamored of Frankie Avalon in *Ski Party* (1965) a sort of teenage *Some Like It Hot* on the ski slopes co-starring Dwayne Hickman and Deborah Walley. "Frankie and Dwayne were hysterical in drag and were like little kids," remarked Bobbi with a laugh. "It was fantasy time. I could not keep a straight face since they were having so much fun with it. Frankie Avalon and I became buddies. He was the sweetest guy."

Perhaps impressed with the success of *The Girls on the Beach* and *Beach Ball*, AIP recruited Gene Corman to produce their first beach party in the snow. He hired Alan Rafkin to direct his first movie after working steadily in television since 1962. The screenplay was by Emmy-nominated TV writer Robert Kaufman whose first movie this was as well. "I don't remember much about Alan Rafkin but I do remember Robert Kaufman. He was on location and I remember talking with him. He was fabulous and very funny—what a terrific sophisticated sense of humor he had."

Though the AIP cadre of actors were present (including Mike Nader, Salli Sachse, Patti Chandler, and Luree Holmes), Corman cast outsiders including Aron Kincaid, Yvonne Craig, Steve Rogers, and Mikki Jamison. Happily for all, everybody seemed to mesh well while filming on location. "We really had a great time up there," said Bobbi. "It was family-like at that point for me. It was very cool working with everybody."

In *Ski Party*, Todd Armstrong (Avalon) and Craig Gamble (Dwayne Hickman) are two average college guys who can't seem to score with pretty coeds Linda (Deborah Walley) and Barbara (Yvonne Craig) unlike suave ladies man Freddie Carter (Aron Kincaid). When they overhear the lothario telling his overly amorous date that she'll get another chance to be alone with him on the upcoming ski trip, the guys, despite their ignorance of skiing, decide to go along.

The ski lodge is run by persnickety hotel manager Mr. Pevney (Robert Q. Lewis) and his star employee is Bobbi Shaw's curvy, blonde Swedish ski instructor Nita ("This was such a fun part to play."). When not on the slopes, Nita likes to glide through the hotel's hallways wearing only a bathing suit to the delight of the male guests. Wanting out of the advanced ski lessons arranged for all the guys, novice skiers Todd and Craig come up with the brainstorm to masquerade as English lasses, Jane and Nora, so they can be instructed by Nita. Taking her aside, the boys ask Nita what she makes of American girls who they say just "play games, games, games" with men's hearts. Nita replies matter-of-factly, "In Sweden it's very different. In Stockholm when a boy and girl meet and they like each other—*no* games and *very little* talk."

During their first lesson, Jane loses control and careens down the hill with Linda in pursuit while Nora skis into Freddie who becomes instantly smitten with the feisty lass. After a sleigh ride together, where Todd and Craig once again strike out with Linda and Barbara, the girls have a slumber party and invite Jane and Nora.

Back on the ski slopes, Todd gets a notion to abandon the plan of becoming ace skiers to impress the girls and instead to make them jealous by dating Nita and her friend Helga. Pretending to be a reporter for the school newspaper, Todd interviews Nita within earshot of a jealous Linda. Todd then makes a date with Nita to meet by the fireplace in the lodge. Sitting around the roaring fire, Freddie moons over the missing Nora, Barbara accuses Craig of seeing Nora behind her back, and Linda sulks while Todd plays cards with his Swedish bombshell. Then out of the blue James Brown and the Famous Flames burst in as the ski patrol and perform "I Got You (I Feel Good)" before going back outdoors. After berating Todd and Craig for their lack of skiing ability, Freddie challenges Todd to enter the next day's ski jump contest. Todd balks but Nita persuades him to change his mind with promises of winning her as well.

Todd straps on a helium tank to give him lift in the jump but it sends him out of control. Craig shoots him down and Todd suffers a broken leg. Despite his injury, a determined Todd wobbles over to Nita's where he is extremely disappointed when the buxom Swede decides that she wants to be treated like her chaste American counterparts with lots of talk and maybe a kiss on the cheek. After being rejected by Barbara, Craig as Nora makes a date with Freddie. He returns and announces to Todd that they are pinned. Fearing for the sanity of his pal, Todd is able to convince Craig to return with him to Malibu where everyone is reunited on the sands except for a heartbroken Freddie who heads out to sea seeking his lost Nora.

The scene where James Brown and the Flames perform is still a standout for all today including for Bobbi. "I absolutely remember filming with James Brown. That was one of my favorite moments because I love music and he was so amazing. It was unbelievable to watch him sing "I Feel Good." We talked and he was just fabulous. What was weird though was that there were no black people in the movie except him and his group. These movies spoke to teenagers so I think having them included helped change attitudes a bit. When they made the new James Brown movie [Get on Up starring Chadwick Boseman] they used a clip of it in the movie. That was so cool and such an honor."

Bobbi Shaw and Frankie Avalon in *Ski Party* (AIP, 1965).

Though the main stream critics ridiculed these movies (the critic in the *Boston Globe* said they are "designed for immature escapists"), *Ski Party* ranks high in the genre. It stands out from the rest of the AIP beach party movies not only because of the change in locale but because of the superior production values. Credit must go to producer Gene Corman and his crew. The film is expertly filmed on location with some awesome ski shots. Alan Rafkin also does a first-rate job of directing and keeps the action moving. He brings some originality in terms of camera angles to the musical numbers as well. Frankie Avalon and Dwayne Hickman are well paired as the wisecracking losers-in-love Todd and Craig and are very believable and amusing as the peppery English lasses, Jane and Nora. But it is the smarmy charm of Aron Kincaid as the pompous Freddie who flips for a guy in drag who steals the movie. Bobbi Shaw does really well too. Trading in her mink bikini for tight ski clothes, she is still a knockout (*Yah! Yah!*). Her funniest scene is at the end when she decides to give up on the Swedish way of free love and adopt the prudish ways of American girls much to an amorous Avalon's dismay.

As AIP did with all of its beach movies, they sent cast members out on tour together to promote the movie and to drum up interest. Accompanying Frankie Avalon, Aron Kincaid, and Mary Hughes, this promotional tour for *Ski Party* was one she never forgot. Shaw explained, "We did a nineteen city tour in thirteen days. They really got their money's worth from all of the actors. I don't think rock 'n' roll bands do that much so quickly. We'd go from one city to another doing interviews and were whisked in and out. I had a tremendous experience happen to me while we were in Texas. I think it was Austin. It kind of blew my mind a bit. We had to do a television interview and answer the same questions they asked in the other thirteen cities. I noticed that in the TV studio the bathrooms and water fountains were marked 'White only.' It just freaked me out.

"During the television interview they asked me how I liked wearing my gold and mink bikini," continued Bobbi. "I replied, 'It was very nice and a lot of fun. Can I ask you a question? How come it says 'White only'? How come you have that here at your studio? What is that all about?' The next thing I know they go to a quick commercial break and I am rushed off the stage into the limousine. I wanted to use my platform to say something but that was not part of the beach party movies. It was just a little bit before its time to stand up for the right thing."

On a more lighthearted note, to take advantage of the popularity of its roster of players, AIP published a magazine called *The Beach Girls* whose cover featured lucky guy Aron Kincaid surrounded by Annette Funicello, Deborah Walley, Bobbi Shaw, and Salli Sachse. It also contained many fabricated stories to perk the interested of the beach party fans. "That magazine had a story of Aron and I having a wild affair," revealed Bobbi. "That was one of my favorite things to read about myself. I'd pick up a newspaper and read in Earl Wilson's column who I was going out with. One time he wrote 'Beach Party star Bobbi Shaw is now dating Tab Hunter.' I didn't even know who he was. Things like that still happen." Shaw was also made TV guest appearances as herself. One that stands out was a local Southern California special titled *The Beatles Are Back* hosted by Sam Riddle that aired in late August 1965. The popular foursome was only shown in a segment taped in London, while Bobbi joined a number of American pop acts in LA.

For her next two AIP movies, it was back to small parts for Bobbi Shaw. In *How to Stuff a Wild Bikini* (1965), she was reunited with Buster Keaton. Hidden under a long black curvy wig, she played a sexy native girl to his potion-mixing witch doctor on a South Seas island where naval reserve officer Frankie Avalon is stationed. This role (which she found to be "really silly") required nothing more than for Shaw to look foxy in a sarong. She traded that for a W.A.F. uniform in the juvenile military service comedy *Sergeant Dead-*

head (1965) where Frankie played an inept astronaut who gets accidentally launched into space with a chimpanzee and on return has switched brain capacities.

Publicity photo of Bobbi Shaw as a Native Girl in *How to Stuff a Wild Bikini* (AIP, 1965).

It was at this point that Bobbi Shaw's time at AIP was becoming not so pleasant. She elaborated, "I really had it and didn't want to do these movies any more. I had a difficult time with a guy in the publicity department who made advances on me. I turned him down and he started saying untrue things about me. It really hurt my feelings and I just didn't want to be around that any more. I was somewhat naïve coming from a sheltered family with high integrity and morals. I was taught to treat everybody the way you wanted to be treated. This was the ugly side of Hollywood with someone coming on really strong."

Bobbi Shaw had one more movie to do for AIP and at least she got to go out with another nice size supporting role without having to do the Swedish accent and wearing the mink bikini. The movie was *The Ghost in the Invisible Bikini* and it was a very troubled production. It began life as *Pajama Party in a Haunted House*, the title of the original screenplay. It was re-titled *Slumber Party in a Haunted House* and then AIP settled on *Bikini Party in a Haunted House* during production. With the box office receipts declining for their beach movies in 1965, this film was AIP's idea to revive the genre. However, Frankie and Annette were no where to be found.

As the movie was to originally open, crooked attorney Reginald Ripper (Basil Rathbone) has summoned the recently departed Hiram Stokely's three heirs—nice guy Chuck Philips (Tommy Kirk), independent-minded redhead Lili Morton (Deborah Walley), and the feisty, older Myrtle Forbush (Patsy Kelly)—to Stokely's creepy mansion for the reading of his will, which reveals that his fortune is hidden somewhere in the house. Myrtle's nephew Bobby (Aron Kincaid), his girlfriend Vicki (Nancy Sinatra), and a gaggle of surfer boys and bikini girls crash the estate and frolic by the pool.

Ripper hatches a scheme to off the heirs with the help from his curvaceous but nearsighted daughter Sinistra (Quinn O'Hara), J. Sinister Hulk (Jesse White), and carnival performers Princess Yolanda (Shaw), her Indian partner Chicken Feather (Benny Rubin filling in for an ill Buster Keaton), and Monstro the gorilla. Unexpected accomplices are Eric Von Zipper (Harvey Lembeck) and his motorcycle gang who encounter Yolanda on the road and follow her to the mansion.

The movie features a search for the hidden fortune, lots of musical numbers around the swimming pool, a hatchet-throwing mummy, and lots of inept attempts to kill the heirs. At the film's end, the rightful folks inherit the fortune, and the movie concludes with the surfer crowd having a pajama party in the chamber of horrors.

Though Bobbi Shaw worked with Harvey Lembeck before, in this movie they spent a lot of time together. "Harvey was amazing and always a joy," exclaimed Bobbi. "You could tell he just loved what he did waking up in the morning and showing up on the set. We always had fun. After we finished making the beach party movies, Harvey started a comedy group and asked me to join. I didn't, but he was always sweet and friendly. His wonderful son Michael directed *Friends* for many years and we are buddies."

She also was enamored with some of the older cast members. "Benny Rubin was adorable and so sweet. Basil Rathbone was a very polite gentleman. I happened to love his Sherlock Holmes movies so meeting Basil was a big deal for me. We talked a little bit. Then there was Boris Karloff. We all had lunch together one day. We spoke briefly. Remember I was very, very young and they were older men so there was really nothing much in common. But it was very cool that AIP was able to get these actors into the movie."

When the picture was completed and delivered to AIP, it was deemed un-releasable. It was then decided to add Susan Hart as an invisible bikinied ghost who is edited into already completed scenes to thwart Ripper's attempts to get the fortune and Boris Karloff as the deceased. Their scenes together were set in a crypt and book ended the movie. This knocked out an elaborate production number filmed with the entire cast (led by Aron Kincaid and Piccola Pupa) singing the then title song "Bikini Party in a Haunted House." The name and the scene were cut and the movie was re-titled *The Ghost in the Invisible Bikini*.

Bobbi's first scene has her Princess Yolanda, clad in a light blue harem-style costume, quarreling with Chicken Feather as they are driving their truck. The Indian is hopelessly lost and turns to Yolanda for help. She quips, "Don't look at me. You're supposed to me the guide, Chicken Fat." They soon run into Erich Von Zipper and his biker gang when their truck and Von Zipper careen into a lake. Yolanda swims over to the drowning Von Zipper and pulls him to shore. The bungling duo finally arrive at the mansion and Yolanda is immediately smitten with Reginald Ripper. She purrs, "Mr. Ripper, I assumed as much. You're like a giant among men—shrewd, forceful, dominating. And *rotten* too! I think we are like birds of a feather—vultures that is!" Unbeknownst to Yolanda, she was secretly followed by an infatuated Von Zipper and his gang.

Ripper expects Yolanda and partners to knock off the heirs before the reading of the will. They fail, due to interference from Cecily the ghost, and a codicil to the will reveals that Stokely's fortune is hidden in the house with the clue "look to the Prince of Love." An irate Ripper finds Yolanda and crew stuffing their faces ("You can't expect us to do what we have to do to do on an empty stomach," she says in protest). He then orders them to find the loot. Once they realize the house is really haunted, Chicken Feather and Yolanda want to hightail it out of there but a gun-toting Ripper won't let them leave. Soon after, Yolanda's gorilla escapes from his cage just as everybody goes on a wild melee of a hunt for the $1 million. Monstro carries off Lily to Stokely's chamber of horrors in the cellar where all the factions converge. Ripper and gang get to Lily first. Bound and gagged, she is tied to a tree headed for a buzz saw. A fight breaks out and feisty Myrtle decks both Yolanda and Hulk. During the ruckus, Sinistra finds the Prince of Love who shoots an arrow releasing the fortune. Just as Ripper pulls a shotgun on everyone, Cecily the plugs the barrel and there is an explosion killing Ripper. She is then shown back with Stokely explaining that the heirs got the deserved money. Obviously the actual scenes that followed were excised and the film finishes with the beach boys and girls shimmying in the chamber of horrors to an instrumental version of "Geronimo" by the Bobby Fuller Four.

Financially the least successful of the *Beach Party* movies, *The Ghost in the Invisible Bikini* put the nail in the coffin for the genre at AIP. After six movies, seven if counting *Ski Party*, the beach films was getting tired and out of step with the times. Though AIP tried to pump life into it by shifting the locale to a creepy mansion and mixing aspects of the beach party formula with the horror genre and populating it with fresh faces, it was not what young audiences were interested in.

The Ghost in the Invisible Bikini was Bobbi Shaw's final film for AIP but not for the decade. That was the hippie comedy *I Love You Alice B Toklas* (1968) where she has nothing more than a walk-on as a bridesmaid at both of Joyce Van Patten's aborted weddings to Peter Sellers. "Paul Mazursky [the film's director] hired me for a week," she recalled. "We shot my scene, but I think it got cut. [It did.] The best part of doing this was having lunch everyday with Peter Sellers in his dressing room. There were three or four of us that would eat with him. He was so amazing and wrote a letter of recommendation for me to study acting at the Royal Academy in London. I would say to him, 'Peter you have so many personalities. I have lunch with a different one every day. Which is the real Peter?' He replied, 'They're all of me.'"

Bobbi Shaw shifted her focus away from screen acting for a few years when she joined Los Angeles' first improvisational comedy troupe The Session. "One of the producers of the beach party movies appreciated my comedy chops," stated the actress. "He told me that

Rob Reiner and Joey Bishop's son Larry were putting together an improvisation group. I met with Rob and Richard Dreyfuss. They hired me on the spot. This was one of the first improve groups and the forerunner to *Saturday Night Live* and others. We set the pace for it and it was well ahead of its time. We were together for almost three years. We performed at the Playboy Club until they kicked us out and then we launched our own club on Sunset Boulevard. On opening night we had Lucille Ball and Carl Reiner in the audience. We were terrific and stayed there for about a year."

Bobbi Shaw returned to moviemaking in the seventies playing colorfully named characters beginning with her role as "Twila Zornes" in the obscure rural shoot-em-up *The Devil and Leroy Bassett* (1973). She then co-starred with the Carradine brothers (David, Keith, and Robert) in *You and Me* (1975) playing a character named "Wynona." In *Pipe Dreams* (1976) Shaw was cast as "Slimy Sue" a hooker peddling her flesh up in Alaska who befriends newcomer Gladys Knight as a woman escaping an abusive relationship. Of the three, *You and Me* is the one she is most proud of because "It was a wonderful film. This was a tremendous experiment because David Carradine [who starred and directed] sort of carried the torch of John Cassavetes with this independent film. This was one of three movies [*Americana* and *Mata Hari* are the other two] he made at the time. It co-starred Barbara Hershey, Robert Carradine, and Gary Busey. I played the girl David falls in love with but he can't stay with her because he is wanted by the police. David used his own money. He was shooting *Kung Fu* at the time and he was editing the movie while working on the series." *You and Me* received a very limited release in 1975 and is ripe for rediscovery on DVD.

Today, Bobbie Shaw Chance is one of Southern California's most respected acting coaches and runs Expressions Unlimited in Los Angeles. Her students have included Brad Pitt, Jennifer Aniston, Drew Barrymore, and Giovanni Ribisi. In 2015 Expressions Unlimited was chosen in to be the first American acting school invited by China to work with some of that country's top actors. The following year Bobbi received the well-deserved Golden Halo Lifetime Achievement Award from the Southern California Motion Picture Council for her contributions to show business.

3. ARLENE CHARLES: THE EPITOME OF THE BIKINI-CLAD STARLET

A STATUESQUE BLONDE WITH A very curvy figure, Arlene Charles was the epitome of the bikini-clad actresses used to decorate the background of many a sixties drive-in movie. She appeared in beach party movies, spy spoofs, and Elvis Presley musicals working four times with the King from a walk-on in *Paradise, Hawaiian Style*, to dancing in the background in *Spinout* and *Speedway*, to a supporting role in *Clambake*. Her biggest role was in the comedy adventure *I Sailed to Tahiti with an All Girl Crew* as one of skipper Gardner McKay's scantily-clad shipmates.

Arlene Charles was born Arlene Gorek in Merrillville, Indiana. She became interested in acting and joined the Gary Players in Gary, Indiana. She appeared in their production of *The Women* playing Crystal Allen made famous by Joan Crawford in the movie version. "I had to take a bath on stage, which was fun, but wore a bikini which nobody could see," she recalled. "For my one and only performance that year I won an award and was quite surprised." This was just the start of many bikini roles to come.

Arlene was also a beauty queen being crowned Miss Junior Indiana in 1961 for the Junior Miss America pageant. Since she was only a high school junior and not a senior as required, she could not fulfill her duties so the First Runner-up got to represent the state in the national competition. Arlene was first runner-up as Miss Indiana for the Miss America pageant, but then in 1964 she was crowned Miss Indiana for the lesser known Miss International Beauty Pageant. Shortly thereafter, she hung up her sashes and crowns and relocated to Hollywood—with her horse! "I only had $300 in my pocket," revealed Arlene laughing. "My father about had a heart attack. He thought I was out of my mind. I told him the horse would keep me grounded and will force me to work harder because of the expense."

Standing 5-foot-9 and sporting a shapely figure measuring 36-25-36, it is not surprising that Arlene quickly snagged an agent. However, he did not think Arlene Gorek would look good on a marquee. Holding firm on keeping her first name, her surname Charles morphed from her nickname Charlie that she got from her coworkers at her job in a Chicago jewelry company that she took after graduating from high school. While working there Hugh Hefner asked her to pose for his *Playboy* magazine but she declined the offer.

The newly crowned Arlene Charles made her film debut in *Winter a-Go-Go* (1965) playing Arlene one of the scantily-clad Winter a-Go-Go girls who are hired by ski lodge owners Jeff (William Wellman, Jr.) and Danny (James Stacy) to waitress and entertain their young skiing clientele. Just as the lodge opens to a full house of guests, Arlene, clad in tight ski pants and fur hat, saunters up to Jeff to congratulate him. She then coos, "I am glad I am working days. They tell me the nights up here are pretty cold." Jeff catches her come on and replies, "Well I never been taken for a foot warmer. You might have a good idea. We'll see how it goes." Arlene then says, "Just remember, all work and no play makes a dull day." He retorts, "Or night." Later, her Arlene is gossiping with the other girls in their room about mantrap Janine (Jill Donohue) when Danny makes his obligatory late night visit once again breaking the rules of fraternizing with the opposite sex in the bedrooms. This leads to a corny scene of the pajama-clad gang having a "Hip Square Dance" sung by James Stacy.

Charles next did two movies for American International Pictures. She played a gold lame bikini-clad robot in the spy spoof *Dr. Goldfoot and the Bikini Machine* (1965) starring Vincent Price as the mad doctor who plans on taking over the world by having his army of Fembots marry and then slay wealthy men but whose plans are bungled do to naïve secret agent Frankie Avalon. As No. 9, Charles' assignment was to lay her claws into a Swiss banker killing him for his dough. She then did a cameo as a Marie Antoinette wax figure in *The Ghost in the Invisible Bikini* (1966) and then faded into the background (Arlene quipped, "$350 a week fine by me!"). For both movies, she was hired to do promotion posing, bikini-clad naturally, for many cheesecake photos and traveling across the U.S. on publicity junkets.

Publicity photo of Arlene Charles in *Dr. Goldfoot
and the Bikini Machine* (AIP, 1965).

After another bit role as a beatnik in the Jerry Lewis comedy *Three on a Couch* (1966), more screen time came Arlene Charles' way when cast as country music star Ferlin Husky's little sister in the low-rent musical *Las Vegas Hillbillys* (1966) infamous for being the battle of the blonde bombshells Jayne Mansfield and Mamie Van Doren whose contract prevented them from being in the same scene together. Next, Charles could be seen but not heard as a "friendly" gal in the western *Alvarez Kelly* (1966). Her lack of lines or screen time did not stop the studio from publicizing the film with photos of Charles and co-star Jan Watson with full cleavage prominently displayed. Arlene remarked, "The studios really pushed sex in those days." *The Oscar* (1966) didn't give her much to do either other than to lounge poolside in a bathing suit.

Publicity photo of Arlene Charles in *Winter a-Go-Go*
(Columbia, 1965). *Courtesy of Arlene Charles*

Next came four films with Elvis Presley. First was a blink-or-you'll-miss-her walk-on in a scene with Presley at a heliport in *Paradise, Hawaiian Style*. This was followed by doing background work in *Spinout* (1966) and finally a supporting role with lines to speak as gold digger Olive in *Clambake* (1967). Arlene was then reduced to no more than an extra for her last Elvis movie *Speedway* (1968). Pushed back into the background, you'd be hard pressed to pick her out from all the gyrating go-go dancers at the club where racecar driver Elvis hangs out while trying to avoid mini-skirted tax collector Nancy Sinatra..

During this period, television offered Charles more of a chance to shine in episodes of *Love on a Rooftop, The Wild Wild West,* and *The Flying Nun*. Rarely receiving credit, which was the unfortunate norm for the sixties, Arlene was the comic foil in skits on many variety shows including *The Bob Hope Show*, *The Red Skelton Hour*, *The Jonathan Winters Show*, *The Steve Allen Show*, and *The Tonight Show Starring Johnny Carson*.

Between doing movies and TV, Arlene Charles was a frequent guest on Johnny Grant's radio program on Armed Forces Radio. This was broadcast to the GIs in Vietnam. Arlene was surprised by the attention she garnered based on the amount of letters she received from servicemen stationed there. She began accompanying Grant on his visits to VA hospitals in San Francisco and then on one of his Vietnam tours.

Back on the big screen, Arlene's last sixties movie was the infamously titled adventure comedy *I Sailed to Tahiti with an All Girl Crew* (1968). It was directed by Richard L. Bare best known for being the sole director for the TV sitcom *Green Acres* and other popular shows from the time. Gardner McKay (best known for starring in the popular TV series *Adventures in Paradise* for three seasons, which is most likely why he was cast) plays a boat owner who bets his rich rival that he can beat him in a race to Tahiti with an all-girl crew. Diane McBain, Edy Williams, Jeanne Rainer, Bebe Louie, and Arlene Charles are the lovelies hired. Bare got the idea for this movie from a trip he took to Nassau in the Bahamas where he spent time with the wealthy Nancy Oakes. He wrote in his memoir *Confessions of a Hollywood Director*, "The next day I joined Nancy on her seventy-foot yacht for a trip around the island. When I came aboard I was surprised to see Nancy and four beautiful women. I was the only male guest and we spent the day leisurely exploring the coves and sandpits that make up the island. Years later I was to write and direct a movie that was inspired by this day. It had to do with a sailor and five beautiful women on a trip to the South Seas and was titled *I Sailed to Tahiti with an All Girl Crew*."

In the movie, Gardner McKay played Terry O'Brien a sea captain who makes his living chartering his sail boat the Samarang. In a drunken moment, he bets rich pompous yachtsman 'Generous' Josh Benson (Fred Clark) that not only can he beat his boat the Sea Witch in a race to Tahiti but he could with an all-girl crew putting the ownership of the Samarang on the line. The next day a sober somber Terry places an ad in the paper for crew members but instead of choosing the more experienced less attractive females, he hires five stunners with very little sailing knowledge—Liz Clark (Diane McBain) a mysterious blonde; buxom Marilyn (Edy Williams) a former topless cocktail waitress; Monique (Jeanne Rainer) a native of Tahiti who just wants a free ride home; and dancer wannabe Tamaya (Bebe Louie). Arlene Charles played the fifth crew member eyeglass wearing grad student Janet who wants to write about the experience in her thesis on oceanography. Stowing aboard is first-rate sailor and teenage tomboy Jimsy (Mary O'Brien) who has a crush on Terry. Before the race begins, the audience sees the wily Benson paying off one of the girls, whose face is not shown, to sabotage Terry's boat. *Green Acres* cast member Put Buttram is also featured playing Blodgett a persistent laconic mystery man on the trail of McBain's Liz Clark.

Actually filmed in the waters around Hawaii during the daytime with the bluest of skies and sea, the sailing sequences are a highlight of the picture. With all the scantily glad beauties on board, Terry uses the same come-on line with all of them to score and seems to hit it off with Monique best as the others have nicknamed him "Captain Bligh" due to his always bellowing orders at them. He gets chummy too with Liz and gets her to confess that she witnessed a murder back home and is on the run because she fears for her life if she testifies.

During the course of the movie, the secret saboteur cuts the sails; drops the anchor; and drains the drinking water forcing Terry to stop at a deserted island so the girls can replenish and also frolic on the sand. Arlene's Janet wanders off only to get her foot caught in the rocks as the tide rolls in. Terry comes to her rescue to the dismay of Jimsy. The crew also loses Tamaya who deserts ship to perform with the band The Baboons.

At one point so fed up with the commandeering Jeff, the girls try to mutiny tying him up to the mast head and later he falls overboard spending the night in the ocean. In both instances Jimsy comes to his rescue. Even with all these setbacks, it is neck-and-neck to the finish line where the Samarang loses by just a few feet in a photo finish.

At Benson's celebratory party, Liz is revealed to be a murdering Black Widow on the run and Blodgett a lawman tasked to bring her to justice. Then a guilt-ridden Monique steps forth as the saboteur. Terry forgives her and they make a date. Benson is disqualified and instead of Terry relishing his victory, the tipsy fool makes a double or nothing bet to race back to Hawaii with five baboons as crew members. The millionaire agrees unaware that those baboons are four burly Hawaiians part of a singing group that Tamaya joined. Terry forgets about Monique when a dolled-up mini-skirted Jimsy gets to him first. The race back to Hawaii begins as Terry bellows commands to his brawny crew with Jimsy by his side and an exasperated Tamaya back in the kitchen.

I Sailed to Tahiti with an All Girl Crew received a limited release slipping into drive-ins in 1969. Trying to capitalize on the catchphrases from the zany and hugely popular TV show *Rowan and Martin's Laugh-In*, the film's poster art included the tag line, "Funk & Wagnall's would describe this naval maneuver as a seven-day SOCK-IT-TO-'EM SKIN-DEEP SAIL-IN." Most mainstream newspapers didn't even review the movie upon its release.

Despite the often belittled title, *I Sailed to Tahiti with an All Girl Crew* is fun light-weight entertainment buoyed by the beautiful cinematography; pretty gals who are just fine in their roles and even finer in their swimsuits; and the affable performance from the normally stoic McKay who talks directly to the audience at times. Not an acting stretch in the least for the talented Diane McBain, her best moment is at the end when her true identity is revealed and she reverts to her thick hillbilly accent. Arlene Charles with her hair more natural, rather than hair sprayed up into a stiff bouffant as it usually was in her Elvis and other teenage drive-in movies, looks simply gorgeous in this and plays her role well though Edy Williams' addled brained waitress has some of the film's funniest lines and scenes. Mindless and amusing, *I Sailed to Tahiti with an All Girl Crew* was perfect for being the bottom-of-a-double-bill summertime feature at the drive-in. When broadcast on television a few years later, *TV Guide* summed the movie up perfectly in one sentence—"Romantic trivia for the pleasure of girl watchers and armchair travelers."

DVD cover art for *I Sailed to Tahiti with an All Girl Crew* (AIP, 1965).

Arlene Charles was *Parade* magazine's cover girl in May 1970 and was still getting press but not so much for her acting career. She modeled fashions on the short-lived syndicated revival of *Queen for a Day* in 1970 with new host Dick Curtis. Arlene remarked, "I wish I had been able to work with Jack Bailey [the original host] as I thought he was fabulous. Dick never listened to the ladies when they told their stories and it made for a lot of embarrassing moments."

Shortly afterwards, in 1971 Arlene co-hosted the local Los Angeles game show *Telefun with Johnny Gilbert and Charlie*. Gilbert, a popular daytime TV presence, is most famous for being the announcer on *Jeopardy* until this day. William Stierwalt produced the program and chose Arlene Charles for his TV special *Hollywood Starlets Most Likely to Succeed*. The actress never got to prove she could when she became involved with and then married heavyweight boxer Jerry Quarry in August 1973 sidelining her career. Though this union kept her from working, her face was splashed across all the media outlets due to her being by her husband's side during his infamous bouts with Muhammad Ali and Joe Frazier. The couple divorced a few years later. In 1999, she was reunited with pop star Mike Smith, lead singer of the Dave Clark Five, whom she dated briefly during the sixties. They wed in Spain two years later where they settled down. The newlyweds planned to move to the U.S. in 2003 when Smith broke his neck in a tragic accident leaving him paralyzed from the chest down. Sadly, he died in 2008 and Arlene Charles eventually returned to the U.S.

How did you get cast in your first movie *Winter a-Go-Go?*
At that time I was still living at the Hollywood Studio Club. It was sort of like a YWCA. A number of starlets lived there. I would always go over to Columbia Studios to see what was happening. I was not under contract, but I was doing a lot of their television shows and they put me into this film.

Were you cast by the film's producers Reno Carell and William Wellman, Jr.?
I don't really remember how I was hired or anything about William Wellman, Jr. Reno Carell though was very, very polite and fun to work with.

What was filming *Winter a-Go-Go* like for you?
We were all a bunch of kids having fun on the set. I never had problems with any of the cast. I was so eager to be working and this was a fabulous experience. I was basically background candy. James Stacy was very nice. I thought he had a brilliant career ahead of him and was very saddened to hear about his motorcycle accident a few years later [the actor lost an arm and a leg]. That was really a shame. Most of the girls on this movie like Julie Parrish and Nancy Czar were so pretty. For me this was the start of the most exciting time of my life. When I had a chance to work I was extremely grateful for any kind of a part I could get.

So you never signed a contract with any studio?

No, I didn't. But it was a very happy time for me because I would go from one studio to the next. I didn't want to be under contract because that way I could work at any studio doing different TV shows or movies. This way nobody could say I couldn't do it. Some of the girls got locked into studio contracts and were paid weekly, which was wonderful. But at the same time they didn't have the opportunities to go out and do other things that I had a chance to do. That was my main reason to not become a contract player.

You then appeared in *Dr. Goldfoot and the Bikini Machine* and *The Ghost in the Invisible Bikini* for American International Pictures.

I did a lot of promotion for AIP. They sent me out on a lot of publicity tours. Even though I was not under contract to the studio, I was treated the same and did what ever the other girls did. And I always got paid for it.

I remember most doing a photo shoot for *Argus Magazine*. I was chosen as one of the girls featured and the story was about us living in this building for single girls only. We were supposed to be having fun helping each other move in. Then they decided to take pictures of us in the pool with the guys having a water fight. I was put on the shoulders of Jody McCrea. I agreed to do it but said, 'Listen I can't swim so if I get tossed into the deep end somebody has to come get me.' They assured me not to worry. We start shooting and Jody and I were one of the last couples remaining. Then boom we get pushed into the deep end and under I go. Nobody comes to help me as I am bobbling up and down in the water. Finally, the photographer yelled, 'I think she was serious. She really can't swim!' Somebody jumped in and saved me. It was a really nice article and they ran a really big picture of me in it. I said it was probably because I almost drowned.

Did you become friendly with any of the beach girls that were contracted to AIP?

No, not really. Mary Hughes though invited me to a party with the Rolling Stones. I declined because I was sort of dating Mike Smith of the Dave Clark Five and said I was not interested. Some of the girls thought I was crazy not to go. I thought Salli Sachse was very pretty but on the reserved side. All the girls had figures to die for and were really beautiful. They all were very nice too. I had a lot of fun working with them.

The leads in *Dr. Goldfoot* were Vincent Price, Frankie Avalon, and Susan Hart. Did you have much interaction with them?

Just with Frankie who was one of the nicest guys you ever want to meet. He was a sweetheart. Years later I ran into him and he still remembered me. Susan Hart was just so pretty. Vincent Price was a such distinguished, charming man. I never learned how to cook because my mother thought that was for other girls and not for me. While we were shooting, Vincent came out with a cookbook. I immediately bought two copies and asked him to autograph them. I still have them and use it constantly. In my mind, he was just so accomplished.

Though she was bikini-clad in the *Beach Party* movies, Salli Sachse felt exploited making *Dr. Goldfoot* parading around in a gold lame bikini and heels. Did you feel the same?

No, not at all did I feel exploited. I knew I had to start somewhere and just being in a picture for American International was a major accomplishment to me at least. At that time I had a horse that I brought out from Indiana and I had horse bills to pay. It was legitimate work and I was happy doing this. Maybe because Salli and the other girls were under contract and were always forced to wear a bikini it became a problem. For me it was exciting and AIP treated us wonderfully.

Did you get to work with Jayne Mansfield or Mamie Van Doren in *Las Vegas Hillbillys*?

No, we were never on the set together. I was originally cast as Ferlin Husky's girlfriend whom he leaves behind to go off to Las Vegas. When Ferlin met me, he said that I was too nice and he wanted me to play his little sister. They had to rewrite the script and I became his sibling. Everything I filmed was in the studio in Hollywood and I didn't go to Las Vegas. Ferlin was such a charmer. He was a very, very nice man and we had much fun filming.

In 2011, I heard that Ferlin was in the hospital and I gave him a call. I said, 'I don't know if you will remember me or not since we haven't spoken in many years, but we did a movie together and I played your younger sister.' He said, 'you bet I remember you kid. How are you doing?' We had a nice chat. Ferlin seemed to be in good spirits and told me he was being released soon. Shortly after that he sadly passed away.

How did you wind up with Elvis Presley in *Paradise, Hawaiian Style*?
I was working with Deanna Lund on the set of the movie *The Oscar* at Paramount Studios. James Shigeta was filming *Paradise, Hawaiian Style* on the lot too. One day during lunch Deanna said, 'I have a surprise for you.' She knew I adored Elvis and told me to come with her to a closed set. Over we go and there in front of me is my hero. I just stood there with my mouth opened. He was so much more handsome and exciting than in his photographs. Elvis came over and Jimmy introduced us. Our lunch break ended and Deanna went back to work, but I couldn't move. I was too mesmerized and returned to *The Oscar* set one hour late. I apologized to everyone and explained what happened. Later as I was leaving they told me that I received a special request to work the next day. I thought it was on *The Oscar* but it was to be on *Paradise, Hawaiian Style*. I just about passed out. I was sent immediately to wardrobe because I was playing the part of a stewardess. I was crying because I was so excited.

Can you recall your first working day with Elvis?
I walked onto the set and there is my hero in this gorgeous outfit. And again I just stood there agape. Elvis and I got along so well that all we did was laugh and laugh. We did so much so that they couldn't use most of the take. I think you barely see me when Elvis and Julie Parrish are at the heliport.

What was it like filming *I Sailed to Tahiti with an All Girl Crew*?
This was so much fun. We were in Hawaii for seven weeks shooting this. The scenes of us on the boat were really filmed on the ocean. The actors and crew were all crammed in on it. I couldn't swim so you'll notice me holding on to poles and railings very tightly. In one scene, Edy Williams and I had to bring the sail over and then let it go. I said to Edy, 'When this sail comes through and we start to come around that wind is going to pick up. I am going to let this thing slide through my fingers and you should do the same. Don't try to hold on to it because you won't be able to.' She said OK. The director yells 'Action' and we start the scene. I let the mast go and Edy holds on. It pulls her right off the boat and into the ocean she goes. I look over and see her two falsies floating on top of the water. I started to laugh hysterically. The frustrated director yells, 'Cut!'

Publicity photo of Arlene Charles in *Dr. Goldfoot and the Bikini Machine* (AIP, 1965). *Courtesy of Arlene Charles*

Another thing I remember is that we filmed daily on the sea and they would provide us a box lunch to eat on the boat every day. It was always a ham sandwich, a hardboiled egg, and an apple. After a few days we were only eating the apple. We couldn't eat breakfast because we knew we were going out on the boat and the worse thing is to eat anything greasy. And we were all wearing bikinis so we didn't want to eat anything heavy anyway. After the day's filming, we were so tired we'd just go to a local club and drink Mai-Tai's.

What did you think of Edy Williams?

Different is the best way to describe her. She wanted stardom so badly and she would go about it a totally different way than the rest of us. Edy wanted to be noticed so if it meant taking her top off she would do it without any qualms. I on the other hand was so prudish it was ridiculous. Edy was friendly but I didn't bond with her.

Edy was comical because we were supposed to wear this body makeup. It was rancid. None of us would wear it except Edy. She'd put it on and boy did it smell. You couldn't escape it on this small boat. Poor Richard Bare, I felt so sorry for him. Here we were a bunch of Hollywood starlets not willing to wear the stinky makeup and he'd say, 'Look Edy is wearing it.' We'd say yes and she stinks! None of us wanted to stand next to her.

In her memoir, Diane McBain described Gardner McKay as "extremely boring." Do you agree?

No, Gardner McKay was extremely nice and loved the girls. He was after every one of us and thought he was the cat's meow. He was a bit full of himself but I think he did make a few conquests. Not me though. I had a horse to take care of.

Did you have any problems shooting this not being able to swim with all this water around you?

One scene called for me to jump off the boat. I said, 'I can't swim! How am I going to jump off the boat?' Richard let me stay on deck, thank goodness. I am the only one who doesn't dive off to push the sailboat.

Did you bond with Diane McBain or any of the other actresses in this?

I didn't get to know Diane very well. We were supposed to go to Vietnam together with Johnny Grant but she cancelled at the last second. Jeanne Rainer was not French but born in New York. She was really nice. We toured the Islands together after we finished shooting. She was writing a book about different religions and asked me to accompany her. We learned a lot about Hawaiian witch doctors.

What was it like to entertain the troops with Bob Hope?
On March 21, 1969, Bob asked me to be 'Miss American Fighter Pilot' and we went to Houston for a big banquet with all the Air Force generals, majors, pilots, and some very prominent dignitaries. It was very exciting. My escort was none other then astronaut Wally Schirra, who was an old friend of mine. After the event, Bob presented me with a photo book of everything that went on that night and obviously it's very special to me.

Why did you decide to visit Vietnam with Johnny Grant instead of Bob Hope?
Johnny Grant ["the unofficial Mayor of Hollywood"] went to all the hospitals and fire support bases. He had more contact with the guys so that is the reason. It was a life changing experience. I have a photo of being in a hospital talking with an injured soldier. That was what the trip was all about for me. It was a very inspiring time and I will be forever grateful to all those soldiers that fought so hard for all of us. Whenever I see anyone wearing a hat or jacket that says they served in Vietnam I thank them profusely for their unselfish efforts and ask them where they served. Most are shocked to hear I was one of the few gals that went over to Nam on a USO tour. Some men are willing to talk about their experiences and others just want to put it behind them and forget they ever went over. I still have my cowboy hat that is covered in pins the guys gave me. I'm very proud of the plaques I received and have them proudly displayed even today.

Do you happen to have a favorite of the movies you appeared in?
I was so busy going from one project to the next that I never watched anything that I did. I was doing commercials and TV shows at the time too. I had no idea I even had any lines in *Winter a-Go-Go*.

***I Sailed to Tahiti with an All Girl Crew* was your last movie in the sixties. Was this planned or did the opportunities just stop?**
At the time I was doing a lot of TV and commercials that kept me very busy. I modeled on *Queen for a Day* for about a year. Then I co-hosted *Telefun with Johnny Gilbert and Charlie*. It was on Channel 13 in Los Angeles. This was sort of a talk/game show. We'd show small portions of an item and the television viewers would call in to guess what it was. While

I was doing this a friend from Palm Springs called me. She had friends over for dinner recently and they were watching my show. One of the guys there wanted to meet me. I asked who it was and she said Jerry Quarry. I knew he was married, but she said he was getting a divorce. I said, 'Yeah, him and about a million other guys.' She convinced me to come out to her house to meet him the next weekend. I drove out there and Jerry was very, very rude. I even told him so. The next day he invited me to a golf tournament. I said yes but he never picked me up and expected me to get there myself. I told him I don't drive myself to dates and he apologized blaming his divorce proceedings. I gave him another chance and the rest is history.

Marsha Bennett, Johnny Grant, Diane McBain,
and Arlene Charles, ca. 1969. *Courtesy of Arlene Charles*

Though your marriage to boxer Jerry Quarry kept you from working, you received a lot of publicity from the media.

I went on the *Today Show* with Barbara Walters and Tom Brokaw. He was suppose to ask me about the upcoming fight with Joe Frazier, but instead he started asking me about our sleeping arrangements as I was the only gal that had ever been permitted to be in a training camp. I couldn't believe how rude Tom was on live TV and finally dismissed his very personal questions with this statement, 'Tom, let's just say Jerry is a very adequate lover, but not anytime before a fight and we will leave it at that.'

My statement ended up in *Time Magazine* and I guess that morning Charles Revson [the founder of Revlon] saw the show. Before the fight, *People Magazine* had been following me around for weeks and published an article about me. A few months later an ad agency in New York told me that Mr. Revson was so impressed by the way that I had handled the interview that he decided to name a perfume 'Charlie' and even copied my signature. The first commercial opened up showing a girl riding a horse (copied from a picture *People* used of me wearing a cowboy hat, Levis, and boots) and then getting out of a limo all dressed up in New York. I laughed and asked why I couldn't do the commercial and they said he didn't want to admit that it was me. I never received any credit for that one but sure would have liked to do one of their commercials!

Your third husband was Mike Smith lead singer of the Dave Clark Five who you dated briefly in the sixties. However, he unfortunately has a terrible accident.

Mike was paralyzed from his upper chest down from a freak accident at our home in Spain. I spent most of my time going back and forth every two weeks from Spain to London. He needed constant care and was in a hospital there for five years. It was the happiest time and yet the saddest time of my life. We thought he was recovering enough to attend the Dave Clark Five's induction into the Rock and Roll Hall of Fame in 2008, but he died suddenly only a few days before.

What is your life like today?

I now live on what they call a 'Hobby Farm' meaning that it's only 3 1/2 acres but I'm raising three black Angus steers; a Tennessee Walking horse and a small miniature pony; ten chickens; and, last but not least, two large German Sheppard dogs. The only thing I don't have is a partridge in a pear tree! It's something I never had the chance to do in the old days but I'm having a ball. I'm close to Chicago, but don't miss the hustle and bustle of L.A.

4. REDISCOVERING STEVEN ROGERS: HEARTTHROB OF THE SIXTIES DRIVE-IN

A NUMBER OF GOOD LOOKING actors appeared in sixties teenage drive-in movies but with his jet black hair and penetrating blues eyes none were quite as handsome as Steven Rogers. When he was on screen you could not keep your eyes off of him. He also had a droll delivery and was perfect to play the wisecracking friend. After a stint on TV's *Combat!*, he hit the big screen where he went from the sandy shores of Malibu in *The Girls on the Beach* to snow-covered mountains in *Ski Party* and *Wild Wild Winter*. In *Angels from Hell* he was too pretty to be a biker so he was cast as a former gang member gone Hollywood. In between, he had the lead in the Albert Zugsmith Grade-Z spoof *Movie Star, American Style: or LSD, How I Hate You!*

Steven Rogers was born Richard Rogers in Chicago. His father was a salesman and radio announcer and his mother's family owned American Linen Company. When a child, the family relocated to Southern California. After graduating high school, Rogers attended college for a short period then left to become a student at Estelle Harman's acting school. His attendance there was interrupted by his call for military service. By this time, the actor was already married with two children. Using his birth name, the striking young actor landed his first professional job with an unbilled bit as a student in the pre-*Death Wish* revenge tale *13 West Street* (1962) starring Alan Ladd (who Rogers found to be "a great guy") as an engineer assaulted by a gang of Beverly Hills punks who decides to hunt the culprits down on his own.

The young actor followed this with some small roles on such TV series as *Cheyenne*, *Lawman*, and *Shannon* before getting his big break when cast in the role of Doc on the new ABC-TV war adventure series *Combat!* beginning in 1962. "I read with a bunch of actors for this and somehow they gave me the role," said Rogers. "I went home after auditioning and later went to get my teeth done. I was at the dentist when I got the call [from his agent] that I got the part. I thought, 'Whoa!' I couldn't believe it! I was really amazed since there were a lot of guys up for it"

Steven Rogers, ca. 1964.

As described by *Combat!* historian and expert Jo Davidsmeyer, the series "is a realistic, mud-splattered World War II drama that presents intimate character studies of men at war. It was the only American television show to feature the frontline infantryman . . . [it] follows the fighting men of King Company's second platoon as they battle their way across Europe from the beaches of Normandy. Second platoon (King Two) is commanded by Lt. Hanley [Rick Jason]. The action often centers around first squad, lead by Sergeant Saunders [Vic Morrow]."

The series was filmed at MGM studios and ABC invested a lot to make it as realistic as possible while making it attractive for the TV audience. Columnist Jack Lloyd visited the set early on and noted, "I get the impression that those behind the show are not averse to taking a few pains to provide that extra touch of quality. There were many takes when a scene did not come off just the way it should have and realism is attempted to almost the point of extreme."

"I loved working with Rick Jason," remarked Rogers. "I saw a lot of him [off the set]. I didn't know much about Vic Morrow because he would come in, do his part, and leave. I worked a lot with Vic early on but after that I did every other show with Rick."

For years *Combat!* fans have been speculating that Rogers changed his name from Rick to Steven not wanting to be confused with Rick Jason. He confirmed that was true. His character was listed in the ABC press kits as "medical aid man Doc Walton" and described as being "a gentle, sensitive youngster who is profoundly affected by his battlefield experiences." The audience was able to see the horror of combat through Doc's eyes. Right from the debut episode, the viewer knew Doc was going to be the show's conscience as he steps in to protect a captured German deserter from being roughed up by a G.I. named Kirby (Jack Hogan) and says defiantly, "He's a human being." Later as the Americans become under siege and need to make an escape Saunders gives an order to Caje (Pierre Jalbert) to kill the German. After their escape by swimming through a canal, Doc asks what happened to the German and Caje lies that the German soldiers shot him. Later Saunders tells Caje to continue with the lie to protect Doc who got to know the German and looked at him more as another man rather than just the enemy. Caje then confesses to Saunders that he couldn't kill the unarmed man and let him live. At first angered, Saunders comes around and says, "You did right." Saunders protectiveness of Doc is one of his endearing qualities and runs throughout the first season.

Rogers was an immediate stand out on the show. With his boyish good looks and touching portrayal, he made Doc one of the series' most popular characters. By mid-season it was reported that the actor was receiving more fan mail then the two leads though some viewers of the macho kind did not take to his character. Pacifist Doc was a bit ahead of his time.

Among the impressive array of directors Rogers got to work with during that first season were Robert Altman, Burt Kennedy, and Boris Sagal. Commenting on them, Rogers said, "Robert Altman was great and had everything to do in shaping the characters. I do not know why he was let go. Working with Burt Kennedy was a whole different thing. He was totally by the book. I didn't like Kennedy as much." The one thing about *Combat!* that Rogers liked no matter who the director was that "each episode was so interesting and different. We weren't doing the same thing so that was really good."

One of Rogers' best episodes was "A Day in June" where in flashbacks it is revealed that his conflicted Doc was nervously apprehensive to go into battle on D-Day as compared to the others in his squad. As a medic he was trained to save lives, not end them. Once again, Vic Morrow's understanding Saunders helps the young medic through the crisis.

Combat! was a modest hit in the ratings its first season and was received warmly by the critics. For instance, Larry Walters of the *Chicago Daily Tribune* called it a "hard-hitting realistic drama." *Variety* found it to be a "first class production" with "good performances by all concerned." Not surprisingly, it was renewed for a second season, but Rogers did not return on his own accord. He explained, "There were a lot of times I could have done other parts but I couldn't get time off. These were good shows too. I realized that I wasn't going anywhere here. There was a lot of action in this show but my character was not part of that. Doc became less and less important. I thought I could do better getting off the show and doing other things so I did. I left on good terms and kept in touch with some of the guys.

"Shecky Green was great and left half way through the season," continued Rogers. "He said, 'Enough of this shit!' I also really liked Pierre Jalbert who was from Canada. Really nice guy to work with and he was a great skier."

With Steven Rogers not returning, his character was dropped from the show without explanation. Conlan Carter joined the cast as the new medic also nicknamed Doc.

Reportedly, Warner Bros. showed interest in signing Steven Rogers to a contract. Rogers revealed that the studio really liked him and tried to put together a medical show with him in the lead but it did not come to be.

Rogers then turned to the big screen. The roles offered to him were usually based on his movie star good looks and ability to deliver a line drolly for a laugh. However, as he demonstrated on *Combat!*, there was a sensitive side to him and he could be quite poignant. Film producers never took advantage of his ability that way though. Eventually, Rogers seem to give in and his last two film appearances had him playing up the image of the matinee idol of yore.

Boxoffice reported that Steven Rogers was up for a lead role in *Summer's Children* directed by James Bruner for Liberty Arts Productions. The title was changed to *The Summer Children* but the actor was not cast.

Rogers copped his first movie lead thanks to his friend, actor Bart Patton, who was hired by brothers Roger and Gene Corman to help cast their new movie. In 1963, *Beach Party* starring Frankie Avalon and Annette Funicello was released and it was a surprise box office hit for American International Pictures. They soon followed up in 1964 with *Muscle Beach Party*, *Bikini Beach*, and *Pajama Party*. Seeing the money to be made off this new genre the major studios got into the act that same year. Soon to be found at drive-ins across the country were *Surf Party* from 20th Century-Fox, *Ride the Wild Surf* from Columbia Pictures, and *For Those Who Think Young* from United Artists. Paramount Pictures waded into the water a bit late and agreed to release the Corman Brothers' beach party knockoff *The Girls on the Beach* (1965).

Steven Rogers, Martin West, and Aron Kincaid as surfers
trying to score with some coeds in *The Girls on the Beach* (Paramount, 1965).

The premise of the movie was simple. Three surfers meet some sorority girls at the local hangout where bands like The Beach Boys and The Crickets perform. They learn that the coeds' sorority mother squandered their mortgage payment and they are going to lose their house if they cannot raise the money. To get the girls' interest, one of the surfers lies that he knows Ringo Starr and soon the girls are selling tickets to a fundraiser head-lined by The Beatles. Realizing they took the prank too far, the guys come clean and in the end some of the gals don Beatles' wigs and perform for the audience saving their home.

Bart Patton was able to get some of his friends cast along with a few newcomers. Noreen Corcoran from the TV series *Bachelor Father* copped the female lead albeit now as a blonde. The three main coeds who surround her were played by Natalie Wood's now grown-up younger sister Lana Wood; TV actress Linda Marshall, and newcomer Gail Ger-ber. Other coeds included Linda Saunders, Anna Capri, and Mary Mitchel. The surfers were played by Martin West and Patton's two friends Aron Kincaid and Rogers.

Commenting on Rogers in *Hollywood Surf and Beach Movies*, Bart Patton said, "Steve was an old friend of mine for years. But he was a bizarre actor. Some of these people were very strange but we had a sort of camaraderie amongst us though."

Another actor cast to do background as a beach boy was Christopher Riordan. Looks-wise Rogers made quite an impression on him. The candid actor remarked, "I remember the first time I saw him on *The Girls on the Beach* and thought, 'Wow, what a good looking guy.' He was really handsome with great skin, beautiful hair, and gorgeous blue eyes. I would sit there and gaze at him thinking, 'God, he is just so chiseled.'"

Aron Kincaid really liked Steven Rogers (who returned the compliment and said, "I had a lot of fun working with him") and they bonded over trying to keep up with scene-stealing Martin West. Kincaid commented about making *The Girls on the Beach* in *Holly-wood Surf and Beach Movies*, "You'd think it was just a bunch of kids slapping around and having a good time. But everybody analyzed every scene that they did. For instance, in the opening scene Martin West is telling Steve Rogers and I what we have to do to pick up these girls at the next table. While he is talking he is playing with a straw. [Director Wil-liam] Witney yelled cut because they had to set up a light differently so I stepped over to the side. Steve said, 'Do you notice what Martin is doing with the straw.' I said, 'Yeah, he's playing with it. He didn't do that in rehearsal.' Steve then said, 'He's doing this to draw all the attention and eyes to him on the screen.' I said, '*We've got to fight back!*'"

Both Aron Kincaid and Gail Gerber relayed how the girls on the beach did not get along so well during production. Per Aron and Gail, they seemed to be jealous of Lana Wood and Anna Capri and ostracized them. This was news to Steven Rogers who said he had no idea what was going on and concentrated on his role. Of the girls on the beach the only one that stands out for him was "Mary Mitchel because she was married to Bart Patton at the time. I knew her personally and really liked her. I remembered watching the scene where she blows up a cake." As for the Beach Boys, Rogers said, "They came on the set, did their part, and left. I never really spoke with them. A few years later I was driving home and Brian Wilson came out of the bushes asking for a cigarette. This was when he was under that psychiatrist's care. I wound up giving him a whole pack."

In the movie, Martin West's Duke was the leader of the trio of surfers, Aron Kincaid's Wayne the questioning follower, and Steven Rogers' Brian the pretty boy who was only interested in scoring with the coeds. Rogers is a standout not only because how good he looks in shorts and swimsuits, but because he gets some of the movies' wittiest lines and delivers them humorously. For instance, at the local college hangout, the Sip 'n' Surf, the Beach Boys are performing on stage while the guys eye pretty blonde Selma (Noreen Corcoran) and her Alpha Beta sorority sisters Cynthia (Linda Marshall), Georgia (Gail Gerber), and Bonnie (Lana Wood). Brian wants to just go over to the girls, but Martin thinks they should concoct a strategy and says, "This is the battle of the sexes. If we are gonna capture the enemy, we gotta fight 'em smart." To which Brian moans, "Yeah, but I don't wanna fight 'em—I want to *fraternize.*"

Later, Duke and the guys while sitting on their surfboards in the ocean are seen spying on the gals sitting on the beach. Wayne and Brian are ready to make their move, but again Duke puts the breaks on them and says, "we've got to learn their weakness." Brian pleads, "Coach, I don't care if I strike out. *I just want to get to bat!*"

The rest of the movie has Rogers' Brian forlorn as he follows Duke's lead to try to undo the damage they caused by tricking the girls into thinking that they knew the Beatles and that the group agreed to perform at their fundraiser. Climbing into one of the top floor bedrooms to retrieve an Western Union telegram from The Beatles management threatening the sorority with a lawsuit, the guys come across an array of wigs. Rogers' character groans, "Oh, no! Our chicks are bald. And they are so young too." To escape without being detected when the gals return home, the guys dress in drag to sneak out of the sorority house in an amusing scene. Having guys in women's clothes was not uncommon in sixties beach movies as it was part of the ending to the follow up *Beach Ball* and was the entire plot of *Ski Party.* Though he didn't mind dressing up, Aron Kincaid didn't think the scene was very realistic as he related in *Hollywood Surf and Beach Movies*. "If three guys did have to do such a thing they would hardly be putting on false eyelashes and lip gloss with a lipstick brush, which is what the make-up man did to us. Everybody said that I looked like Lana Wood. I swore that Steve Rogers looked like Lizabeth Scott and Martin West resembled Rose Marie of *The Dick Van Dyke Show*."

Martin West, Aron Kincaid, and Steven Rogers in drag trying
to sneak out of a sorority house in *The Girls on the Beach* (Paramount, 1965).

The cads come clean to the coeds just before show time leaving the girls in a major fix with paid customers screaming for The Beatles. They then don wigs and impersonate the singing group—badly. But this being a beach movie, the audience is satisfied after Duke sticks up for the masquerading sorority gals. Waiting off-stage with a pleading look on their faces, the gals forgive the guys and are reunited.

The Girls on the Beach is one of the better *Beach Party* clones. *Variety* called it "pleasant" and felt the male actors did "well enough" in their roles. The film is enhanced by some funny dialog; attractive young people; and outstanding musical performances by the Beach Boys. The fact it is their sole appearance in this genre makes the film still memorable to this day. While the entire cast is good, Steven Rogers, Aron Kincaid, and Gail Gerber as man-hungry, drag-racing Georgia are the comedic standouts. It is no surprise then that Gene Corman cast Kincaid and Gerber in his next Hollywood surf movie *Beach Ball*, but it is disappointing that Steven Rogers was excluded. Perhaps to make up for the slight, Corman hired Rogers for his following teenage movie.

After its success with the beach milieu, AIP was the first studio to switch the party from the sandy shores of Malibu to the ski sloops of Sun Valley with *Ski Party* though the movie concludes back on the beach. Two average college guys, who are unlucky when it comes to the ladies, masquerade as English lasses on a ski trip to discover why the coeds dig suave athlete Freddie and what they really want in a guy. Complications ensue when the pompous ladies man falls in love with one of the guy's female incarnation.

Ski Party was produced by AIP outsider Gene Corman. Of course, he was limited to the studio's roster of players for the leads and supporting roles, but he succeeded in nixing AIP's John Ashley as Freddie (too similar in looks and stature to leading actors Frankie Avalon and Dwayne Hickman) and instead prevailed with the more suitable taller, blonde Aron Kincaid in the role. He was also able to sneak into the film Mikki Jamison from *Beach Ball* and Steven Rogers. Their parts were small compared to their leading roles in Corman's previous movies, but at least Rogers had lines and received prominent billing. Jamison was reduced to a background player.

"Yes, I got this due to Gene Corman," commented Rogers. "He was a really interesting guy and wore interesting clothes. Whenever I got a part it was a great thing because it was hard getting work. Everybody was up for the roles I played so if I got it I was lucky. This was fun. I would just say hello to Frankie Avalon but that was it. He was usually by himself."

Steven Rogers (now billed as Steve Rogers) played Gene and was paired with Mike Nader as Bobby in the movie. Their girl chasing characters provide a few fleeting humorous moments. For the most part though Rogers could be seen but not heard and his screen time unfortunately is limited. He gets to dance too but not so well per Christopher Riordan who did background work and assisted with the choreography. "I was assigned to Steve Rogers by the choreographer Jack Baker to make him move," revealed Riordan. "I would ask him to do something choreographically and he'd make a semi-attempt." It is true that Rogers never looks comfortable dancing in the film and doesn't shake his booty the way Mike Nader does. Rogers cops to this and frankly admits, "I hated dancing in these movies!"

Rogers is first spotted in an all-boys sex class, taught by a comely professor (Annette Funicello making a cameo appearance), sitting behind class losers-in-love Todd (Avalon) and Craig (Hickman). Hearing that the gals they like Linda (Deborah Walley) and Barbara (Yvonne Craig) on headed on a ski holiday with some classmates, the guys decide to go along even if they cannot ski. On the bus ride up to the mountains, Rogers is seated, with popular AIP beach bunny Patti Chandler, two rows behind the film's leads and they dance in their seats to Lesley Gore singing "Sunshine, Lollipops, and Rainbows." At the ski lodge, Roger's Gene and the rest of the gang are seen reacting to the screwball antics of Todd and Greg who mess with the unstable manager (Robert Q. Lewis). When sexy bathing suit clad ski instructor Nita (Bobbi Shaw) strolls by, Gene is the first one to ask, "Where are our bathing suits Bobby?" The boys then head to change in their rooms and meet at the pool.

After Avalon's Todd finishes performing his pool side number "Lots, Lots More," the camera focuses in on the seated Gene and Bobby with Nita between them as they whisper in her ear. Each time she replies with "yah, yah." An excited Bobby exclaims, "Gene, she says yes to everything!" He replies, "Yea, I know!" But then drolly adds, "Something's wrong. What's your name honey?" When she says in her thick Swedish accent that her name is Nita, Gene says, "No wonder she is so friendly. She's a Southerner!" This was Rogers best moment in the movie but soon Nita turns her attention towards Todd. Rogers' Gene then returns to the background with the rest of the AIP contingent around the lodge's fireplace. He is seen dancing with Salli Sachse's Indian and then listening and clapping along to the film's iconic moment when James Brown & His Famous Flames come in from the snow to perform "I Got You (I Feel Good)," before hitting the ski jump as one of Todd's competitors. He and the rest of the gang finish up the movie dancing on the shores of Malibu to The Hondells after all the romantic misunderstandings are resolved for the obligatory happy ending except for poor love struck Freddie who is led to believe that Craig's female persona Nora has swam off to farther shores.

Regarding James Brown, Rogers remarked, "This was a really weird and very strange scene. Afterwards, I tried to get James Brown to talk but he was not very friendly at all."

Ski Party was one of the best in the beach party genre even with the locale switch to the snow. Frankie Avalon, Dwayne Hickman, Bobbi Shaw, and especially Aron Kincaid are standouts with their amusing performances. As for Steven Rogers, he is basically just eye candy here along with Mike Nader and the scantily clad beach girls.

Steven Rogers and Linda Marshall in *The Girls on the Beach* (Paramount, 1965).

Steven Rogers' next movie sent him back to the snow. Ironically, he admitted, "I wasn't a skier at that time. Later I learn to ski." The actor was cast thanks again to friend Bart Patton. Impressed with footage of the yet to be released *Beach Ball* shown to studio head Lew Wasserman, Universal Pictures signed producer Bart Patton and director Lennie Weinrib to a two-picture deal. The studio was almost the last to get in on the teenage beach party craze and wanted the team to replicate their prior movie. Following the lead of AIP with *Ski Party* and Columbia Pictures with *Winter a-Go-Go*, they decided to set it in the snow. Sam Locke still working under the pseudonym of David Malcom was recruited to write the screenplay. The film's working title was *Snow Ball* but it was changed at the last minute by Universal to *Wild Wild Winter* with the tag line "a surfin' snow ball." The film was budgeted at approximately $220,000 and finished under budget by $5,000.

According to Bart Patton in *Hollywood Surf and Beach Movies*, "We shot this at Sam Goldwyn Studios and not on the Universal lot. We were considered a sort of independent film so we were allowed to cast actors of our choosing and were not limited to Universal's contract players...Once the studio approved the leading actor, we had pretty much autonomy." Gary Clarke from TV's hit television western *The Virginian* was tapped for the male lead. From *Beach Ball*, Patton rehired Chris Noel as the female lead, Anna Lavelle in a small bit, and Don Edmonds as one of Clarke's two best friends. Rogers (again billed as Steve Rogers) was cast in the fourth buddy role. Rogers only knew Edmonds previously because "we were friends from acting school."

In the book *Wild Beyond Belief!*, Patton told writer Brian Albright, "We shot the interiors first, because the weather was too bad up there, then went up to Lake Tahoe and shot the snow stuff. Don Edmonds went snow blind the first day and had to wear shades the rest of the movie."

Steven Rogers concurs about the rough conditions shooting on location. "There were a lot of problems because the weather kept changing. For the cast and crew it was hard because you'd do a scene and then rain or snow would come in. They'd have to change the lights and things. It was a mess. How he [cinematographer Frank Phillips] managed I'll never know."

Don Edmonds and Steven Rogers in *Wild Wild Winter* (Universal, 1966).
Billy Rose Theatre Collection, The New York Public Library for the Performing Arts

Wild Wild Winter is one of the lesser beach party-type movies released during the mid-sixties though the guest musical performers help greatly. Two college guys keep striking out with shapely coeds due to their prudish sorority leader, Susan. They coax surfer and ladies' man Ronnie away from the beach bunnies in Malibu to attend their school to melt the icy veneer from Susan. To do that, he pretends to be a rich boy in hiding and makes time with Susan who agrees to teach him to ski and then plants a story that he is a championship skier when that plan goes awry. He continually butts heads with Susan's pompous ace skier boyfriend. Steven Rogers plays frat boy Benton who finances Ronnie with his scheme hoping Susan's sorority sisters will finally loosen up.

All the ingredients are here to make a successful beach-party type movie—nicely photographed ski footage, romantic misunderstandings, lots of pretty girls and good-looking guys, and an array of musical guest stars including Jay and the Americans, the Beau Brummels, and Dick and Dee who perform because their singing helps Ronnie devise his next scheme in the film's running joke. However, *Wild Wild Winter* is severely hurt by the casting of the much too long-in-the-tooth Gary Clarke (32 at the time) as Ronnie and, as his rival, Steve Franken (a year older than Clarke) who look more like college professors than students. Or as Suzie Kaye quipped about Clarke in *Drive-In Dream Girls*, "He looks like our father!" Granted a lot of the actors in these movies were in their late twenties or pushing thirty (i.e. Rogers, Aron Kincaid, Gail Gerber, Frankie Avalon, etc.) but they at least had a young vibrant attitude about them and could pass for early twenties. Clarke and Franken look like dirty old men when fighting over the nubile Chris Noel as Susan.

Steven Rogers' character Benton is a popular self-confident rich college boy (the actor looks and fits the part to a tee) who knows his way around the campus. Though Rogers technically has the fourth male lead, he is on screen continuously with flattering close-ups and even may have more lines than Edmonds and Brown. The actor first appears on screen just after the opening credits finish and Benton is seen greeting his newly enrolled friends, Burt (Don Edmonds) and Perry (Les Brown, Jr.). As Benton bestows the wonders of the majestic Alpine Mountains, the guys are ogling ski bunnies Sandy (Suzie Kaye) and Dot (Vicky Albright). Benton advises to forget about them because they are members of the Zeta Theta sorority whose leader, "professional goodie-goodie" Susan Benchley (Noel), thinks men should not be trusted or dated.

Trying to impress the sorority girls, Burt and Perry lie and tell them that their fathers are in the television and motion picture industry. They make a date for dinner but it is spoiled when Susan looks up their records and learns the truth—Burt's father owns a TV repair shop and Perry's dad is a film projectionist. Burt and Perry are livid with Susan's meddling. Benton acts out for them in an exaggerated manner how Susan probably scolded the girls mimicking her exact words, "Remember girls, boys are all alike. They are not interested in love and marriage. All they care about is a hi and a goodbye. And will do anything to get it—lie, cheat, anything." When the guys erupt about how terrible that is too say, Benton replies, "And the most terrible thing is—it's the truth." Benton is skeptical when Burt comes up with a plan to entice their fraternity brother Ronnie Duke (Clarke) to enroll in school and win over Susan even though as Benton warns she has a fiancé named John (Franken speaking with an annoying nasal snooty voice) the college's top skier.

Benton agrees to pay a small portion of Ronnie's expenses with the frat's money. However, as he spies the affect Duke has on a hot blonde after only an hour bus ride, he forks over the frat's entire stash to Burt believing the lothario can distract Susan breaking her hold on her sorority sisters. Duke comes up with a scenario to trick Susan to think he is the son of a millionaire pineapple cannery owner trying to hide being wealthy. The rest of the movie is a slapdash affair with Ronnie trying to woo a smitten Susan away from the pompous suspicious John who keeps trying to expose him as a phony. Meanwhile the Dean has inadvertently put the university in hoc to the mob now looking to collect their money. Benton and the guys keep tabs on Ronnie and help him when their plans go awry due to meddling John. Of course, in a convoluted away, it ends with a happy ending as Ronnie comes clean and wins Susan and accidentally saves the school all due to a rampaging bear. Don't ask.

Wild Wild Winter is one of the less successful beach party movies. Gary Clarke tries as Ronnie, but he and Franken are totally miscast as college students. The ridiculous ending of Clarke being chased by a guy in a bear costume doesn't help. At least the other players help buoy the film from being a total bummer. Chris Noel, Suzie Kaye, and Vicky Albright are perky, Don Edmonds does some decent clowning, and Steven Rogers exudes charisma throughout and has some funny moments. He is particularly shot well here and when on screen you cannot but help be drawn to him. The musical performers are also quite good. Jay and the Americans rock on the rousing "Two of a Kind" as the entire cast dances at the fade out. A surreal musical highlight is Jackie and Gayle singing about their love snowballing while on the sandy shores of Malibu with swimsuit clad boys and girls gyrating around them. The Beau Brummels and The Astronauts perform too, but it is Dick and Dee, looking like Sonny and Cher-lite, who stand out with their rendition of "Heartbeats."

Steven Rogers bid for major stardom may have rested with his next movie the Grade-Z satire (or as it called itself "high camp") *Movie Star, American Style; Or LSD, I Hate You!* from director Albert Zugsmith, king of the exploitation movies. Most of his prior movies from the late fifties onward, which he also produced, starred platinum blonde sexpot Mamie Van Doren in such wildly titled films as *High School Confidential; The Beat Generation; Girls Town; Sex Kittens Go to College;* and *College Confidential.*

Movie Star, American Style poked fun at celebrities and the developing fascination with the drug LSD. Substituting in for Van Doren was another platinum blonde named Paula Lane, who built a career out of impersonating Marilyn Monroe. Here she is Honey Bunny a breathless movie star sent to a "rest home" after her umpteenth suicide attempt. It is run by a Dr. Horatio (Del Moore who appeared in many Jerry Lewis comedies) who treats his patients with LSD. Steven Rogers gives his all parodying his movie star persona ("I tried—that is true," he quips) as a big time film idol named Barry James, Super Star also being treated by the wacko doctor. Other patients include female impersonator T.C. Jones as a fashion designer, Frank Delfino as a midget photographer, and others as Hollywood producers and directors.

"I have never seen this," revealed Rogers. "This was a whole weird thing, man. It was a bad experience. I don't remember how I got cast by Albert Zugsmith but somebody backed out of the movie and I did the part. He was a bad guy. Afterwards he wanted to get me in another film [most likely *The Chinese Room* starring Elizabeth Campbell]. It was shot in Mexico. I called the Actors Guild and they said don't go down there."

Movie Star, American Style was filmed in black-and-white, but includes color tinted LSD tripping scenes. One of the film's promotional gimmicks was to have the audience guess who were the real actors the characters were based on. This was highlighted in the film's trailer and poster art asking, "Who am I?" After Paula Lane as Honey Bunny speaks, clips from the movie of Barry James are shown as Steven Rogers says, "Who am I? I'm that big star who took LSD. See me in *Movie Star, American Style* and see how LSD changed my life."

Though this was bare bones filmmaking (and cannot even be found on DVD until this day) at the time the reviews were not overly bad. *Boxoffice* remarked, "Gratifyingly, the film is played for laugh effects and doesn't attempt any significant soul-searching. Zugsmith has directed with wryly winning touches stressing at all time constant move-ment..." Margaret Harford of the *Los Angeles Times* was less generous to the movie though calling it "a not very lucid parody...not very funny, either." In a number of cities, the film went out on a double bill with another sexploiter from Albert Zugsmith called *The Sexual Revolution* about wife swapping in the suburbs. Not surprisingly, this movie did not help propel Steven Rogers to major stardom.

Steven Rogers, Gary Clarke, Don Edmonds, and Les Brown, Jr. in *Wild Wild Winter* (Universal, 1966).

In his last motion picture, Steven Rogers once again was cast as a matinee idol but this time in a violent biker film and he doesn't play it for laughs. ("I was offered the part out of the blue one day and said fuck yeah I'll do that.") With his hair on the bit of the shaggy side befitting the style worn by young guys in 1968, Rogers had a supporting role in *Angels from Hell* (1968) directed by Bruce Kessler for producer Joe Solomon's Fanfare Productions. Too pretty to be a rough and tough biker, Roger's character Dude Marshall is an ex-biker gone Hollywood who left the open road behind a few years prior to become a big movie star. Rogers' personable charm that he projected in his prior movies is no where to be found here as his character frets the entire time on screen suspicious of why the biker gang tracked him down.

"I have to tell you that they hired real bikers for this," said Rogers." I remember I was looking at one guy before we were about to shoot and he had this hook like thing in his face."

Shot on location in Bakersfield, California, *Angels from Hell* starred Tom Stern as Mike, a disillusioned GI just returning from Vietnam, out to combat the establishment for sending him off to war. He heads for a new town where his buddy Smiley (Ted Markland) and his other former gang members are part of a new biker club, the Madcaps that are at peace with the law to Mike's consternation. Backed by his military experience, Mike takes out the club's leader and beds the mini-skirted Ginger (Arlene Martel), who lets the bikers hang out at her farm because "they amuse her." Seeking revenge against "the man" for making him fight in Vietnam, Mike wants the gang to join with other bikers to take down the man. First though he wants to recruit his former friend Danny who is now a movie star named Dude Marshall. "Don't you go to drive-ins any more," says Mike. "Dude Marshall is the biggest thing to hit Hollywood since Elvis." "Elvis who," asks one gang member. This was a jab at Presley to show by 1968 he had become uncool in the eyes of the drive-in crowd. With Ginger and a few others in tow, Mike heads to Hollywood to look up his old buddy.

Steven Rogers gives a very low-key performance here as compared to his previous movies. He first appears on screen as Dude listens while producer Saul Joseph (an uncredited Joe Solomon) is on the phone negotiating a deal for him to star in a Japanese science-fiction film for a hefty $150,000 fee. Dude is disturbed by his nervous girlfriend Jennifer (Susan Holloway) who whispers something to him but he shoos her away. With a second thought, he follows her to the front door where he sees his former biker gang outside. Hesitantly, he invites the gang into his home and at poolside introduces them to Saul by adding not very enthusiastically, "these are some buddies of mine from my flaming youth days." He offers them some joints while cigar-chomping Saul goes gaga over the guys with the idea to produce a motorcycle gang picture. While a reluctant Jennifer shows the biker chicks around and Saul chats with the interested Madcaps. Mike takes Dude aside to talk. He notices how uptight Dude is and promises that they are not there to hassle him. Dude admits he was taken aback by their surprise drop in. The gang just wants to see if he wants back in and Mike says to his former pal, "Don't you miss the bugs in your teeth tripping down the highway with the wind blowing in your face?" With enticement like that it is no wonder Dude takes a pass. As a parting gift, he gives Mike the rest of his marijuana stash. The Madcaps ride off with Saul promising to keep in touch about the movie.

During the course of the rest of the film, the Madcaps drink beer, smoke pot, make love and tangle with "the squares." Mike's power as leader of the gang goes to his head as he dreams to unite all the biker gangs, after biker Speed (Stephen Oliver) is "accidentally" killed by the police. When an innocent flower child is raped and murdered by one of the drugged-out bikers (Paul Bertoya as Nutty), the police close in as Mike tries to cover it up. Now out of control, an enraged Mike calls for an all-out war against the cops only to die defiantly opposing the oppression of the establishment.

Angels from Hell was distributed by American International Pictures throughout the drive-ins across America. It was a financial success bringing in $1.25 million at the box office and was the third highest grossing biker film of 1968 after *The Mini-Skirt Mob* and *The Savage Seven*. It was Rogers' swan song from acting as he moved to the other side of the camera teaming up with former co-star Don Edmonds with a production company.

The late Edmunds revealed in *Hollywood Surf and Beach Movies*, "Rick and I had these great offices on Brighton Way in Beverly Hills and we wore suits to lunch at La Scala. But we weren't making any movies. We walked around with business cards convincing ourselves that we were producers for about a year and a half. Finally, I said, 'Rick, we're bullshit! We're looking good and doing nothing!' He didn't care because he was wealthy and living up on Stone Canyon in a colonial mansion with his wife and two children. His family owned American Linen Supply Company and Steiner Products. I'm over there on Orchid Avenue in an $85.00 a month pad and I can't make the rent. I told him we were going to go out and make a tits and ass movie. He said, 'My wife would never allow me to make a tits and ass movie.' I said, 'Yes, she will.' And that's how we made *Wild Honey*."

Edmonds directed and wrote the sexy comedy released in 1972 about a country girl who comes to the big city and gets in all sorts of trouble. Rogers was credited as producer. But he and Rogers had a falling out due to "creative differences" and stopped speaking. "It was a terrible experience," admitted Rogers.

Steven Rogers disappeared from show business. He revealed, "I realized I wasn't going anywhere. I kept playing the same old shit. I thought it was stupid and I couldn't get the parts I really wanted. After years of doing this I thought I would do something else. After *Wild Honey*, I got very depressed and sat in a room for about four days. I didn't know what to do with myself. I started sewing and I got really good at it. Then I went to this famous designer who showed me how to do different things. Gradually, I began sewing for people. I designed jackets for Cher and Sammy Davis, Jr. that were all hand-embroidered. Later I went to UCLA and took courses in their design and architectural school."

With his new wife Carmen, Richard Rogers relocated to Park City, Utah where he helped save the Egyptian Theatre and began appearing on stage before suffering a stroke in the late 2000s. Almost eight years later, he is still fighting the affects and attending regular therapy.

Arguably one of the most handsome men ever to grace the drive-in movie screen, Steven Rogers should have had more lead roles. He had the looks for sure and proved that he was a versatile actor who could play sensitive as in *Combat!* and comedic as in his beach party movies. Still, super stardom for him never came to be. Even so, he remains one of the standout actors of teenage drive-in movies during the sixties.

5. SLAYGIRL JAN WATSON CELEBRATES THE MATT HELM SPY SPOOFS

SHE WAS KNOWN AS "THE girl with the perfect figure" so it is not unexpected that this brunette beauty was scantily clad and the joke of the double entendre playing Slaygirls in three swinging Matt Helm spy spoofs *The Silencers*; *Murderers' Row*; and *The Ambushers*. Her whole short career was one pin-up photo session, which did not bother her in the least since she was having such a good time. Even in her other movies, she was invariably always chosen to pose scantily clad for photos to help promote them even if she didn't even have a speaking part.

Janet Helen Watson was born in New York but raised in Los Angeles after her parents divorced. Her father was hockey legend Phil Watson who played for and later managed the New York Rangers and her mother a Powers model. In 1961, Jan was crowned Miss Hollywood and later in the year placed first runner-up in the Miss California contest. She assumed the winner's duties when her predecessor forfeited the tiara by getting married. With an alluring smile and a figure measuring 36-23-35, it is no surprise movies beckoned for this beauty queen and she happily answered the call. At the time, she credited her mother's advice for her successful entre into show business. Watson told columnist Lydia Lane of the *Los Angeles Times*, "Models must have poise and confidence. This keeps them from being obviously nervous or trying to hard to make an impression."

Jan Watson made her film debut as an anonymous bikini-clad robot in *Dr. Goldfoot and the Bikini Machine* (1965). She is noticed most toward the end of the movie as one of the curvy robots serving at the dinner party Dr. Goldfoot throws for his prisoners. Her screen time is minimal, but she was featured prominently in publicity ads and promotional appearances.

The actress was next selected to play one of the original three Slaygirls, then called Slaymates, in *The Silencers* (1966) starring Dean Martin as secret agent Matt Helm. The other two chosen were Barbara Burgess and Marilyn Tindall. *The Silencers'* tagline exclaimed, "Follow his secret from bedroom to bedlam, with guns, girls and dynamite!" For once the studio's PR department did not over hype. Based on a series of novels by Donald Hamilton, Matt Helm is a boozing, philandering rake of a spy, now a playboy photographer, enticed out of retirement by his ex-partner Tina Batori (Daliah Lavi). Their assignment is to travel to Phoenix to thwart Tung-Tze (Victor Buono) the leader of the Big O organization from starting WWIII by sabotaging an atomic missile—Operation Fall Out. Stella Stevens played red-haired Gail Hendrix the innocent, wide-eyed girlfriend of Big O operative Sam Gunther (Robert Webber) who innocently ends up with a computer tape that both the good and bad guys want.

Jan Watson and the other Slaymates make a fleeting appearance though the way the gals were used in promoting the movie fans thought they had much more screen time. Clad in a black bikini top and black lacy leotard with fishnet stockings, Jan appears in one of Helm's three erotic dreams. Though she is holding a fencing sword, the amorous Helm wants to make love not war as they begin kissing.

Publicity photo of Jan Watson in *The Swinger* (Paramount, 1966).

During a tacked on promo for the film's sequel *Murderers' Row*, Watson is snuggled up next to Dean Martin on a rotating bed chock full of Slaygirls—Burgess, Tindall, and added to the mix Susan Holloway, Karen Joy, Mary Jane Mangler, Margie Nelson, Margaret Teele, and Larri Thomas, amongst others. It was reported that it took over four hours to shoot. Though Martin kissed all the girls only the first impromptu smooch with Jan Watson remained in the final print. The girls were interviewed by Jack Altshul of *Newsday* while on tour doing promotion for the movie in New York. They stated that after all the kissing Dean quipped, "And my wife thinks acting is fun." Watson went on to say, "We bought him chap sticks for his lips."

In *Murderers' Row* (1966) Jan was back again as a Slaygirl (Miss July) along with Burgess (Miss December) and Tindall (Miss May). They were joined by Corinne Cole (Miss January who tries to assassinate Helm at the film's start) and nine others to round out the calendar. It was reported that Earl Wilson helped producer Irving Allen make his selections, which included *Beach Party* castoff Mary Hughes, Mary Jane Mangler, Amadee Chabot, Dee Duffy, and Rena Horten.

In this sequel, a squealing Ann-Margret is the innocent this time playing Suzie, the swinging daughter of kidnapped scientist Dr. Norman Solaris (Richard Eastham) who has invented a helio-beam capable of destroying the world using the sun's rays and has disappeared. Arch villain Julian Wall (Karl Malden) plans to use it to decimate Washington D.C. ("Operation Scorch"). He orders his top agent Ironhead (Tom Reese) to orchestrate the assassinations of all of ICE's agents including Helm. However, Matt survives the explosion rigged in his home. Presumed dead, he poses as a hit man named James A. Peters and heads for the Riviera where he discovers that his contact has been murdered and stuffed into her refrigerator. It is there at a discotheque where he meets Suzie and they join forces to find Wall and her father. After a series of car chases, fistfights, explosions (caused by Suzie's hairpin), and a hovercraft pursuit, Ironhead and Wall are killed, Solaris is rescued, and Washington D.C. is saved. The film ends with Matt Helm and Suzie taking the plunge from his bed into his enormous bathtub surrounded by his Slaygirls.

Murderers' Row was a better showcase for Jan than *The Silencers* since this time she got lines to recite! Miss July arrives early wearing a very form-fitting floral patterned dress with blue gloves and picture hat to her photo shoot with Dean Martin's Matt Helm who tells her that they will be doing the Spirit of 76. The naïve Slaygirl retorts, "76? *Are you kidding?* I'm only a 44." Later she leads the other Slaygirls in a toast to Helm after believing that he was killed by the bomb planted by Miss January and appears in the film's finale wearing a velvet red, white and blue star-studded bikini topped with sapphires in her chestnut brown hair.

Pin-up photos of Jan Watson from the Matt Helm movies found there way into the overseas edition of *Stars and Stripes* that was read by many a G.I. in Vietnam. It was reported that Jan was swamped with thousands of letters from servicemen whose requests ranged from asking for romantic advice to requesting autographed photos. Watson remarked in the *Hollywood Citizen News*, "Some of the letters really get to you. Most of them are just plain lonely. I intend to open and read each and every letter."

Watson's third and final appearance as a Slaygirl was in *The Ambushers* where she began being billed as "Jann Watson." In this silly adventure yarn, Matt investigates the disappearance of a U.S. space craft. He is aided by Sheila Sommers (an out of place Janice Rule) the aircraft's pilot (it can only be flown by females due to some cockamamie reason) who was raped and left for dead in the desert when it was taken. They pose as husband and wife photographers when the culprit is believed to be beer magnate Jose Ortega (Albert Salmi) who is hosting a fashion show in Acapulco as a cover in trying to sell the spaceship to the highest bidder. Matt also has to deal with seductive enemy agent Francesca Madeiros (Senta Berger) working for the Big O organization one of the interested parties.

Of all the Matt Helm films, this gave the most screen time to the delectable Slaygirls whose scenes at their training headquarters and later at a fashion show in Acapulco are the film's highlights. Though Jan is seen more she has fewer lines than in the previous movie. After appearing with the other heavily made-up girls throughout the opening montage clad in mod sixties fashions on the hunt for potential mates as the title tune is sung by Tommy Boyce and Bobby Hart over the credits, Watson with her brown hair grown long is one of the Slaygirls at ICE's rehabilitation center getting a refresher course on the newest gadgets developed by the spy organization. Clad in a low-cut halter top with matching shorts, she rides up to Dean Martin's Matt Helm and offers him a ride on her Vesper. After he hops on, she quips, "I go pretty fast. Better find something to hang on to." With a nod to the audience, he reaches for her breasts as the scene fades out.

Later Watson and the other Slaygirls are undercover at an Acapulco resort modeling fashions by Oleg Cassini while "photographers" Matt and Sheila try to determine where the spacecraft has been hidden. Jan can be seen wearing a light blue patterned dress as she circles the pool area during a cocktail party with the other girls.

Jan Watson, ca. 1966.

In between Matt Helm movies, Watson snuck in some minor movie roles. She appears briefly in the Ann-Margret comedy *The Swinger* as one of *Girl Lure* magazine's international models introduced to reporters at an outdoor press reception by editor, Tony Franciosa. She had more of a wardrobe and a line to recite as a whore in the western *Alvarez Kelly* (1966) starring William Holden and Richard Widmark. As with *Dr. Goldfoot* and the Matt Helm movies, Watson (along with co-whore Arlene Charles) was selected to help publicize this film by appearing in numerous pin-up photos published in newspapers and magazines worldwide giving the illusion that their roles in the film were bigger than they actually were.

Watson also turned up as a model (what else?) in "A Piece of the Action" on *Batman*, and had a bigger role on *I Dream of Jeannie* in "My Master, the Swinging Bachelor." She played Roger Healey's perky date Polly the skydiver who accompanies him to Major Nelson's house for a dinner party sabotaged by Jeannie, of course. Jan looks stunning in a lime green chiffon cocktail dress and is quite amusing. The oblivious Polly downs a Bloody Mary thinking it is just tomato juice and hungrily eats her spaghetti whose sauce is laced with loads of salt and other condiments by Jeannie while the other guests gasp for water. Unfairly, Watson did not receive screen credit for this.

After playing a secretary in the serious secret agent thriller *Panic in the City* (1968), Watson married director Henry Levin whom she worked with on *Murderers' Row* and *The Ambushers* on June 21, 1968. He announced their engagement at the wrap party for *The Ambushers*. Following in the footsteps of many a sixties glamour girl, she left acting to raise a family when her son Anthony J. Levin was born.

In *Dr. Goldfoot and the Bikini Machine*
if you blinked you missed you.

That's because I resembled Susan Hart too much who was the star of the movie and wife of the studio head at American International Pictures. I just had a little scene because of that. I worked again with China Lee and Pamela Rodgers [in *The Swinger*]. We were usually part of the little groups of pretty girls hired to play models or whatever to decorate the scene.

How did you wind up in *The Silencers*?

When I graduated high school, I was modeling and doing TV commercials but I [also] had to have a steady job as a receptionist at an advertising agency. They were very generous with me and would allow me to go on modeling and acting interviews as long as I had someone to cover for me. Guess who I hired to sit in for me—Linda Gray from TV's *Dallas*. I paid her $2.00 an hour. She was married to a record producer named Ed Thrasher at the time. She was very sweet and such a lovely girl.

I was with the William Morris Agency for about a year. They wanted a Natalie Wood-type, but they didn't get me any work. I switched to an agent named Dale Garrett at a small agency. He was known for representing pretty girls—model and beauty queen types. He was responsible for changing my life forever when he got me an interview at Columbia Pictures with producer Irving Allen for a picture starring Dean Martin titled *The Silencers*. It was supposed to be one day's work as a model. My agent told me to dress sexy. I went on the interview and within a day or too learned that I had the job. I thought I was supposed to go right to the set, but they wanted to photograph me first. In the movie, there are three pictures above Dean's bed. They chose about twelve girls to be Slaymates and they wanted only three for the pictures. So one day's work now stretched to a week.

What was the first day of filming like?

When we got on the set, they first filmed Barbara Burgess as the cowgirl. Marilyn Tindall was next as the fishing girl. And my bit as the Slaymate fencing with Dean Martin came last. He and I really connected and there was a spark between us. When we finished, Dean asked me to sit with him and have a cigarette. He then called the director Phil Karlson over and said, "I would like Jan to play my secretary Lovey." Karlson told him that they already signed Beverly Adams.

So that was your only day on the set?

No, I had to come back for one more photo shoot. On that day, I am standing on the side with the other girls. Dean comes over and kisses me hello. I am told we are going to do this promo piece on this round bed. Some girls are on the bed and others are standing behind. I am the only one propped up lying right next to Dean. He says his lines and then surprises me with another kiss. He says, "Oh, my God." I start laughing and they left it in. As a result of all that everybody at Columbia knew that there was a connection between Dean and me. And that picture on the round bed was run full page in *The Hollywood Reporter*. I saw it while reading the paper as I was standing on the unemployment line. It was also used on the cover of the film's soundtrack LP.

You were also hired to promote the movie around the country.
Yes, they sent Barbara, Marilyn, me, and three others to New York to do publicity. That is where I met Sam Jaffe who was the head of Columbia Pictures at the time and a number of other executives. It was a real whirlwind kind of a situation. We were wined and dined. I even got to see my first Broadway show, *The Unsinkable Molly Brown*. At some point we appeared on *The Merv Griffin Show*. Merv was an absolutely wonderful man. Barbara choreographed this little dance for us to do on his show. The result of this was that Columbia was so impressed that three days later we were on our way to Europe. They treated us like queens. We went to Rome, Paris, Munich, and London where we attended *The Silencers* premiere. I have a picture with Paul McCartney from that. This was all so flabbergasting to me because what was suppose to be one day's work turned into months of work and was a life changer for me.

How did you get along with Barbara Burgess and Marilyn Tindall.
Barbara was my roommate and we were friends. At the time, I got along very well with Marilyn who was fine to work with. We don't get along now and I have nothing to do with her. I met her prior to *The Silencers* in the Miss California contest. I knew her, but we were not friends and I didn't see her again until *The Silencers*. We all got along well especially the six of us who did all the traveling. There was never any problem.

Any of the other Slaymates stand out for you?
Margaret Teele was very sweet. I met her when we did the round bed shoot. She wore a man's shirt. I don't think she was in the movie though. Mary Jane Mangler was one of the girls in the opening scene and she went on tour with us. Then they began switching girls in and out. Pamela Rodgers joined us in Chicago. In Europe, Inga Nielsen was part of the six. She played the statue who came alive during the nightclub scene. She was very nice.

Publicity photo from *The Silencers* (Columbia, 1966) with (*1ˢᵗ row lying on bed*) Marilyn Tindall, Barbara Burgess, Dean Martin, and Jan Watson; (*2ⁿᵈ row kneeling on bed*) Mary Jane Mangler, Margie Nelson, and Larri Thomas; (*3rd row standing*) Susan Holloway, Margaret Teele, unidentified actress, and Karen Joy

What did you think of producer Irving Allen?

He was fine and a lot of fun. He had a good sense of humor. He wore these big eyeglasses. Dean wore them in the movie when Matt Helm would be examining the film he just shot.

And director Phil Karlson?

He was a doll. He sent Barbara, Marilyn, and me each a bouquet of flowers on our first day of filming. He took us in to meet Cyd Charisse and she was just lovely.

My time working on *The Silencers* was an absolutely positive experience from Phil Karlson, to the girls, to the crew, to anybody we worked with. Nobody made a sexual play for me or exhibited any rude behavior.

The Silencers was a huge hit and a sequel ***Murderers' Row*** was put into production. Were you surprised to be invited back?

No, I wasn't. After *The Silencers*, I had a small part in the western *Alvarez Kelly* for Columbia Pictures. They liked my line reading. When Bill Holden walks into the saloon I stare at him and a guy says, "Do you know him?" I respond, "No, but I wish I did!" The studio sent me to New Orleans to promote the picture.

Columbia also put me in their studio acting school for contract consideration. I was earning $350 a month at the ad agency and now at Columbia Pictures I was making $350 a week. My acting partner at the school was this good looking guy named Harrison Ford. I told him that he looked like Paul Newman. He said that he was married with two sons and was a carpenter. He was not the best actor but wanted to make a better living. Columbia dropped him after six months.

In ***Murderers' Row*** you got a bigger part with lines and have an amusing scene with Dean Martin and Beverly Adams.

This was fun. Beverly Adams was a doll and we became good friends. All the girls just adored Beverly. I saw her in London after she married Vidal Sassoon. She and her husband visited Henry and I at our home after my son Tony was born.

How was it to work with Dean Martin a second time?

Dean was still great to work with. He was a truly wonderful, easy-going man. A total professional and he didn't drink. That was all an act. I also appeared on his variety show a few times. Nothing got him upset. He just rolled with the tide.

Frank Sinatra was known for not wanting to do more than one or two takes tops while making a movie. Was Dean Martin like that?

Dean Martin was nothing like that. He was very relaxed and it didn't bother him. He probably didn't like having to do more takes, but never objected. With his TV show, he would not even rehearse. He'd come on Sundays and just do the show. He had a good time with it and ad-libbed a lot. On the movies however he stuck to the script.

Publicity photo of Slaygirls Dee Duffy, Jan Watson, Dale Brown,
and Mary Hughes in *Murderers' Row* (Columbia, 1966).

Henry Levin was brought in to direct *Murderers' Row*. Professionally, how did his directing style compare to Phil Karlson's?

I thought they were very much the same. Both were easy-going, nice directors. They weren't demanding. They were both kind men. I met Henry on the set, and after awhile he started calling me J.W., which I thought was kind of weird. He didn't ask me out to dinner until after I was done filming. We went to this very quaint intimate little place in Santa Monica, which was a favorite of people in show business because it was off the beaten path and there were never any paparazzi. We went there a lot and then travelled together to promote the movie.

Does anything stand out for you while on this promotional tour?
The executives at Columbia found out that my father was a former player and coach of the New York Rangers. They asked me to contact the hockey team to see if we could take publicity photos with them and promote the movie at one of their home games at Madison Square Garden. They said no to that, but my father stepped in and they said we could take some pictures with the team. The six Slaygirls wore black trench coats and they put us in a goalie's net with some of the Rangers behind us. We looked like a big puck. It ran on the back page of either the *New York Daily News* or *New York Post*. Columbia was very pleased with the publicity it drummed up.

Slaymates or Slaygirls?
In *The Silencers* we were called Slaymates. However, Hugh Hefner objected because it was too close to his Playboy Playmates, so they changed them to Slaygirls for the next two movies. I think Hefner was going to sue them if they didn't stop using that name..

Ann-Margret co-starred in *Murderers' Row* and you also had a small part in her comedy *The Swinger.* Did you get to meet or talk with her?
No, I didn't. But the thing that is interesting is that for *The Swinger* director George Sidney had about fifty girls in a room interviewing us to play models. I found it odd that Ann-Margret was sitting there on the side watching and didn't say a word. I couldn't understand why the star of the movie even cared because none of these were speaking parts.

On *Murderers' Row*, the one scene we had together was at the end when Dean and Ann-Margret slide into the pool and the Slaygirls are around it. But they shot us separately, so even though I was on the set with her, we never met.

The *Los Angeles Times* reported about the trouble Oleg Cassini and Henry Levin had with the international models picked to be Slaygirls for *The Ambushers*. In particular it singled out Karin Fedderson who complained about having to go bra less; Annabella Incontrera who was upset because she thought she would have a main role; Terri Hughes who felt Cassini was not paying her enough attention; and Kyra Bester who threatened to quit because she thought there was to be only six Slaygirls. Were you aware of any of this?

I did not know that Oleg Cassini and Henry were experiencing problems with the international models on the set. Henry and I were engaged at the time, and were living together in our own bungalow at the Las Brisas Resort. Therefore, I really didn't spend much time with the other models once the filming had concluded each day, and Henry certainly didn't mention anything to me personally.

Do you remember any of these new Slaygirls?

To be honest, I didn't know many of the girls all that well, and was more familiar with them by reference of the countries that they came from. Annabella Incontrea was from Italy, and she had a scene in the swimming pool where Dean asks the resort manager "who is that?" to which the manager replies, "That's my wife!" Terri Hughes was from Australia, and from what I can recall, her part consisted mostly of dancing around the swimming pool. I don't think she had her own individual scene. I'm surprised to learn that she said Oleg Cassini was not paying enough attention to her. Kyra Bester, who I believe was from France, had her own scene in the movie where she was fencing with Dean. My guess is that Kyra thought there would only be six Slaygirls based on the fact that there were six of us who went on tour in Europe to promote *The Silencers*. I don't recall Karin Fedderson. After all, it has been forty-two years since then!

Dee Duffy stands out for me though. She was in *Murderers' Row* and came into *The Ambushers* later for the Acapulco scenes. She was very sweet and we became good friends. Both of us lived in Beverly Hills and she married David May of the May Company. Our children went to the same elementary school.

Inga Neilsen is also mentioned in the article and she was perturbed because she was a "leftover" and not picked to be one of the twelve main Slaygirls. She refuses to speak about making *The Ambushers*.

That is very surprising. I'm not sure why she referred to herself as being "a leftover." I don't know anything about that. I did work with Inga on this and remembered that she did have a speaking part at the spy school and in Acapulco.

What was it like to wear clothes by Oleg Cassini?

He was the one who said I had the perfect figure. He also told me that I reminded him of his ex-wife Gene Tierney. He was very nice and designed the clothes specifically for each of us. We had no say in what we were to wear.

Did you have any off-screen interaction with *The Ambushers'* leading ladies Senta Berger or Janice Rule?

I really didn't get to know either of them, but remember that Henry gave Janice an extra line to say. When she and Dean are getting into the car after Matt realizes that Sheila has had her memory back for awhile, he says that she fooled a lot of people. She replies, "That was the idea, Dr. Watson." That was for me.

The Matt Helm movies seem to have been only a positive experience for you.

Making all three of those movies was a wonderfully glorious time for me. It changed my life because Henry Levin became the love of my life. After filming *Murderers' Row*, Henry returned to Rome where he lived. When he came back to Hollywood, he had a diamond engagement ring and asked to marry me. I said yes. This was just before we began filming *The Ambushers*.

On the Matt Helm movies we were like family. Jerry Siegel was the assistant director on *Murderers' Row* and Henry wanted him for *The Ambushers*. It was just a very tight knit group. If you are lucky enough to work in a series of films like this people want to stick together. They usually like hiring the same people because they can trust them. They know their work and don't have to worry about any problems. That's how it was with the Matt Helm movies.

Jan Watson and Dean Martin in *The Ambushers* (Columbia, 1967). *Courtesy of Lee Pfeiffer*

Do you have a favorite Matt Helm movie?
The Ambushers was probably my favorite. I had more to do and we were on location in Mexico. I was in love with the director. What more can you ask for.

How come you aren't in the fourth Matt Helm movie, *The Wrecking Crew*?
My agent called me and asked if I wanted to be in *The Wrecking Crew*. At that point I had such a good relationship with producer Irving Allen and Columbia Pictures that I did not have to interview for it. I said no because Henry and I had just gotten married and my life was with him. None of the Slaygirls from the prior movies are in it and neither was Beverly Adams as Lovey. They brought back Phil Karlson as the director, but I do not know why the others were not in it. Sharon Tate was in this and she was tragically murdered sometime after making it a sad situation.

In your later films you are billed as Jann.
That is because when I did *The Dean Martin Show* someone made a typographical error and spelled it that way on my contract. I looked at it and thought "that's great," so I changed it. You have to be original!

Any special memories about your TV work?
I had no interaction with any of the cast members on *Batman*. I came in to do my bit as the fashion model and left. When I did *I Dream of Jeannie* Larry Hagman and Barbara Eden were really nice to me, so were Bill Daily and Hayden Rorke. They both invited me to have lunch with them. We had just done an eating scene so all I ordered was chicken broth. I was a cheap date!

Did you miss show business once you stopped acting?
No, I didn't miss it. I never had a hunger to be famous. For me, it was a means for an income.

6. IRENE TSU RETURNS TO *Paradise,* *Hawaiian Style*

DURING ELVIS' ACTIVE PERIOD MAKING his films for MGM between 1963 and 1968, he snuck in three movies for producer Hal B. Wallis and Paramount Pictures. *Paradise, Hawaiian Style* (1966) was the last of them and his final film for Wallis. Trying to ape the earlier success of *Blue Hawaii* and *Girls! Girls! Girls!*, Elvis was sent back to the lush tropical islands to recapture his former glory and was surrounded by five lovely lasses. One of them was Chinese starlet Irene Tsu.

During the 1960's, Irene Tsu played a variety of "native" girls in a number of popular drive-in films. Irene was born in Shanghai. When the Communists took over in 1949, she and her family fled first to Formosa and then to Hong Kong where they remained for six years before immigrating to New York. Once in the U.S., Tsu began ballet training, which was her steppingstone into the performing arts. At the tender age of fourteen, she borrowed her aunt's cheongsam and got the role of Gwenny in the road company of *The World of Susie Wong*. Her friendship with the play's star Nancy Kwan led to a small part as one of the teenage dancers in the film version of the Rodgers and Hammerstein musical *Flower Drum Song* (1961) starring Kwan and James Shigeta. Soon after, she traveled to Rome to be one of Elizabeth Taylor's handmaidens in *Cleopatra* (1963).

Back in Hollywood, Irene appeared as a French speaking actress in the Sandra Dee comedy *Take Her, She's Mine* (1963). More exotic supporting roles followed in *John Goldfarb, Please Come Home* (1964), *The Pleasure Seekers* (1964) and *Sword of Ali Baba* (1965). In 1965's *How to Stuff a Wild Bikini* (the last official *Beach Party* movie), Irene played a native girl who romances Frankie Avalon while he is on reserve duty away from Annette Funicello. Irene then went from a leading role in the sci-fi cheapie *Women of the Prehistoric*

Planet (1966) to a supporting part in the big budget epic *Seven Women* (1966) directed by John Ford. Her next stop—*Paradise, Hawaiian Style*.

The screenplay for *Paradise, Hawaiian Style* (originally titled *Hawaiian Paradise*) was credited to Allan Weiss (based on his story) and John Lawrence. Weiss had previously scripted *Blue Hawaii* and *Girls! Girls! Girls!,* among other Elvis movies, so he was an obvious choice for Wallis to hire to pen another Hawaiian set musical for the King. Co-writer Lawrence previously worked with Weiss on the screenplay for *Roustabout*.

Hired to direct was Michael D. Moore, a former child actor in silent films (as Mickey Moore), who had been working as an assistant director since the late forties mostly at Paramount Studios. He previously worked with Elvis Presley on all his Wallis-produced movies beginning with *King Creole* in 1958 through *Roustabout* in 1964. This was his first feature as director.

Paradise, Hawaiian Style featured not one, not two, but five leading female roles. The character of Judy Hudson was the main love interest for Elvis' amorous flyboy. She is an ace pilot too, but because she is a woman has a hard time landing jobs. Needing to support herself, she becomes the office manager for Elvis' charter service but pretends to be married to keep him at bay. High profile actresses for the time such as Yvette Mimieux, Sandra Dee, Pamela Tiffin, Carol Lynley, Ann-Margret, Elizabeth Ashley, and Tuesday Weld were considered for the part. According to a memo dated June 24, 1965 written by Paul Nathan to Paramount's legal department, "they are either unavailable or far out of reach on price. Most of this list ranges from $50,000 to $250,000." He went on to note that a number of "less known girls" were tested including Marianna Hill, Julie Parrish, Diana Millay, Yvonne Craig, Brenda Benet, Mary Mitchel, Joan Staley, Julie Sommars, Andrea Dromm, Michele Carey, and Chris Noel but they were all found unsuitable to play Judy.

Pretty blonde Suzanna Leigh was cast as Judy Hudson the main love interest for Elvis and was his first British leading lady. Paul Nathan wrote in the same memo above, "We want to use Suzanna Leigh in the Presley picture *Hawaiian Paradise*, because she co-stars with Tony Curtis and Jerry Lewis in *Boeing, Boeing* and because we think she will come off as an important star in that picture. In addition, she is blonde, twenty and absolutely ideal for the part of Judy..." In her autobiography *Paradise, Suzanna Style*, Leigh boasts erroneously that she was Elvis' first non-American leading lady. Actually, Juliet Prowse (born in India) from *G.I. Blues* has that distinction followed by Ursula Andress, Ann-

Margret, Jocelyn Lane, and then Leigh. A minor problem did arise in regards to Leigh's actual age. There was confusion if she was going to turn twenty or twenty-one on July 26, 1965. The producers thought the latter based on what the actress was stating in the press, but her mother set the record straight. She wrote to Paramount that her daughter was turning twenty and that she expected a chaperon to be hired.

Promotional poster art for *Paradise, Hawaiian Style* (Paramount, 1966).

Raquel Welch was the first choice to play the second female lead entertainer Lani Kaimana. Others tested included Nobu McCarthy and Miko Mayama. However, Welch's agent was Jack Gilardi and he asked for a salary of $17,500. In a memo to Hal Wallis dated June 17, 1965, Paul Nathan wrote that "I told him good luck and tell her we are not interested." The role then went to Marianna Hill who was rejected as Judy. She had a bit part in Elvis' *Roustabout* and just wowed the critics with her performance as a French tease in Howard Hawks' racecar drama *Red Line 7000* for Paramount Pictures in which she signed a contract with an option for one picture a year for five years. *Paradise, Hawaiian Style* would be her first film under this pact and she agreed to be paid $1,000 per week (rather than the stated $1,500 per her contract) with a ten week guarantee. She also relented to co-star billing with her name listed below the title with "no size or position guaranteed" per a memo from casting director Edward R. Morse.

The competition was fierce for the remaining three roles in the audition phase as many young actresses vied for the chance to act opposite Elvis on location in the Hawaiian Islands. Irene Tsu recalled, "I heard about the movie and wanted to work with Elvis so badly that I even went to an acting coach for help. I was very nervous during my audition. Hal Wallis loved my test. He was undecided if I should play Pua or Lehua. He was very open and I ended up with Pua [the role she wanted] who was featured in one of the film's most lavish production numbers. All the roles were different degrees of girlfriends of Elvis."

Actress Julie Parrish (who passed away in 2006) was a huge Elvis Presley fan and also desperately wanted to work with the King. After blowing her audition to play the female lead, she begged Hal Wallis for a second chance. He gave it to her and her reading went much better resulting in her being cast as Joanna over Joan Staley. Though she was elated, things quickly became unpleasant for her as the insistent producer kissed her once in his office and began putting pressure on her to go out with him. She recalled in *Fantasy Femmes of Sixties Cinema*, "Mr. Wallis, who was married, was an old *letch*. I think he felt there was an unspoken promise that I would sleep with him since he allowed me to re-test for the part. On the day before filming began, he called me into his office, led me over to the sofa, and briefly kissed me on the mouth. He said, 'Little girl, we're going to have a long talk about your future.' I made up any excuse to get out of there."

Parrish wasn't the only starlet who had a problem with Wallis. Laurel Goodwin almost did too previously on *Girls! Girls! Girls!* "Hal Wallis made me a little nervous," commented Goodwin in *Drive-in Dream Girls*. "But by the time that we were in a position where there might have been a problem for me he had a personal crisis. Wallis then had to leave the shoot in Hawaii and return to the mainland. I took a sigh of relief and really didn't have to face that issue but I saw it coming around the corner, so to speak. He was always a gentleman with me but I knew what was lurking." Maybe it was something in the tropical air that made the old dude horny.

Elvis Presley and Irene Tsu in *Paradise, Hawaiian Style* (Paramount, 1966).

Lastly, sultry Korean actress Linda Wong, a former beauty queen, was cast as Lehua beating out, among others, Nobu McCarthy and Linda Ho. She was originally in the running to play Lani and the producers thought Lehua was a better fit. Her prior films included *Five Gates to Hell*; *Wake Me When It's Over* (1960); *The Nun and the Sergeant*; and

The Horizontal Lieutenant. Other starlets cast in smaller roles included Jan Shepard as the wife of Presley's partner; Gigi Verone as a flight attendant; Deanna Lund as a nurse; and Edy Williams, China Lee, Chanin Hale, and Ann Morell as secretarial candidates.

What is interesting to learn is that during the casting process none of the actresses auditioned with Elvis. Hal Wallis and his team just had to go with their gut feelings and hope the actresses would have some chemistry with the actor. Irene Tsu confirmed, "I didn't meet Elvis until my first day of shooting in Hawaii. It was a very hot day and the air conditioner in my trailer was broken. I went to Elvis' dressing room, which was in this huge hut to escape the heat. One of Elvis' bodyguards let me rest in an extra bedroom. I dozed off and was woken by Elvis himself. We became very good friends after that. Elvis was such a nice guy. At that time, he also was very spiritual."

Paradise, Hawaiian Style reportedly began filming on July 26, 1965 in beautiful tropical locations, mainly in Kauai and Maui, though all was not paradise on the set. According to Julie Parrish, Elvis despised the song "It's a Dog's Life" that he had to sing to her in a helicopter surrounded by a bunch of rowdy mutts and couldn't stop laughing while filming. And her battle with the amorous Hal Wallis continued in the islands. She said in *Fantasy Femmes of Sixties Cinema*, "While on location he was constantly calling me and asking me out. It was quite annoying and insulting. He called me one last time in Hawaii and said, 'little girl, you'd better think again.' I knew I would probably never work for him again, but that was fine with me. This whole incident highly offended me. I'm not claiming to have been an innocent, but when I make mistakes, I like them to be due to choices of my own."

Irene Tsu had no knowledge of Parrish's problems with Wallis or that she was a huge fan of Elvis, but she commented, "Julie Parrish and I had the same agent. She did the usual 'starlet' thing at the time. I am not sure if she had a thing with Elvis, but she did with others."

While Parrish was fighting off Wallis, Elvis had a jealous leading lady who was demanding to boot. Suzanna Leigh admits in her autobiography that she became miffed when she realized that she was not going to be the only blonde in the movie. She claimed that she used her on-set affair with Elvis to have co-star Marianna Hill don a long black wig—an ill-fitting one at that. She even freely admitted that she was jealous of Hill's musical duet "Scratch My Back" with Elvis and tried to interfere with the shooting of it by sitting next to the cameraman. "This was the sexy bit of the film and I saw it as a threat to me—childish, I know…I wanted his attention all the time; I didn't want to share him with anyone," she said in *Paradise, Suzanna Style*. She went on to write that Elvis sang his portion of the song directly at her. However, this is wishful thinking on her part. Watching the film, Elvis is concentrating on Hill alone and not looking off-camera. Despite Leigh's unsuccessful intention to sabotage, the sultry and highly talented Marianna Hill's pairing with Elvis makes this one of the movie's most memorable musical numbers.

Regarding the British actress' claims, Irene Tsu commented, "Suzanna Leigh was sort of standoffish because she was the leading lady. I really didn't have much interaction with her. I saw no signs of an affair with Elvis, but maybe in private they were hooking up." As for her own relationship with Elvis, Tsu said, "A number of times I was invited back to have dinner with him, but it was very uncomfortable. He would be sitting there with Colonel Parker and his entourage. Nobody really had a conversation—it was more like trying to say something to entertain Elvis. It was horrible and I felt sorry for Elvis so I stopped going."

As for the rest of the cast, Tsu commented, "Now Marianna Hill is a good friend of mine. On the set we kept to ourselves though she did warn me that my dinner invitation with Elvis would not be with him alone. Our friendship I think started after making this movie. Linda Wong was Korean and was very beautiful. She was a lot older than me and I looked up to her. When we filmed *Paradise, Hawaiian Style*, she was already engaged to some financier, I think. She was kind of reserved and spoke English with an accent. She was very poised and may have been a model. I met James Shigeta when I worked on *Flower Drum Song*. He was the nicest guy. I really didn't have a lot to do on location with him, but later on we became friends."

Irene Tsu didn't have any problems with the cast or Hal Wallis whom she described as being "very hands on and on the set a lot." Luckily for her, his hands were not on her. However, she was so *not* impressed with director Michael Moore. "He was kind of a novice," she recalled. "Hal Wallis let him direct this because he was the assistant director on a couple of Wallis' other films. The guy was terrified of everybody most of all Elvis. He never directed Elvis at all and let him do whatever he wanted.

"Michael Moore was just trying to please Elvis," continued Tsu. "He was like some of the TV directors I worked with who were brought in to do a show where the star is so strong that the star basically knows exactly what they want to do. The director is really there directing traffic. Michael was constantly asking Elvis, 'Are you comfortable with that? Are you okay with this?' He basically set up the shots and then ran it by Elvis for his approval. There was no attempt by him to help us with our performances. It was basically hit your mark so they could shoot it fast." Suzanna Leigh concurred with this and wrote in her autobiography *Paradise, Suzanna Style*, "Mickey had little or no control over Elvis." Julie Parrish, on the other hand, was more impressed with the director especially when working on the "It's a Dog's Life" number and remarked in *Fantasy Femmes of Sixties Cinema*, "I think...Michael Moore did a good job with this scene."

Moore's lackadaisical directing style really irked Irene Tsu when it came time to film the big production number "Drums of the Islands" the sole reason she pushed for the part of Pua. "This was a very lavish production number for this or any Elvis movie," remarked Tsu. "Elvis and I come down a river in a canoe as he's singing "Drums of the Islands." This turned out to be difficult because we never rehearsed it. I found that very strange. The only instructions I got were that some natives would help me onto the barge and they pointed out where I should sit as it floats down river to a spot where we were to run to once we got off it. There we were to exchange lines of dialog, but since there were helicopters with camera men shooting from above they said even if we can't hear you don't worry we'll loop the dialog later. As the scene started they blasted the song from these huge boom boxes hidden along the banks of the river. At first I thought it was just going to be the background music. We sailed along, as Elvis just lip-synched to the song. I was really shocked and nobody told me that he was going to sing to me. So I decided to just sit there and look pretty. Our heads kept going back and forth. Elvis was looking one way and I was looking another. It looks pretty silly. Our characters liked each other but you couldn't tell that from this scene. As an actress, it was one of my most awkward moments on screen. I was so embarrassed when I saw it at the screening.

"It was shot all in one long take," continued Irene. "We didn't even do close-ups for it. That is one of the reasons I wasn't very happy with Michael Moore as a director. I am sure he worked it out technically, but they left me on my own. The setup was so elaborate with lots of extras as natives you would have thought they would have told me exactly what to do. Of course, I was too green and didn't ask any questions."

Some of Tsu's criticisms are most likely true. In Michael Moore's autobiography *My Magic Carpet of Films—A Personal Journey*, Moore expounds on the technical difficulties with regards to shooting *Paradise, Hawaiian Style*. He recounts surveying the island locations and creating storyboards for all the scenes; the problems he had with the helicopters needed to shoot high above the islands including footage shot at Waimea Canyon; and coordinating hundreds of dancers and extras for two major scenes including the "Drums of the Islands" production number at the Polynesian Cultural Center. He never writes about working with the actors or what he did to help them with their performances..

Of course, the one actor from *Paradise, Hawaiian Style* Moore mentions in his book is Elvis Presley. He opined, "The Elvis I worked with was always a hard worker, never too tired to put out his best, even if he had an early call. He was always polite, even a bit formal... Nevertheless, he could be very loose and relaxed on the set."

Marianna Hill, on the other had, had a totally different opinion of Elvis. When back in Hollywood after filming was completed, the starlet opened up about her frustrations with Presley in an interview she granted writer Tony Taylor of *Motion Picture Magazine* in 1966. She had a few complimentary things to say about the King, but unlike most of his co-stars, took him to task and described him as being "unprofessional." She went on to explain, "He's always competing with the leading ladies. He doesn't seem to want you to get serious with your work because he knows you're better trained than he. So he likes to break up all the time and throw the scene. He doesn't concentrate on what he's doing. He acts as though he cares, but he doesn't. I never care about anybody turning up late. However, it's very difficult to work with people when they're not trying and not doing what they have to do. But the apathy on the set is quite discouraging."

When asked if she thinks Marianna Hill actually said those things, Irene Tsu replied, "Yes, because it would be something she would do because of her personality. She probably did it just to cause a sensation. She is a nice person, but could act crazy. We both practiced yoga with Bikram Choudhury. I am one of the core members and have been one of his teachers for many years. Marianna would always come to class. She is extremely funny and was always cracking jokes in class and got away with it. She would call Bikram 'Biggie baby.' Nobody else would dare call him that but he would laugh every time. She was always a rebel and kooky. We would hang out after class and she was always getting herself into mega trouble. She was the mistress of some married Hollywood big shot for a long time. We would go out to dinner and she would climb on top of the table and start singing. It was always the same song so I would sing along with her."

In *Paradise, Hawaiian Style*, Elvis Presley played pilot and ladies man Greg "Rick" Richards. He returns to Hawaii after losing his commercial piloting job due to his fraternization with a stewardess mid-flight (she was the one smoldering in the galley). While visiting with his married buddy and charter pilot Danny Kohana (James Shigeta) and his family, Rick bonds with his five kids and sings a duet with the precociously annoying Donna Butterworth as eldest daughter Jan. The next day Rick accompanies Danny and passenger Mr. Cubberson (Grady Sutton) to the Maui Sheraton Hotel, but they make a pit stop for Rick to pitch going into a personal helicopter service business with Danny. He already has the connection with an investor to put up the two helicopters and wants Danny to be his partner providing the service. Danny is skeptical and still needs convincing. At the hotel, Rick introduces Danny to an old girlfriend named Lehua (Linda Wong). The miffed beauty reminds the flyboy about their missed date two years ago. She then goes on to insult Rick and agrees to another date—two years from today. Though Irene passed on this role, Lehua has the wittiest lines and Wong is so wonderfully droll. Rick tries to convince her to help recommend customers to their new charter helicopter business but she refuses until Rick charms her with kisses and hugs ("make bigger circles," the amorous Lehua moans). They are interrupted by Cubberson who realizes that they are at the wrong hotel and island.

The next stop is the Hanalei Plantation where coincidentally another old flame of Rick's works. She is entertainer Lani Kaimana (Marianna Hill) who performs at the Piki Niki. Rick gives her the same come-on as he did with Lehua and she agrees to help out after a promised romantic getaway. They then sing a duet "Scratch My Back." With two gals lined up to drive customers their way, Danny agrees to go into business with Rick. Danrick Airways is formed and the first thing Rick does is to line up a few nubile girls (including China Lee, Ann Morell, and Edy Williams) and a brainy blonde (Chanin Hale) for the job of Girl Friday (in which Danny quips, "Sure it is not a little something for Saturday and Sunday?") since he and Danny will be in the air most of the time. They settle on Judy Hudson (Suzanna Leigh) a frustrated pilot who can't get many jobs because of her gender and needs to make some money. On advice from Danny, she pretends to be married to keep lascivious Rick at bay and focused on business.

Rick next heads to the Polynesian Cultural Center (highlighted by stunning aerial shots of the natives dancing and singing below) to meet up with Irene Tsu's Pua (who has the least amount of lines compared to the other girls). Unlike Lehua, Pua doesn't need much convincing to help Rick out as she is ecstatic to see him again. The native show for the tourists begins and he accompanies Pua on a large canoe paddled by six islanders that sails down stream as he sings "Drums of the Islands." Tsu is correct that it does look a bit awkward as she and Elvis are not in synch with their head turns and their waving to the crowds on shore. There is no connection between the two like Elvis had with Wong and Hill. However, the song is one of the best in the movie and the production is so lavishly produced and staged that it really isn't much of a detriment. Once they debark, the number continues with Rick and Pua surrounded by male and female hula dancers.

Elvis Presley sings "Drums of the Islands" while Irene Tsu looks on in *Paradise, Hawaiian Style* (Paramount, 1966).

Needing the business, Judy agrees to have Danrick Airways transport four uncrated show dogs to Kauai. Rick heads to the Kauai Hilton where Joanna (Julie Parrish), yet another former flame, works. She agrees to come along because "I want to see what I'm selling," While transporting the misbehaving barking dogs, Rick sings the corny "It's a Dog's Life." Watching you can tell Elvis found this number ridiculous as he laughs and is startled here and there by the rowdy dogs. Joanna rolls her eyes in frustration trying to keep the dogs calm. She fails and Rick loses control of his chopper and unknowingly forces a car driven by FAA regional director Donald Belden (John Doucette) off the road. As promised and for surviving the outing, Rick takes the cleaned up Joanna out to dinner and runs into Judy on a date with a man named Andy (Dan Collier). Thinking she is stepping out on her husband, Rick makes some comments to the brutish Andy who starts to paw Judy liking the fact that she married. A brawl breaks out, Joanna flees after getting a face full of fruit salad, and Rick escorts Judy back home still thinking she is wed.

Due to Rick's doggie adventure, Danny has to break a date with Jan after an irate Belden calls and is threatening to have Rick's license suspended. He goes to see if he can fix things while Danny takes Jan to Lani's hotel where she has a pair of newlyweds needing a copter ride back to the airport. Unfortunately, instead of dropping Butterworth's Jan in the nearest volcano we are subjected to more warbling from her as she again duets with the King this time on "Datin'. Thankfully, the song is brief. Learning they have five hours before the honeymooners need to get to the airport, Rick flies Lani and Jan to Moonlight Beach. Here we are treated to the glorious sights of Waimea Canyon. The trio spends the day lunching and swimming. Miffed that she didn't get any alone time with Rick, Lani tosses the key to the helicopter when it is time to leave. The passionate gal gets a quick make out session with the pilot in exchange for it, but they can't find where she threw it. Figuring Rick would take Kani to Moonlight Beach, Danny heads over there the next morning and arrives just as they find the key. Furious, he takes off with this daughter but not before ending his partnership with the irresponsible Rick.

Back at the airport, Rick learns his license is suspended by the FAA for thirty days and that Danny and Jan never returned. Rick risks his livelihood and flies in search of them. He rescues the pair who crashed on a deserted ocean cliff. With Danny now with a broken leg and Rick's license suspended for a longer period of time, they are in danger of losing their business. Rick decides to crash a Polynesian Festival he knows Belden will be attending to try to have his suspension lifted. Judy accompanies him and there Rick notices Lani, Lehua, and then Pua are in attendance. He tries to avoid them, but when Joanna arrives he gives up and performs the song "Stop Where You Are" on stage with a bevy of dancing beauties. Afterwards, he goes to track down Belden, but the girls, led by Pua, stop him in his tracks. Pua says, "No wonder you are too busy to come see me." Lehua quips, "You took the words right out of my mouth." As he tries to leave, Pua stops him and says, "I've got business to settle with you first." The girls then realize that they all have been sending him customers and say in unison, "You scratch my back and I'll scratch yours." He then offers to pay them a percentage. They agree after he promises to put it in writing and they all return to their dates. Finding Belden, the FAA director agrees to recommend to the Board not to suspend Rick's license since he saved his friend in an emergency. Celebrating with Danny and Judy, Rick also admits he knew all along that Judy was single and didn't want to spoil her fun. As he is about to kiss her, Hawaiian dancers rush him outside to perform "This Is My Heaven" and then a reprise of "Drums of the Islands."

Paradise, Hawaiian Style opened in most parts of the country in June or July 1966 just in time for drive-in movie going. The poster art tag line boasted, "His Newest! His Biggest! All ELVIS breaks loose in the Swinging Swaying Luau-ing South Seas!" Unfortunately, the mainstream press was not as enthusiastic, but did not trash it as they did with some of his prior movies such as *Harum Scarum* and *Tickle Me*. Sara Davidson in the *Boston Globe* commented that the film "is a light, bright, tuneful piece of nothing." Kevin Thomas of the *Los Angeles Times* called it a "pleasant hot-weather diversion." The reviewer in *The Washington Post* concurred with Thomas and stated. "the result is pleasant and unsensational." *Variety* called it a "gaily garbed and flowing musical."

Not surprisingly, Irene Tsu was rarely mentioned in the reviews having to compete with so many actresses and not really having much to do other than look pretty. The one performer who stood out for some of the critics was not Suzanna Leigh but unbelievably ten year old Donna Butterworth. Perhaps the British lass should have been trying to sabotage her instead of Marianna Hill.

At the box office, *Paradise, Hawaiian Style* grossed approximately $2.5 million—more than half a million dollars more than Elvis' previous movie *Frankie and Johnny*. But still its box office take was lower than *Blue Hawaii* (1961) and even *Girls! Girls! Girls!* (1962). This may not have been that the movie was lesser quality but that by 1966 times they were a changin' and Elvis Presley was losing his luster with younger hip moviegoers.

Years later, *Paradise, Hawaiian Style* found disfavor with a number of Elvis Presley movie historians and fans alike. Most felt it was very inferior to *Blue Hawaii* and *Girls! Girls! Girls!* They felt producer Hal Wallis got lazy and commissioned a retread of those movies with nothing original added except a lot more girls. Jerry Hopkins writing in *Aloha Elvis* said, "Of the three movies, *Paradise, Hawaiian Style* had "the thinnest and most preposterous plot." Paul Lichter, author of *Elvis in Hollywood*, called it a "a really poor film featuring a very poor soundtrack." *Paradise* co-star Julie Parrish commented in *Fantasy Femmes of Sixties Hollywood*, "I don't think any of Elvis' later movies are all that good so I can't really judge *Paradise, Hawaiian Style*. I have had fan mail saying it is their favorite Elvis film. But I don't know if they are just saying that. I love *Jailhouse Rock* and *King Creole*. They were before he started his association with Hal Wallis. The Colonel and Wallis were just making money off of Elvis who was much better than his material. He didn't deserve to have that done to him."

Paradise, Hawaiian Style may not have been as popular as the other two movies, but arguably it is better than *Girls! Girls! Girls!* The plot moves swiftly; the girls are stunning; Elvis seems to be enjoying himself; most of the songs are more than pleasant; and the island paradise is beautifully highlighted. This is where Michael Moore deserves much of the credit. He convinced Hal Wallis to hire a third helicopter and special cameraman to shoot and it truly pays off with same stunning shots of the islands. The movie features picturesque helicopter rides over jungles, through canyons; and above white sandy beaches; and lively musical production numbers with many local dancers and musicians. The standouts being Elvis' duet with sultry Marianna Hill on "Scratch My Back" and the lavish "Drums of the Islands" featuring a song that according *Elvis Films FAQ* was "based on the old Tongan chant 'Bula Lai.'" Even "Queenie Wahine's Papaya" had a traditional Hawaiian song feel to it. The one minor flaw is too much screen time for irksome Donna Butterworth. Less of her would have been better.

Asked what she thought of *Paradise, Hawaiian Style*. Irene Tsu responded, "I haven't seen it in a long time, but it looked like a Hawaiian travelogue. They just wanted to show beautiful scenery and pretty girls and built a story loosely around it. It isn't a great movie at any sorts."

7. MIMSY FARMER: FROM AIP TO ITALY

CULT SIXTIES ICON MIMSY FARMER was a pretty hazel-eyed blonde with the fragile features of an Yvette Mimieux and the independent streak of a Tuesday Weld. After playing the ingénue in a few movies and on TV, she became Queen of the drive-in movie circuit playing restless youth roles in a string of exploitation drive-in movies (*Hot Rods to Hell; Devil's Angels; Riot on the Sunset Strip;* and *The Wild Racers*) in the late sixties. Farmer then relocated to Europe, where with a whole new look, she became an international sensation in 1969 due to her mesmerizing performance as a heroin addict in *More*. Thereafter she worked mostly in Italy playing the unbalanced, blank-faced heroine (ala Carol Lynley in *Bunny Lake Is Missing* or Catherine Denueve in *Repulsion*) in a series of popular European giallos and horror films.

Mimsy Farmer was born Merle Farmer in Chicago. Her parents, Arch and Suzette Farmer, were reporters for the *Chicago Herald Tribune*. The nickname Mimsy purportedly came from her mother who took it from the poem "The Jabberwocky" used in *Alice in Wonderland*. When their daughter was about four years old, the Farmers moved to Hollywood when Mimsy's father took a job writing news for NBC-TV's Los Angeles affiliate. While attending Hollywood High, the lovely teenager was discovered by an agent and almost immediately landed roles on TV's *My Three Sons* and *The Donna Reed Show*.

Mimsy auditioned to replace Sandra Dee as Gidget in *Gidget Goes Hawaiian* (1961), but the producers opted for Deborah Walley. As consolation, they gave her a bit role entering an elevator where she greeted whoever was there. Her official film debut was in the heartwarming or mawkish (depending on your taste—there is no in-between) family drama *Spencer's Mountain* (1963) based on the novel by Earl Hamner, Jr. (who later created the popular television drama, *The Waltons*) and set in scenic Wyoming with the majestic mountain peaks of the Grand Teton Range as background. Farmer read for her role opposite actor Christopher Connelly who was testing to play her love interest. She got the part, but he lost out to James MacArthur. "When we made *Spencer's Mountain* I was sixteen," said Mimsy. "I was accompanied by my mother and a teacher, and spent most of my time with them (or riding horseback) when I wasn't working."

Recalling her castmates and director, Farmer commented, "I didn't have many scenes with Henry Fonda who seemed pretty miserable and spent most of his time at the local café, or Maureen O'Hara who was also fairly distant. James MacArthur, who was quite a bit older than me, was nice but the person I felt most comfortable with was Wally Cox who seemed to take me more seriously and taught me some lovely Elizabethan songs, which I still remember. Delmer Daves [the director] was more concerned about my weight than about my acting, unfortunately, and kept telling me, 'watch your bottom honey.'" Farmer is not a fan of the movie and agrees with Henry Fonda that it is not very good.

In *Spencer's Mountain,* Mimsy played Claris the girl friend of Clayboy (James MacArthur), the eldest son of hard drinkin' and hard livin' Clay Spencer (Henry Fonda) and his long-suffering formidable religious wife Olivia (Maureen O'Hara). Clay dreams of building a house for his wife big enough for their huge brood but when Clayboy has an opportunity to become the first Spencer to go to college, Clay has an important decision to make.

For the time, Farmer's teenage Claris is surprisingly very amorous and sexually-charged (the character spent a lot of time outside the small mountain community so she thinks she is more worldly in regards to love and marriage) compared to the typical Tammy's and Gidget's that bounced across the silver screen at the time. Within her first few minutes on screen, after riding up to Clayboy on horseback, Claris (Farmer is unfortunately saddled with an unflattering head band that pushes her curly blonde locks back and up making her resemble a younger Faye Dunaway sans the cold cream in *Mommie Dearest*) boasts of her grown up measurements, demonstrates to Clayboy calisthenics bending over provocatively in his direction, and exclaims that her favorite class at her all-girls school is marriage and the family. She later enjoys showing the embarrassed Clayboy all the dirty words she underlined in her dictionary. This atypical teenage love interest was just the start for the roles Mimsy would play in the future as she rarely was cast as the sweet ingénue despite her demure appearance.

Some critics took offense to her language and behavior calling the film "salacious." This criticism really disturbed Delmer Daves who told Marjory Adams of the *Boston Globe*,

"All my scripts are read and commented on by 23-year-old daughter and 21-year-old son...They told me that girls really do talk today the way Claris does in the picture." Other reviewers on the opposite side of the spectrum frowned on the folksiness and one dubbed it a "marshmallow *Tobacco Road*." Seems Daves could not satisfy all with this one.

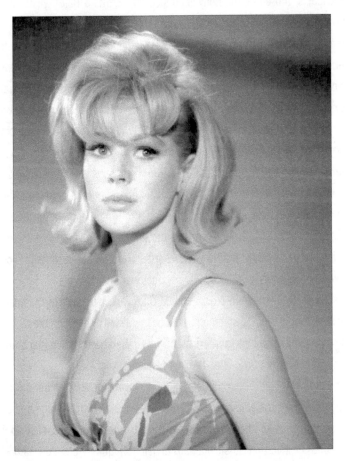

Publicity photo of Mimsy Farmer in *Hot Rods to Hell* (MGM, 1967).

Farmer received mixed reviews for her performance. One of the better notices came from John L. Scott of the *Los Angeles Times* who dubbed her "an attractive ingénue" and said she "showed promise in her film debut." Extolling her dislike being labeled an ingénue and determined to become an actress and not a teen idol, ala Sandra Dee or Annette Funicello, Farmer commented to the *Chicago Tribune*, "I don't want to appeal to the teen-aged mentality. The ones that do are only stars, not actors—and they're good for only a few years. Teen stars can't handle the fame." This most likely disturbed Warner Bros. who wanted to groom her to be their next Connie Stevens and began by choosing her as their candidate to be a 1963 Hollywood Deb Star. From a field of 80 young actresses, Farmer was one of the fourteen winners, chosen by the Hollywood Make-Up Artists & Hair Stylists, along with Joan Freeman, Lori Martin, Susan Seaforth, and Barbara Parkins, among others.

Unhappy with her performance in *Spencer's Mountain*, Mimsy began studying with esteemed acting coach Jeff Corey who taught her about improvisation and helped her get over her shyness. Despite keeping busy on television including guest appearances on *The Outer Limits*, *Honey West*, *My Three Sons*, and *Perry Mason*, Farmer kept her job selling candy at a local movie theater. She finally left it when she returned to the big screen in the soapy *Bus Riley's Back in Town* (1965) directed by Harvey Hart from a screenplay by William Inge who had his name removed from the credits when Universal ordered a script re-write to make the film more of a vehicle for Ann-Margret. Aping James Dean, the brooding Michael Parks played a disillusioned sailor returning home after three years at sea. He finds his sultry ex-girlfriend (Ann-Margret) unhappily married to a wealthy older man, his job prospects bleak, and his younger sister (Farmer) has become the town tart. The film was not well-received though Farmer does well with her role.

Not surprisingly neither Ann-Margret nor Michael Parks had much of an impact on the serious actress. Farmer said, "I just remember being impressed by being on the same set with Jocelyn Brando [who played her mother], as much as if she'd been Marlon [her brother]."

For alienated youth movie fans, 1967 was a banner year for Mimsy Farmer who had three films in release and became Queen of drive-in cinema. Despite her ambition not to become an idol for the young, she became very popular with teenage audiences for a short period of time and began her ascension to cult movie actress. First up was the explosive youth exploitation classic *Hot Rods to Hell* from quickie producer Sam Katzman for MGM and directed by John Brahm whom Mimsy liked a lot. She found him to be a soft-spoken gentleman and credited him for teaching her the trick to crying on screen, without using menthol or glycerin, but by staring wide-eyed at something without blinking until the eyes start to hurt causing tears to begin swelling up.

Originally made for television as *52 Miles to Terror*, the movie was deemed to violent and released to drive-ins throughout the country instead with the more exploitative title *Hot*

Rods to Hell. In some places it went out on the bottom of a double bill with the Italian production *Wild, Wild Planet*. This was Farmer's first real bad girl role after playing mostly ingénues. The worried actress remarked to columnist Dick Kleiner that she was cast by her looks alone and hoped she wasn't going to now be typecast as the bad girl. Even so, she accepted the part because "I needed to work and couldn't wait for a better offer. I also thought, 'If Dana Andrews and Jeanne Crain had accepted who the hell was I to be so finicky?'"

Hot Rods to Hell is great camp fun. After almost dying in a car crash, traumatized Tom Phillips (Dana Andrews) moves his wife Peg (Jeanne Crain) and children, teenaged Tina (Laurie Mock) and Jamie (Tim Stafford, son of actress Anna Lee), from New England to the California desert to take over a motel and roadhouse. Unbeknownst to them, the place is a hangout for underage troublemaking hot rodders and hoodlums (albeit the most clean-cut looking set of thugs to ever hit the silver screen). Mimsy Farmer played a wild reckless thrill seeker named Gloria first seen standing in the back of what looks like a souped-up dune buggy holding on to the roll bar yelling, "Run him off the road Duke! Run him off the road!" as she eggs on her drag racing boyfriend Duke (Paul Bertoya). Their wild antics elicits from Andrews' Tom, "What kind of animals are those?" They're the kind that is out for kicks—racing, having sex, drinking beer, and harassing the townsfolk. Farmer is effective first eliciting sympathy as the easy lay who wants to find a better life but then lets her inner bitch get the better of her tormenting good girl Tina whom she sees as her rival for self-centered Duke, no prize he. Since this was an MGM production, the film ends with the family triumphing and the teenagers repenting for their misguided ways.

Actor Christopher Riordan had a small role in *Hot Rods to Hell* as one of the roadhouse denizens and was unfortunately not impressed with Mimsy or the young actors who played her tough-talking friends. He opined, "They were taking themselves so dreadfully serious it was really stupid and they wasted a lot of time in their so called preparation and their attitude. Whereas I am from the old school and thought, 'Why don't you just act?' They were professional but everybody was wishing that they would calm down and do the part as written hoping it would work out. Unfortunately it didn't if you saw the movie."

Not surprisingly, the critics dismissed *Hot Rods to Hell* and offered condolences to Dana Andrews and Jeanne Crain for their career slides into exploitation while simultaneously slamming them for their hammy performances. John Brahm however did get praised for trying to get a little more out of the pedestrian script. As for Mimsy, the best review she could muster came from the critic in *Variety* who remarked, "Miss Farmer has a few frantic moments as the town plaything..."

Mimsy Farmer next did three youth-oriented movies in a row for American International Pictures. She explained, "I did not have a contract with AIP but I was supporting my first husband [a cowboy from Brooklyn who could not find work as a stuntman in Hollywood] and a bunch of animals on our quasi-ranch. The better directors were not lining up in front of my door pleading for me to be in their movies. They didn't even know I existed."

Mimsy Farmer and Schuyler Hayden at an LSD party in *Riot on Sunset Strip* (AIP, 1967).

First up for Mimsy was her most notorious movie from this period, *Riot on Sunset Strip* (1967) produced by Sam Katzman. Also trying to capitalize on the latest teenage trend, Katzman rushed this movie into production while real riots were actually happening on the Sunset Strip. The actress was skeptical about doing his but she said her agent suggested if this movie was good enough for Aldo Ray to do, it should be good enough for her. She was reteamed with Laurie Mock from *Hot Rods to Hell*. However, the roles were switched as Mock was cast as the out-for-kicks Liz-Ann friend of Farmer's more conservative Andy who hailed from a broken home. She was described in the press book as "a real swinger, who took her first 'trip'...all the way to Hell and back!" All the ingredients were present—hippies, LSD, protestors, free love, mod fashions, police brutality— to make *Riot on Sunset Strip* a camp classic of the alienated youth movie genre.

Riot on Sunset Strip was supposed to be released by MGM but they couldn't get it into theaters quick enough for Katzman. The wily producer then sold it to AIP, which was better equipped with fast drive-in distribution.

The movie opens with young people milling about on the Sunset Strip with deadly serious voiceover narration that describes the kids as, "Irresponsible, wild, beat, protest youths with nowhere to go, nothing to do, no goal in life." Hanging out at a club called Pandora's Box, underage high school kids Andy, Liz-Ann, and their boyfriends get involved in a brawl and are hauled off to jail for breaking curfew. Andy's estranged police detective father (Aldo Ray) who hasn't seen his daughter in four years has been informed of her arrest. When Liz-Ann and the gang decide to return to the strip the following night, Andy declines but when she finds her mother in another alcoholic stupor she changes her mind. There she hooks up again with the wild Liz-Ann and Schuyler Hayden as Herby, the bored son of a movie star. He gets a bunch of kids to break into an abandoned house on the Strip where drinking leads to marijuana then to LSD, which Herby spikes the unaware Andy's coke with saying, "Grass is fast, but acid is like lightning, man." Strung out, Andy begins to freak out and is then led upstairs to a bedroom by Herby where the poor thing gets gang raped. When the police raid the house, all the kids get out except Andy and Liz-Ann who fingers the guys who assaulted her friend. Andy's father beats Herby to a pulp with cries of "police brutality" in his ears, but he is able to stave off the impending riot.

The movie's standout scene is Farmer's wild LSD freak out dance where she writhes around the floor in her mod mini-dress gazing in wonder at her hands and feet. She then begins dancing around shaking her wild mane of hair ala Ann-Margret (critic Clifford Terry described it as "a dry-land water ballet"). Whatever you label it, it has become a YouTube favorite much to Farmer's bemusement. "That 'great LSD freak-out scene,' which I took very seriously at the time, has since become for me a source of amusement tinged with embarrassment," she remarked. "Somewhere on the Internet someone said, 'that scene is so bad, that it's hilarious.' I agree. I was pretty naive back then and so earnest!"

The biker film *Devil's Angels* (1967), AIP's in-name only sequel to its mega hit *The Wild Angels*, was directed by Daniel Haller and featured Mimsy Farmer playing another bored small town girl. The ad copy exclaimed, "Violence is their God... Lust the law they live by. They hunt in a pack... Like Rabid Dogs." John Cassavetes starred as Cody the leader of an outlaw biker gang called The Skulls, whose members included Beverly Adams, Russ Bender, Marc Cavell, Salli Sachse (a former *Beach Party* regular), Nai Bonet, Buck Kartalian, Leo Gordon, and Kipp Whitman.

"I really liked Daniel Haller who was a very nice man," remarked Mimsy. "I also admired John Cassavetes, also a very nice guy and great acting partner. All Cassavetes and I talked about though was how much he missed his wife. Actually, I mostly listened. Anyway, doing a movie with him, even though he wasn't directing it, was a step in the right direction."

John Craig, Mimsy Farmer, and John Cassavetes in *Devil's Angels* (AIP, 1967).

The toned-down, as compared to other biker films of the time, *Devil's Angels* follows a motorcycle gang called the Skulls led by idealistic Cody (John Cassavetes) on their way to find an idyllic life in the "Hole-in-the-Wall" when they stop in the town of Brookville to attend a local carnival. Farmer's Marianne is the only girl in the Kissing Booth who will smooch any of the bikers. Roy (Kipp Whitman) is the lucky winner. Flirty Marianne then gets him to take her on a joyride and he heads straight to his gang who are partying along the shores of a lake. After smoking pot and drinking many beers (this is definitely not your typical Frankie and Annette beach party), things get out of hand as Roy fiercely kisses Marianne and begins to pass her around to his friends. The terrified disheveled girl flees into the night and the sheriff and mayor think she has been raped, which she denies. Her debauchery leads to an all out war between the townspeople and the bikers. The Skulls emerge victorious and take over the town putting Marianne, the sheriff and Mayor on trial leading to more violence. Despite their triumph, Cody is sickened by his gang's actions and rides off alone deserting them and his girl Lynn (Beverly Adams).

Devil's Angels was a huge drive-in hit though it did not gross as much as *The Wild Angels*. Reviews were on the positive side as well. Screenwriter Charles Griffith received praise for trying to take a balanced approach with the antics of the biker gang versus the sanctimonious townspeople. Both commit contributing acts that result in the violent showdown. Farmer is quite good as the foolish Marianne. Howard Thompson of the *New York Times* singled her and co-star Leo Gordon out for their "solid performances."

Unhappy with her wannabe stuntman husband and her career in Hollywood, Mimsy headed for Canada on advice from actor Peter Brown who told her about Hollywood Hospital in New Westminster, British Columbia near Vancouver where they experimented with LSD and psychotherapy. After her own session, she announced she was quitting show business to train as a psychedelic therapeutic assistant. She quipped in *Variety*, "I'm leaving work in one 'nut' factory to toil in another" and then added "If I ever do come back to Hollywood it would be for roles with substance where there is an area of 'freedom of expression.'" Mimsy began working there but left when she realized the hospital never followed up with their patients after their "treatment."

Still in Vancouver, Farmer received a life changing phone call from Daniel Haller (one of her favorite directors) who wanted her for the female lead in his new movie *The Wild Racers* (1968). However, it was not to a return to Hollywood. The film's story following a racecar driver on the Grand Prix circuit was going to be shot on location throughout Europe "My experience working at the Canadian hospital was enlightening but disappointing," opined Mimsy. "When Daniel Haller contacted me, I jumped at the chance to go to Europe and also to see my brother Philip, who was living in London at the time. It was the best move I'd made up to then and I loved traveling in France, Spain, and Holland." She also didn't mind starring opposite handsome former singing sensation Fabian who she had a nice time working with.

The Wild Racers stars Fabian as arrogant race car driver Joe Joe Quillico who calls himself "Joe Joe Quillico, King of the Hillico. They call me Joe Joe, because I have the mojo." After being banned from NASCAR racing in the U.S. due to an accident he caused, he has moved abroad to compete in Formula One and sports car prototype racing on the European Grand Prix circuit. Determined to win races because he is tired of finishing out of the money and points earned, he sends his French and then his British girlfriends packing and vows no more serious relationships just a casual fling or two. It is a promise he seems to keep making then breaking.

In Italy, Joe Joe and his mechanic Charlie (Warwick Sims) follow American tourists Katherine (Mimsy) and her friend June (Talia Coppola) until the girls finally agree to have dinner with them. Later Katherine stays on to watch Joe Joe drive a sports car in a race outside of the Grand Prix circuit while June departs for Venice. Joe Joe finally wins his first race and is determined to go back to the Formula One racing in the Grand Prix. He loses at the Dutch Grand Prix, but surprises everyone with a win at the Spanish Grand Prix due to an accident that takes out his teammate and rival Ian (David Landar). He finally gets all the attention and adulation he always desired, but it makes Katherine uncomfortable even though he does introduce her to all the reporters as "his girl." Later at a celebration, Joe Joe gets caught up in the festivities and ignores a peeved Katherine as he dances with a bevy of beautiful senoritas. Joe Joe's lack of compassion for the injured Ian, out of racing for at least six months, also dismays her. Even so, she sticks by him as they head to Paris where Joe Joe makes a TV commercial and prepares for his next race. He promises Katherine a wonderful time, but instead she sits idly by in silence as he takes her to a business meeting where he negotiated with a car manufacturer about putting his name on one of their new designs or to one of umpteen press interviews. Despite his professions of love, Katherine remains unhappy and the self-centered Joe Joe can't understand why. While making love, he says,

"Don't you just love when I call you baby?" Katherine replies stoically, "I hate when you call me baby." The next scene has Joe Joe leaving Katherine at the train station as she follows in the footsteps of his girlfriends before her. While a melancholy Katherine stares aimlessly out the train's windows, Joe Joe continues racing without a look back. Winning the French Grand Prix, Joe Joe's life goes on with lots of new partying and girls.

Mimsy Farmer and Fabian in *Wild Racers* (AIP, 1968).

This was the only film Mimsy Farmer did for AIP that was not a hit with the drive-in crowd. Farmer's three previous movies brought in between $1.2 million and $1.75 million at the box office and were in the Top 50 highest grossing movies of 1967. *The Wild Racers* did not break the $1 million mark. In an interview with the *Oakland Tribune*, Haller opined that it was a picture "too esoteric in its treatment to make as much money as it should have." Though featuring great racing sequences comparable to *Grand Prix* and *Le Mans*, the film may have been too artsy for the typically teenage and drive-in audience aimed for by American International Pictures. The quick edits and off-camera conversations over nicely shot racing footage may have been bit much for them. However, this stylized approach is what makes the movie way above average. It is also buoyed by the interesting mix of French pop songs by Pierre Vassiliu with a bouncy music score by Mike Curb, and from the fine performances from the two leads. Fabian, who with his boyish looks, makes Joe Joe likable despite his self-centered attitude and Mimsy Farmer, with her short hair worn in a small pony tail, is adorably sweet and innocent as the girl who almost tames him.

Deciding to remain in Europe, Farmer sought out work there and landed the female lead in *More* (1969), first time director Barbet Schroeder's cautionary tale of drug taking (based on his own original story about a German student who is introduced to pot and then heroin by an American girl) with a song score by Pink Floyd. The actress was recommended to Schroeder by *The Wild Racers'* cinematographer Nestor Almendros and associate producer Pierre Cottrell. "Pierre had produced Eric Rohmer's films and was going to produce *More*," revealed Farmer. "He talked to Barbet Schroeder about me."

Asked by writer Elliot Stein why he cast Mimsy Farmer, Schroeder answered in *Film Comment*, "I saw her in a film made by Roger Corman. In every picture of hers I saw, even the worst ones, she had at least five extraordinary shots. The...thing that really excited me was that she had quit acting to become a nurse in a hospital, in a very special hospital where they were treating alcoholics with acid...I wanted to create the character of a new kind of vamp, someone you would never think was a vamp, someone innocently perverse, like a strange nurse."

Though not completely happy with the script or things her character had to do in it, Farmer accepted the role in part because she would get to work with her two friends again. Even the required nude scenes did not deter her unlike they did for other sixties starlets of the time. "Nudity was an integral part of the movies in which I appeared naked," explained Farmer. "Being flat-chested and boyish helped a lot and, I hope, there was nothing vulgar or lewd about these scenes." It also helped that these scenes were shot with a small crew consisting of the director, his assistant, the cinematographer, and an electrician.

More was filmed on a shoestring budget, but you would never guess that when watching the movie thanks to the gorgeous photography by Almendros. With a stylish short haircut ala Mia Farrow, Farmer gives an entrancing performance as Estelle an offbeat American expatriate living in Paris who meets German college graduate Stefan (Klaus Grunberg who spoke no English and had to learn his line phonetically) who has been warned to stay away from her by his friend Charlie (Michael Chanderli) who says, "She has already destroyed two men—do you want to be the third?" Ignoring the advice, Stefan spends a few days with the girl smoking pot and having sex. In love, he then follows her to the sunny island of Ibiza where they live an idyllic life nude sunbathing and taking LSD. However, things begin to go awry when they graduate to shooting up heroin and become entangled with the island's leading drug dealer an ex-Nazi (Heinz Englemann) whose mistress turns out to be Estelle. Stefan's love for the secretive American becomes obsessive and abusive as his crave for heroin increases, which leads to tragedy despite the appearance of Charlie who tries to help his addicted friend. In an odd twist, Grunberg's character is sometimes unlikable because of the demands he puts on Estelle though you do feel sorry for him, while Farmer makes her Estelle more sympathetic than she should be despite her cavalier treatment of Stefan.

In 1969 an honest, outspoken Farmer opined about *More* to Judy Klemesrud in the *New York Times*, "I think the hip people will put the film down…the idea that smoking marijuana leads to heroin is ridiculous. A lot of people will just be bored by the whole thing." She also went on to say that she wasn't thrilled with director Barbet Schroeder regarding the scene where Grunberg runs his hand up her dress and remarked that he "misrepresented the way he was going to shoot it."

"Well, I think now, that I was silly to berate Barbet and his movie at the time," admitted Mimsy, "but I still think that it's naive and moralistic and some of the scenes were an embarrassment to do, all the 'Zen' and 'Lotus' shots and the 'unexplored brain' nonsense. What I didn't say though was that his movie was pretty daring and unconventional for those years, in Europe anyway, and that he was a better than average director.

"It's true that I said, and still believe, that smoking grass does not in itself lead to shooting heroin," continued Mimsy. "I know many people who light up a joint from time to time who have never touched anything harder and never will, myself included (though now I prefer a good glass of wine)."

Promotional lobby card for *More* (Cinema V, 1969).

More made a huge splash at the Cannes Film Festival and was an international sensation. The reviewer in *Variety* raved that Mimsy "reveals a potent personality and gives her role of the girl a tension, inner hurt and alienation, tempered by her ability to love although her moral outlooks bypass conventionality." Gene Siskel of the *Chicago Tribune* called it "important" and said Mimsy is "curiously charming... [Her] words are whispered, but one listens." Some American critics however were not as enthused with her or the movie with a number feeling it glamorized drug taking. Raymond A. Sokolov in *Newsweek* was particularly mean-spirited and said about Mimsy, "If her facial expressions number only two, so do her nipples, and she provides a few moments of cinematic interest with them..."

Farmer laughs off bad reviews and recalled one that she remembers to this day for *Il maestro and Margherita*. Coincidentally it also came from *Newsweek*. "Of me, *Newsweek* said, 'She acts the range of emotions from A to B.' Bette Davis once said, 'Old age ain't for sissies.' I say, neither is being an actor!"

More really clicked with young people of the time and helped to kick off Mimsy Farmer's European career, which lasted for over 20 years. When asked if she thought *More* was her best movie, Farmer responded, "I don't think so, though the role was interesting and Nestor Almendros' photography was gorgeous. It was, though, very important for my career, both in the positive and in the negative sense. Its success in France was huge and overnight I became a 'star' but, as is often the case, I became 'type cast' and most of the roles directors offered me subsequently were those of neurotic or outright mad young women. Well, I can't complain."

Farmer next co-starred with John Philip Law (who she just remembers for his immense height and for his bluest of blue eyes) in the international co-production *Strogoff* (1970) based on the Jules Verne novel *Michel Strogoff*. Filmed in Bulgaria, Farmer had to deal with a case of hepatitis and then discovered she was pregnant by her new husband writer Vincenzo Cerami.

Director Georges Lautner specifically wanted Farmer to star in the interesting but hard to find nowadays film *Road to Salina* (1970) but she was not familiar with his work. After screening his movie *Fleur d'oseille* and knowing she would be filming in the Canary Islands with Rita Hayworth, Robert Walker, and Academy Award winner Ed Begley, the actress said yes. Again, the nudity required did not deter her in the least.

Road to Salina was filmed on the island of Lanzarote 100 miles off the coast of North Africa, doubling for Mexico. A true international co-production, the actors were American, the director and crew French, and the extras Spanish. Mimsy had a nice interaction with Walker off-camera as he brought his wife and brood of children on location. She did not have that much contact with Hayworth. "Rita Hayworth was a splendid actress," remarked Farmer. "She was still very beautiful and a lovely partner. I didn't get much of a chance to know her well because she kept very much to herself and retired to her room on the top floor of the little house, which was our 'set,' after each shot."

In the movie, Walker played a drifter named Jonas who turns up at a roadhouse owned by Mara (Rita Hayworth) who immediately mistakes the boy for her long lost son Rocky who disappeared four years prior. Living with Mara is her promiscuous daughter Billie (Farmer) who accepts her mother's assertion and then immediately hops into the sack with Jonas. "So it's starting all over again," sighs Mara. Jonas knows he is not the son, but he cannot tell if Billie believes that or not, making her character the oddest of the bunch. Providing narration, Jonas says, "I began to suspect that I'd be caught up in some kind of trap." Soon flashback scenes reveal what really went on with Billie and her brother

Rocky who supposedly jilted the daughter of Mara's beau Warren (Ed Begley in his last film appearance) before vanishing. When Jonas' hippie friends finally catch up with him, they try to tear him away but the silly boy decides to stay.

Road to Salina was not well-received with a lot of the criticism for the flashbacks, which most critics felt marred the rest of the movie, including the denouement. One nice review though came from Joseph Gelmis, of *Newsday,* who called the film "strange" (but in a good way) and found the best things about it were the direction and "the neurotic, almost carnivorous, energetic intensity of the…predatory Mimsy Farmer." For her performance, Mimsy was bestowed a special David di Donotello Award, Italy's equivalent to the Oscar. Looking back on the movie, she complimented Lautner for trying to make a good movie, but found the actions of the hero unbelievable. For her, the motivations of why this young man would hang around the two crazy women, even if he was in love, was not realistic

The second phase of Mimsy Farmer's career as a cult Italian horror film actress began with the Dario Argento giallo *Four Flies on Grey Velvet / 4 mosche di velluto grigio* (1971) co-starring Michael Brandon (reportedly Michael York was originally cast but had to bow out due to a scheduling conflict). It was rumored the director cast Mimsy (over such beauties as Florinda Bolkan, Claudia Cardinale, and Lisa Gastoni) because she reminded him of his blonde and waifish wife. According to Louis Paul, writing in his book *Italian Horror Film Directors*, "The title of the film stems from a police test on an eyeball of a murdered victim done with a laser. Apparently, under the pretext that a victim's killer's image is retained on the retina of the eye, the laser photographs the image, which looks like four flies on grey velvet." This permeates throughout the movie.

When filming began Mimsy Farmer quickly discovered that Argento liked to work his cast hard. "Dario Argento is a good craftsman and knows what he's doing," stated Farmer. "As a person, he's a funny sort of man, doing his best to appear neurotic and genial. I liked him enough and had a good time making that movie, especially the four-minute mono-logue at the end which we shot at four in the morning with three cameras. He allowed my input on this and we worked together." All were satisfied with the result.

As much as she respected Dario, Mimsy felt no respect for his father Salvatore Ar-gento who produced the movie. When a car crash stunt when terribly wrong and the stunt man wound up afire, the producer was more worried about going over budget than the welfare of the man in flames who was rushed to the hospital. Thankfully, he lived.

Farmer also liked working with her leading man, Michael Brandon, though later she found out the feeling was not entirely mutual. "I got along fine with Michael though I read somewhere that he complained about me not socializing during off hours," she revealed. "Oh well. All I wanted to do after work was get back home to my husband and baby daughter, which strikes me as natural."

In this classic thriller, Mimsy played somber Nina, the wife of rock musician Roberto (Michael Brandon) who, after being followed by a mysterious man in dark glasses for a week confronts his stalker at an empty theater where he accidentally stabs him to death...or does he? Someone in the balcony witnesses the crime and takes photos, which are used to blackmail Roberto. The drummer reveals what happened to his doubting wife, who suggests he get help. She believes her husband after the blackmailer begins terrorizing the couple, breaking into their home leaving threatening notes and pictures. After their maid is murdered, a terrified Nina abandons Roberto, irritated that he won't leave. She surprises him the night after her nubile cousin Dalia is murdered in the house. A retina scan reveals the last thing Dalia saw were four flies. Guess who is wearing a fly pendant around the neck? Fleeing the house after shooting and wounding Roberto, the killer's slow motion decapitation scene crashing a car into the back of a truck is typical stylized Argento.

In America, the mainstream critics were taken with the dazzling color photography, pacing, and handsome production values, but were not with the plot and denouement, finding it "far-fetched," old," or "banal"—just some of the adjectives thrown its way. Louis Paul wrote in *Italian Horror Film Directors*, "If it were to be compared with Argento's other thrillers, surely this film will pale by comparison. Still it's an interesting thriller with a notably weird twist ending."

Though she is not a fan of horror films, Mimsy truly likes this due to Dario Argento. "The monologue in *Four Flies on Grey Velvet* was a real collaboration between Dario and me," she said. "Even my then husband, Vincenzo Cerami, helped me work on it at home. It is two of the five horror movies I made, that as a spectator, I don't mind watching. The other is parts of *Il Profumo della Signora in Nero*."

Despite critics' disappointment with *Four Flies on Grey Velvet*, it is arguably Mimsy Farmer's most famous foreign movie. Mimsy though goes on to clarify that it "is my best known foreign movie *in* the United States. In France, it's practically unknown, as are my

American movies."That aside, no matter what you label it, the notoriety the movie brought kept the actress working steadily in Italy and France especially in the thriller genre for another fifteen years or so. She even got to work with another master of horror, Lucio Fulci, on *The Black Cat* (1981). Comparing Fulci with Dario Argento, Farmer remarked, "I'd never seen a movie by Lucio Fulci but had been told that he was a good and respected craftsman—which he was. I liked him very much. Behind his gruffness and despite the sort of films he put out, he was very gentle, intelligent and cultured. *The Black Cat* isn't a good movie but I'm not at all sorry to have done it.

"I haven't really seen enough of either of their movies to talk about style," continues Mimsy. "Maybe though, Argento was more ambitious. He certainly had more money (thanks to his father) and was younger and took himself more seriously. Both were open to suggestions but in *The Black Cat* there wasn't a hell of a lot to suggest."

Asked why she never returned to Hollywood after the success of *More* and *Four Flies on Grey Velvet*, Mimsy replied, "I was, and still am, much happier in Europe. Of course, it's been many years now since I left the U.S., and I'm sure that working methods have changed a lot since then, but at the time, my experiences were almost always frustrating. In Europe, actors were not shuffled off to their trailers between shots and were invited to participate and collaborate with the director and other crew members. It was so different. Nobody was anxious about my 'bottom' (admittedly much diminished) and nobody was redesigning my eyebrows and curling my hair. I just had the feeling that nobody wanted me to act or look like anyone but myself—such a relief."

Though she achieved personal peace living in Europe, Farmer was pragmatic about being a working American actor there. She opined, "On the whole, when you've decided to live and work in a foreign country, *you* are the foreigner, and if you're an actor there are limits to which and how many roles you're going to be offered. If you're working to make a living, you can't be too choosey and you're mostly grateful when you can work."This last statement probably refers to some of the bad movies she appeared in and that most of her films were never released in the U.S., including her three favorite movies.

The well-received *Il maestro e Margherita / The Master and Margarita* (1972), an Italian/Yugoslavian co-production directed by Aleksandar Petrovic and loosely based on ideas from the novel by Mikhail Bulgakov is a strange mixture of serious drama and fantasy as it tackles the subjects of the existence of God and the evils of censorship to protect the masses in mid-1920s Russia. Ugo Tognazzi is a playwright whose new play about Pontius Pilate enrages the Communists of the Proletarian Writers Guild who refuse to allow it to open due to its religious and anti-authority themes. They pressure him to redraw it and go to Yalta on holiday instead. He refuses, deciding to stay to write a novel about Satan who is roaming the streets of Moscow killing off the Guild writers who doubt that God exists. Farmer played Margarita of the title, a mysterious married young woman infatuated with the Maestro, who appears in his life just as his strife with the play begins. Loving him, she agrees to move in with him but when she returns he is gone and all traces of him erased. Distraught and desperate to find him, the Devil appears to her and promises patience. But is it too late?

Mimsy Farmer in *Four Flies on Grey Velvet* (Paramount, 1972).

In *Allonsanfàn* (1974) she played the jealous lover of "ageing and reluctant revolutionary" Marcello Mastroiannai who betrays him during the 1816 Restoration and in the violent revenge film *La traque* (1975) she played a rape victim who turns the tables on her attackers.

Commenting on some of her leading men, Farmer gushed, "Ugo Tognazzi was a lot of fun and a great cook. Marcello Mastroianni was a wonderful actor and a great guy! As a kid I was in love with him and to work with him was so exciting! I was completely star struck when I met him. I've never known an actor as modest as Marcello was. He told me, and he really believed it, that he wasn't such a good actor, that he had no real personality and that the times he'd been good, had been when he'd had a good director. I guess he'd had only very good directors because as far as I can tell, he'd always been magnificent. In France there is an exceptional actor named Michele Bouquet with whom I worked with twice in *Deux hommes dans la ville* [1973] and *Les suspects* [1974]. He was a favorite of [director Claude] Chabrols' and is still hugely popular in the theatre. I also admired Patrick Magee and was happy to work with him in *The Black Cat* (1981)." As for a comment about James Franciscus whom she'd co-starred with in *Concorde Affaire '79*, all she'd say was that "he was a blonde."

When asked if it was difficult acting in films where the cast and crew spoke many different languages and if that had an effect on her performance, she answered, "I worked in French and then in Italian films. At the beginning, my French wasn't so hot! Eventually my French got better and I was able to act in French (sometimes changing the dialogue to substitute impossible to pronounce words for easier ones). In Italy it took me a year and several weeks of intense Italian classes before mustering up the courage to utter a few sentences. Later, my Italian was good enough to act in (*The Master and Margherita*) but unlike the French, Italians couldn't tolerate any kind of accent, not even local ones, and dubbed everything by professionals. There was no direct sound track. It was frustrating but some times I was able to demand that a very good actress named Ludovica Modugno dub me. The only time I did act in Italian with direct sound—I'd studied my part with a coach for weeks until I could recite my dialogue in perfect Florentine (the equivalent of the BBC accent)—was a TV mini series about Clara Schuman. My Italian was perfect but so monotone and my acting was terrible. Each time I opened my mouth it would take me forever to wrap my tongue around the words and my expression was blank and a little bit terrified."

Mimsy Farmer kept acting into the early nineties in European features and TV mini-series most of which never made it to these shores. Her last acting credit is the Italian TV-movie *Safari* (1991) for director Roger Vadim. Today, Mimsy concentrates on her art (displayed on her web site www.mimsyfarmer.com) and sculpture work, which can be seen in such movies as *Blueberry* (2004), *Troy* (2004), *Marie Antoinette* (2006), *The Golden Compass* (2007), and *Clash of the Titans* (2010).

8.   A FLINT GIRL NAMED BOND...DIANE BOND

DIANE BOND WAS A REAL looker with long straight auburn hair, a charming smile, and a curvaceous figure similar to many of the young actresses of the day. However, the fact that she was extremely athletic and worked as a stuntwoman made her an atypical starlet. A shapely beauty (the press book for *A Swingin' Summer* extolled her measurements as being "36-23-36"), Bond was bikini-clad in practically all her film appearances, from *Pajama Party* with Annette Funicello, to *Tickle Me* with Elvis Presley, *to A Swingin' Summer* as "The Girl in the Pink Polka Dot Bikini." However, her most memorable movie was the spy spoof *In Like Flint* playing one of the three shapely beauties (bikini-clad, of course) who work for super cool spy Derek Flint (James Coburn). Bond didn't take advantage of the movie's success and moved to Rome, ala Mimsy Farmer, where she made a few films including *House of a 1,000 Dolls* with Vincent Price.

Diane Bond was born in Los Angeles but spent her childhood growing up on her father's ranch in the mountains of Colorado. The athletic Bond quickly became an expert skier, skater, and horse rider. In her mid-teens an executive of the Rose Marie Reid Bathing Suit firm spotted her on the beach at Malibu and offered her a job as a model. Between modeling assignments, the shapely brunette began working with a troupe of trapeze artists. Describing her time there, Diane commented in her autobiographical piece titled "Trapezeasy:"

> I eyed the rig, rising above the treetops not far off from the freeway I
> daily traveled to work on...It was obvious that it was for trapeze and I
> was to fly on it. Little old Dell, in his purple leotard, answered the door.
> He must have been no taller than my shoulder but with all his trapeze
> muscles where they should be. He had a big nose, scraggly thinning

grey hair and crooked teeth and he probably thought the gods had answered his call when I knocked on the door.

He had in mind a project to create an all-girl flying act and if I would be interested? The gods *had* answered his call as I didn't need convincing, or so it seemed to me, as I was led into a strange maze where this little Spiderman in leotards easily caught me in his net.

The atmosphere in the 'group' wasn't actually Snow White and the Seven Dwarfs but a change about to a Dwarf and Seven Snow Whites. I left home and went to live with the circus gang. Kitty and Pug, and Kitty's small girl, lived with Spiderman. Tootsie and I roomed in the back guesthouse and in between stood the mighty RIG. What went on in the big house was not of our concern and all my stout blonde roommate Toots and I had to do, was fly from the bar but not lie on his bed, which was quite satisfactory to the two of us, considering also that Kitty and Pug were jealous of Spiderman's bsd* which you could very well see through his purple leotards.

*bsd=big swinging dick

Though the troupe persevered, their dream of "an all-girl flying act" was not destined to become a reality. However, they were hired to play trapeze artists in a number of episodes of the 1963-64 TV series *The Greatest Show on Earth* starring Jack Palance as the circus' manager. It was the first DesiLu production to be broadcast in color. Diane quipped, "So one can say I flew into the studios and my acting career." She left the series before the end of the season and made her film debut in 1964 as one of the anonymous beach girls in *Pajama Party*. It is here where she met actress Lori Williams. The two became fast friends and would work together many times.

As with Williams, Bond also began doing stunt work (and squeezing in acting lessons) between movie roles where, according to the *A Swingin' Summer* press book, she was tagged "Hollywood's prettiest stunt girl." Among the films she worked on were *The War Lord* with Charlton Heston and *Texas Across the River* with Dean Martin and Alain Delon. She did the latter after playing a nurse on the TV series *Run for Your Life* and elicited this comment from Dean Martin in the *Chicago Daily Defender*, "What a girl! From bronchitis-busting to bronc-busting!"

Publicity photo of Diane Bond in *A Swingin' Summer* (United Screen Arts, 1965). *Courtesy of Joel Gibson*

Diane Bond's next acting role was in *A Swingin' Summer* (1965) where she received featured billing as "The Girl in the Pink Polka Dot Bikini." The swinging beach movie starred James Stacy, William Wellman, Jr., and Quinn O'Hara as college students who take summer jobs operating a dance pavilion at Lake Arrowhead. As the film's opening credits roll,

Diane in her signature pink and white polka-dot bikini is doing a water-ski Watusi on Lake Arrowhead to the surf-rock instrumental composed by Harry Betts. She and the "Swingin' Summer girls" (including Lori Williams, Irene Sale, and Diane Swanson), were bikini-clad vacationers who are romanced by handsome lothario Mickey (James Stacy). He first joins them on the shore as they toss around a beach ball. Feigning an injury, he gets the bevy of beauties to fawn all over him. Later he lures Bond and the rest to allow him to take their measurements for the Miss Lake Arrowhead beauty contest. This is just a pretext to get his forlorn friend Rick (William Wellman, Jr.) interested in them after being dumped by his girl Cindy (Quinn O'Hara). Rick appreciates the effort but declines dating any of the girls, though Mickey does cop a few feels for his trouble. Though Diane Bond filled out her swimsuit nicely, she only received a modicum of attention, as all eyes seem to focus on a buxom newcomer named Raquel Welch, playing a bookworm who learns to groove.

Like most young actresses of the mid-sixties, Bond also got to work with the Elvis Presley. She joined Lori Williams, Francine York, Linda Rogers, Ann Morell, and a myriad of other starlets playing essentially themselves—young actresses and models at a spa for women who flip over handyman Presley in *Tickle Me* (1965) but he only has eyes for yoga instructor Jocelyn Lane. Bikini-clad Bond has much less to do than in her previous movie and is seen only in the scenes around the pool. With all the nubile actresses working on this, Diane Bond never got any "alone time" with the King to her dismay.

In John Frankenheimer's cult fantasy thriller *Seconds* (1966), she played a stewardess who encounters a middle-aged banker named Wilson (Rock Hudson) on a plane. "My part lasted a matter of seconds," joked Diane. Unhappy with his life, Wilson has faked his death and now has a new handsome face and identity. En route to start his new life in Malibu, she freaks him out when speaking her only line, "Pillow, Mr. Wilson?" and he flees into the restroom. After doubling for Claudia Cardinale in *Blindfold* (1966), Diane scored her most notable role.

Bond beat out hundreds of young actresses to play Jan, one of debonair secret agent Derek Flint's three consorts, in her best known film *In Like Flint* (1967), the successful sequel to the extremely popular *Our Man Flint* (1966). None of the actresses who played Flint Girls returned in the new film and the number dropped from four to three. Diane Bond, blonde Jacki Ray as Denise, and dark-haired Mary Michael as Terry were costumed in mod fashions just as their predecessors were, but they did not fawn over Flint as overtly as the girls did in the original.

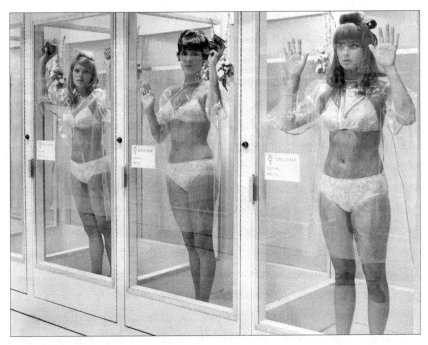

Jacki Ray, Mary Michael, and Diane Bond are frozen in the crogenics lab in *In Like Flint* (20th Century-Fox 1967). *Billy Rose Theatre Collection, The New York Public Library for the Performing Arts*

The witty spoof was released with the tag line: "Flint's back. In action...In danger...In the Virgin Islands...Where the bad guys...*Are girls!*" It opens memorably with an erotic, red tinted montage of women being pampered at a spa. As the title credits roll, the tint dissipates and the camera focuses on the stunning Jean Hale, dressed in a white mid-riff, wordlessly making her way through the resort to the accompaniment of Jerry Goldsmith's catchy theme. Flint (James Coburn), who is still working with Z.O.W.I.E., must thwart a secret society of women who are plotting to take over the world. Led by Lisa Norton (Hale) and the world's three top female fashion leaders they operate from a lavish spa in the Virgin Islands called Fabulous Faces. Their plan is to take over a space station that controls nuclear weapons. To reach their goal, they disguise two of their women as golf caddies and kidnap the President of the U.S. right off the golf course, as he plays with the Head of Z.O.W.I.E. Lloyd Kramden (Lee J. Cobb), and replace him with imposter Trent (Andrew Duggan). However, Kramden was using his stop watch to time the president and after the incident is perplexed about a missing three minutes. He decides to go to Flint for help unaware that he is being spied on by a colleague, Colonel Carter (Steve Ihnat), working for the women. When the ladies of Fabulous Faces ask if Flint has a weakness, the answer is "three of them."

Thinking Flint is away, Lisa arrives at his penthouse to lure "the weaknesses" Jan, Denise, and Terry to the island. They are interrupted by Kramden who arrives unexpectedly. Lisa is pleasantly surprised to hear that Flint is home. Jan leads Kramden to the indoor pool where the secret agent is trying to communicate with his dolphin. After discussing with his boss about the three unaccountable minutes on his watch, Flint introduces himself to Lisa and agrees to let his girls spend the week at the spa. Unbeknownst to them, the clientele get "brain and hair washing at the same time" as a way to get the rest of the female population to support their nefarious plot. However, the brainwashing doesn't take on the three bikini-clad charmers. Realizing that Flint has too strong a hold on them, Lisa orders her ladies to take Jan and the others to the cryogenics lab. The Flint Girls struggle, but are no match for the team of Amazons sent to obtain them and are frozen. While investigating what happened to Kramden, including his being set up by Lisa and Carter causing him to lose his job, the trail leads Flint to Fabulous Faces and he realizes his girls were lured there on purpose. After a long chase through the spa, Flint is captured and then has to listen as Lisa and her bosses boast of their misguided plans while they lead him to join his frozen beauties. Trent turns on the women with the help of Colonel Carter. Flint, Lisa and the rest are thrown into the cryogenics lab. With the help of sound waves from his belt, Flint is able to burst the glass and escape. He frees everyone including Jan, Denise, and Terry. Realizing their plot is ruined by the men who betrayed their cause, Lisa and the women join forces with Flint to stop Trent. In a wonderfully comical scene they all board various types of small boats to get to the island with the rocket. The gals then launch Operation Smooch, whereby they distract Carter's men by kissing and caressing them. Flint ends up on a rocket with Carter and prevents him from destroying the world. As the end credits roll, two female astronauts rescue Flint and they float in space as "Your Zowie Face" plays on the soundtrack.

In Like Flint did not receive an enthusiastic reception from the critics. Most found it inferior to the original *Our Man Flint*. However, that did not keep the fans away and it was a box office hit grossing an estimated $5 million. It ranked #18 in the biggest movie rentals of 1967. However, Diane Bond never got to go on tour to promote the movie or revel in its success. Before it was ever released, she had already relocated to Rome after accepting an offer to work from Academy Award- nominated screenwriter Pasquale Festa Campanile in a film, but it fell through.

Since she didn't speak Italian, acting roles were scarce for Diane. She didn't have name recognition like non-Italian speaking actresses Pamela Tiffin or Carroll Baker who had recently come to the Eternal City and landed lead roles. Her agent got Bond to do background work on director Roger Vadim's *Barbarella* (1968) starring Jane Fonda and then a small part in AIP's *House of 1,000 Dolls* (1968) starring Vincent Price as a mad magician and Martha Hyer as his willing assistant who work out of a sleazy club. When sexy women volunteer to be in their act, they disappear and are sold into white slavery. Hypnotized, the gals are bound and put into a casket. Then they are shipped to a Kasbah brothel. Bond played Liza, one of the scantily-clad captives, who is shackled and whipped. George Nader is the hero. *House of 1,000 Dolls* was produced by Harry Alan Towers just before his infamous association with director Jess Franco. This movie was set in Tangiers, but filmed in Spain and was released on a double-bill with either the teen exploitation film, *Maryjane* or another George Nader film for Towers, *The Million Eyes of Su-Muru*.

House of 1,000 Dolls was such a horrible experience for Diane Bond due to Harry Alan Towers. Louis P. Heyward was Towers' co-producer and was there to keep an eye on things for distributor American International Pictures. In the book *Harry Alan Towers: The Transnational Career of a Cinematic Contrarian*, he revealed that "we had some horny scenes" and one day there on the set is a guy dressed as Abraham Lincoln. Towers explained that to keep the Spanish censors away he submitted a script for *Abraham Lincoln in Illinois*. Towers also angered a number of his stars on other movies, such as Christopher Lee and Vincent Price, who only found out after they shot their scenes of the sexually exploitative ones that were being edited into their films. However, in *House of 1,000 Dolls* the S&M and torture is kept to a bare minimum and is referred to more often than shown except for Diane Bond's infamous flogging scene.

Disgusted with her experience on *House of 1,000 Dolls*, Bond left Italy and returned to her home in California. Shortly after, she went back, where she attended the Accademia di Belle Arti di Brera of Milan and the School of Fine Arts at the Sforza Castle. She worked as a model, photographer, and then became a writer of Feminist issues never acting again. Now an artist, her web site is www.dianebond.info.

How did appearing as a trapeze artist on the TV series *The Greatest Show on Earth* lead to stunt work for you?

I received my SEG [Screen Extras Guild] card for *The Greatest Show on Earth*. I was an experienced horsewoman, and also skated and water skied. My body was perfect except for my appendix scar, which then (later modeling too) was a major problem. It was the sixties and plastic surgery wasn't in vogue, but taking the 'Pill' was. It made my breasts quite voluptuous. It was for my breasts then that I got into SAG [Screen Actors Guild]. My first 'stunt job' was showing my tits on a tower in *The War Lord* with Charlton Heston.

What was it like working with Charlton Heston?

I have to laugh now, but for years I loathed him for copping a feel under the cloak. I gave him my elbow in his stomach, which hurt me more since he was wearing armor. The footage rolled and I couldn't flinch. Thank God they didn't do a retake.

Any of your other stunt work jobs stand out for you?

The one that gave me the most pleasure was due to my horsemanship. I love horses and have always had them in my life, as a child in Colorado and later in Italy. I was hired to ride with Alain Delon in his first U.S. movie *Texas Across the River*. Tina Aumont couldn't ride a horse so I doubled her and had to hang onto Alain on the back of his horse for half of the film. Now this stunt was to turn into a 'set affair.' He would pick me up in his limo. We would go on location together and dine on Bordeaux wine and fresh baguettes. That was my easiest and most joyful stunt!

Doing stunts you worked for some big name directors like Michael Gordon and Philip Dunne. Did you have much interaction with them?

No, not really. My contact in those situations was more with the stunt people. The director is saying when to stop and when to go but you really don't have direct contact. The stunts are already pre-designed. The director really doesn't talk directly to the stunt person.

Did you get to know Claudia Cardinale well while being her stand-in on *Blindfold*?

Oh, yes. We spent quite a bit of time together as we filmed in New York and Florida. I didn't become friends with her though. She was always busy doing her English lessons or having massages because of her weight. Sometime later in the seventies when I was already living in Milan, I ran into her in Rome at a rally to legalize abortion. She said, 'Oh my God, what are YOU doing here!?!' We had a little chat.

Publicity photo of Diane Bond (*at right*) and unidentified actresses in
A Swingin' Summer (United Screen Arts, 1965). *Courtesy of Joel Gibson*

What do you remember most about *Pajama Party* your film debut?

Pajama Party was another 'good times' set dancing, drinking, swimming, and playing like we were having fun, which we were. It's a film where I am hardly seen at all due to the amount of extras in it.

On the set, did you find you were treated differently when doing stunts versus playing small roles?

Well I think that feeling comes from within yourself. What you are given when you are acting is more attention—like a chair and make-up artists always completely around you. Doing stunts, you don't really have all that attention and is quite different.

What was your experience like working in *A Swingin' Summer*?

A Swingin' Summer was a happy experience and we all had a grand time. I started out only doing stunts, but they liked me and they picked me out of the crowd for a speaking part. Normally you don't get billing for this, but I did for doing the Watusi on the water skis at the beginning of the movie. Reno Carell [the producer] really liked me so I think he did this to try to help me out.

Regarding working with Raquel Welch, William Wellman, Jr. admired her professionalism; Quinn O'Hara found her merely OK; and Lori Williams called her "a bitch." Where do you fall on the Raquel meter?

As for Raquel, she was really immersed in herself and acted the part on and off the filming—haughty and above it all. I have no reason to call her a bitch and didn't at all envy the stretch marks she had all over her from childbirth although her figure seems perfect. She didn't converse with any of us, as she was too engrossed in her role. Now she is all mushy mushy, but back then at the moment she was only into the fame thing.

Publicity photo of Diane Bond, Mary Michael, and Jacki Ray in *In Like Flint* (20th Century-Fox, 1967). *Courtesy of Diane Bond*

Do you have any special memories of the film's leads, William Wellman, Jr., James Stacy, Martin West, or Quinn O'Hara?

I only really remember James Stacy because he was fucking my roommate, so I got to know him even after Lake Arrowhead. This was really hush-hush since he was married to Connie Stevens. I think they broke up shortly after. I didn't pass much time with Jim, but he was a nice guy—friendly and easy going. What else to say—except that he had a lot of bad luck and admirably kept his dignity.

How did you land the role of Jan in *In Like Flint*?

I have a great sense of humor and I obtained many jobs because I was funny. I was always telling jokes and made people laugh, which is how I got the part in *Flint*. Lori Williams told me years later that she was in the outer office when I arrived and she said I looked like shit, which can very well be as I had been on a weekend in Mexico drinking Tequila at the seaside. Upon my return, my agent was on the phone screaming at me to get over to 20th Century-Fox as they were closing the interviews for the three Flint girls. I was the last person director Gordon Douglas met with. I remember walking in, evidentially with bags under my eyes and my hair who knows, and I see his huge desk in total disarray with tons of pictures strewn everywhere on top. I threw my manila envelop, with the few photos of me inside, on his desk and I said, 'I'm last, but not least.' I plopped down in the big chesterfield chair and told him a few jokes that made him laugh. I got the contract and they dyed my hair red. He was always very nice to me.

How was James Coburn to work with?
Was he approachable off-camera?

We passed a lot of time together and he was a splendid, jovial person, always joking. He was very down-to-Earth and you could even tell that from his body language. When there were rain showers in the afternoon, which was quite often, a group of us with Coburn would sit on someone's veranda at the super resort we were staying and puff on Jamaica Gold. We'd all laugh. He never made a pass at any of us, or not to my knowledge—a cool guy.

Did you get along and work well with Jacki Ray and Mary Michael?
The three of us were all in it together and luckily we all got along with each other. We shared a huge spacious suite in that paradise so there was nothing to complain about. I don't recall any bad words or situations among us and we passed a lot of time together when we weren't needed on the set. We all got untied on several drinking bouts, with makeup artists included, all very innocent.

Considering how many actresses tested for *In Like Flint*, the casting of Jacki Ray and Mary Michael is surprising. How do you think they did in the film?
Jacki was quite rigid and unsexy. To me, her body language was stiff and not very sensuous. Gordon Douglas really didn't give Jacki many lines. Mary was a bit older and was more limber. I think she was hooked up to someone to get this part because when we got to Jamaica she took us with her to Billy Rose's mansion over looking Montego Bay. The house was bizarrely decorated with musical instruments. I know she was going with some older gentleman at the time.

It must have been glorious filming in Jamaica.
The whole atmosphere was absolutely exotic with all the palms and flowers everywhere. It was my first time in the Caribbean and staying at a dream resort—wow! The film troupe took over the whole hotel, which was also where we did all the filming. The sea water was such a turquoise blue with colored fish everywhere. It was like a dream.

Do you have any memories of leading lady Jean Hale or the Glamazons such Thordis Brandt, Inga Neilsen or Marilyn Hanold?
I just know none of the Amazons were with Coburn and our group getting high on the veranda so I really had no contact with them off-camera. Jean Hale was really unsexy and I thought someone better could have been the lead.

Mary Michael, Jacki Ray, Diane Bond, Inga Neilsen,
and James Coburn with in *In Like Flint* (20th Century-Fox 1967).

Did you know Fox studio head Richard Zanuck wanted Catherine Deneuve but producer Saul David was pushing for Hale?

There you go. Jean Hale was also not very sensuous and not really interesting because I really have no memories of her at all.

Hal Fimberg's screenplay was rather interesting for a spy spoof and foreshadowed an actor as president and women in charge. What did you think of the script?

It is far from any of my feminist standpoints as these women are just photocopying men and their ways of thinking. It really doesn't reflect anything but an excuse for a story. Jacki, Mary, and me are suppose to be the 'sex images' because Flint had three! But sex had really little to do with the scheme of power and play.

Do you have a favorite scene?

For sure in the beginning when I am introducing Lee J. Cobb to Coburn and he kisses me. Lee J. Cobb was very professional and was a funny guy, too. I can say that Gordon Douglas gave me the most footage of us three as you can denote in the film.

What made you decide to relocate to Italy?

While working on *In Like Flint*, I met Pasquale Festa Campanile and he offered me a part in his forthcoming film with Tony Curtis and Monica Vitti in Rome called *The Chastity Belt*. After *Flint*, I was not convinced of a further contract with Fox and I let it fall, taking off for Italy. Nothing was for sure, but my decision to leave was a need for adventure, I guess. And adventure I found in Italy where I have lived ever since.

How did you wind up playing one of the many prostitutes in *Barbarella*? What was that experience like working with Roger Vadim and Jane Fonda?

The Festa Campanile project continued to be postponed because of script problems and my funky agent did what he could, since I spoke only English so it wasn't really happening. I ended up in *Barbarella* and there I discovered Cinecittà Studios and how they worked in Rome. This was more extra work than acting.

The set was more than bizarre. The quantity of costumes that were discarded by Roger Vadim was an everyday amusement or tragedy, as the costume designers appeared with ten new designs and he chose maybe one, or none, and alè!—back to make new ones. I remember also how we were transfixed on the crotch of Vadim as his 'bsd' [big swinging dick] was soooo visible and long, plus all the gossip about his extravagant sex life made it all very curious. And Jane was so smiling and sweet and pretty in her crazy outfits. She seemed so naïve and was, although I never really got to speak with her.

Your last movie was *House of 1,000 Dolls* with Vincent Price and George Nader. How was it to work on this?

Horrendous due to madman producer Harry Alan Towers, a real sleaze of a person I came to find out once I arrived. He never touched me, but his reputation among some of the girls was really 'watch out.' Some of them worked on a film for him in Hong Kong and he took away their passports to make them prostitute themselves. I heard all kinds of crap about him. Even later Vincent Price complained how he was deceived by this man. Everything Towers did was to skimp and cheat and not have all the cards in the right place.

Towers' wife Maria Rohm had a part in this. How was she to work with?

I don't know how she was. She was one of those little actresses who think they have a really big role and it goes to their heads. It was like Raquel Welch on *A Swingin' Summer*.

You have a very infamous scene of being whipped. Do you recall shooting this?

Do I! The whips were supposed to be fake but there were only a couple and the rest were real. That's what the thug mistakenly picked up as the film was rolling. I screamed and the director Jerry Summers must have thought what a great actress. After the second time, I started swearing and by the third strike they saw the blood. It was obvious I wasn't acting. Finally, he yelled, 'Cut!' My back received three lashes all real, but by then it was too late! Luckily, getting beat with a real whip in my *infamous* scene enabled me to break my contract and I never went back again.

Vincent Price always claimed that additional scenes were being shot with nudity for the European release. Did you know anything about that?

I don't know how true that is. He may have said that to distance himself from the film because we didn't do any nude shots at all. Even when they beat me with the whip I am wearing panties and a brassiere like a bikini. However, it is possible. I wouldn't put it past that bastard Towers. He was a real sleaze.

What made you decide to stay in Italy?

Actually, I went back home to Los Angeles for a time but knew I was not going to stay. Rome was not happening and I was undecided between New York and Milan. I chose Milan. By 1976 I had graduated from Academy of Belli Arti di Brera and the School of Applied Arts of Castello Sforzesco where I studied painting and photography. I modeled and later married, and also wrote a book about thirty years ago called *Pictures in Peach Pit*, which is a really long story on all the Italian women artists from the 14th century to the 19th century. It is all in English so I never got it published.

9. NICOLETTA MACHIAVELLI: HEROINE OF THE SPAGHETTI WEST

A CLASSIC BEAUTY WITH DARK hair and olive skin, sultry Italian-born Nicoletta Machiavelli made a name for herself in the popular spaghetti westerns of the time, usually playing Native Americans or Mexicans. With her wind-blown long mane of hair, dust on her clothes, and stunning vistas of Spain's Almeria desert behind her, Nicoletta was visually perfect for the genre. She also spoke English fluently, which was a great asset since she was cast opposite many American actors. *The Hills Run Red* was her first, but the movie most remembered in the U.S. was *Navajo Joe* starring Burt Reynolds as the title character, out for revenge with Nicoletta as a helpful Indian. It never received much of a release in America, but became infamous from all the bad-mouthing Reynolds has given it over the years. More spaghetti westerns followed including *Hate Thy Neighbor*; *A Minute to Pray, a Second to Die*; and *Garter Colt*. Nicoletta proved talented and versatile enough to work in other genres including very popular mid-sixties spy spoofs such as *Kiss the Girls and Make Them Die* and *Matchless*.

Nicoletta Machiavelli was born to an American mother and Italian father who was a descendant of the Florentine politician/historian/philosopher/writer Niccolò di Bernardo dei Machiavelli. Her parents separated when she was a child, so she experienced a more Bohemian way of life with her mother and high society cultured ways with her father. She was studying painting at Accademia D'Arte in Florence when discovered by renowned film producer Dino De Laurentiis. Nicoletta explained, "Oscar winning set and costume designer Piero Gherardi who worked with Federico Fellini on *La Dolce Vita* and *8 ½* knew my mother. He suggested I select pictures of myself and send to De Laurentiis who offered me a seven-year contract. I was a minor so my father had to sign it. I hated him for doing that because I wanted to stay in school. At that time De Laurentiis was trying to ape the Star System in Hollywood. I was sent to acting and dancing classes because he wanted to make me a star."

The role that De Laurentiis chose to launch Nicoletta's international career was that of Eve in his sumptuous production *The Bible...in the Beginning*. However, there was one person standing in his way—director John Huston. The producer tried valiantly to push his newest protégé onto the director with auditions and photo shoots to no avail. "I met a number of times with Huston who was a nice guy but he didn't like my look," said the actress. "He thought me too Mediterranean. Years later I discovered that I reminded him too much of his daughter." With Nicoletta out of the running, the part went to the unknown, then and now, Ulla Bergryd.

Nicoletta Machiavelli in *A Minute to Pray, a Second to Die* (Cinerama Releasing, 1968).

Before Nicoletta became ensconced in spaghetti westerns she co-starred opposite legendary comic actor Ugo Tognazzi in *Una questione d'onore* (1965) shot on location in Sardinia. Describing the plot to writer Francesco Mennella in *The Sun*, Nicoletta said in 1966, "[It] is about the hot rivalry between two families in an old-fashioned world where 'honor' can be at stake even over matters that would be considered inconsequential or futile elsewhere. Sardinia, like Corsica, is a place where family hatreds are often passed on from one generation to another." Being new in the business and shy at the time, the inexperienced actress did not take advantage of getting to know Ugo Tognazzi though she commented, "He was a nice guy. I was totally not a good actress and I had no idea what to do."

Commenting on Nicoletta Machiavelli's film career and her appearance in *Una questione d'onore*, Roberto Curti a renowned film historian and author (whose books include *Italian Gothic Horror Films, 1957-1969*) opined, "In the crowded realm that was Italian cinema in the 1960s, Nicoletta Machiavelli is a very peculiar figure. The beautiful Emilian actress' career was serpentine and unpredictable, wavering between genre and auteur films, and the bizarre thing is that perhaps she is now most remembered for the films she cared for less—such as the Westerns she had to play in while under contract with Dino De Laurentiis. [These] allowed her to display not only her exceptional good looks, but also her acting chops—as proven by her first important role, as the unfortunate Domenicangela, the victim of Southern Italy's sexist and oppressive subculture, in Luigi Zampa's *Una questione d'onore*, a grotesque comedy very much in the mould of Pietro Germi's *Divorce—Italian Style* (1961) and *Seduced and Abandoned* (1964). Machiavelli's impressive turn, alongside Ugo Tognazzi, may have been partially clouded by the film's tepid critical fortunes, and failed to launch her as an alternative to such affirmed divas as Stefania Sandrelli. Still, the film gave her notoriety and led to more comedies (*Thrilling* and *I nostri mariti*) where she displayed her good comical qualities."

The spy genre also took advantage of the talented actress. The stylish and praised *Kiss the Girls and Make Them Die* (1966) was beautifully photographed on location in Brazil and stars the excellent Mike Connors as a CIA agent in Brazil investigating wealthy industrialist Mr. Ardonian (Raf Vallone). Nicoletta appears briefly as ill-fated Sylvia, one of a bevy of beauties (including Margaret Lee, Marilu Tolo, and Beverly Adams) Ardonian plans to repopulate the U.S. with after his satellite emitting ultrasonic waves has destroyed the sex drive of the world's population. This was an experience Nicoletta would never forget.

"I only worked with Raf Vallone," she revealed. "I had a small part but I loved doing this because I got to visit Rio de Janeiro. Dino De Laurentiis hated me because I came to Brazil with my-then Italian boyfriend. I only had one day of shooting and I was there for I think almost three months because the city was completed submerged by monsoons. I stayed in the part of the city called Copacabana and got pneumonia because I wasn't used to air conditioning. I was able to listen to all the songs by Jorge Ben Jor and others and basically learned Portuguese from them while recuperating in my hotel room. After I got well, I visited all the Samba clubs with live music. I am so happy to have done that because I do not think that *that* Rio exists anymore."

Machiavelli landed a tad bigger role in the not well-received spy spoof *Matchless* (aka *Mission Top Secret*, 1966). This was the first of three color pictures that Dino De Laurentiis produced for his distribution deal with United Artists. *Navajo Joe* was also part of this package. In *Matchless*, Patrick O'Neal is American columnist Perry Liston (who writes under the name "Matchless") mistaken for a spy in China and then put in prison, where an inmate gives him a jade ring that gives him the power of invisibility for a twenty minute stretch. Liston is then recruited as a real spy to retrieve some lethal vials from the film's villain (Donald Pleasence) though it is never made clear just what he plans to do with them. Nicoletta played a seductive mystery woman who shares a cab with Matchless in London and then turns up scantily clad rolling around on his bed later that night. She is stopped from shooting him by another agent (Ira von Furstenberg) but her intent is never revealed in this not very coherent spy film.

What Machiavelli remembers most about this movie is working with Princess Ira von Furstenberg. "This was one of her first movies. She was just a young girl with no experience. I had already been working about four years in the profession. We had a scene together [with Patrick O'Neal] where we had to get out of the frame and had to do this on the set while the camera was moving. The director told us to go behind the bed so they wouldn't see us. As soon as we were in hiding, she starting giggling and this was a movie where they shot sound. The director called cut so many times because she wouldn't stop laughing."

When told how a future co-star Pamela Tiffin was snubbed by the Princess at their wrap party, Nicoletta was not surprised and emphatically states, "This aristocracy is like shit in Italy. I grew up in an aristocratic family on my father's side. I did everything to get out of that life. But Italy, it is different and Ira was so much into that world. She was already benefitting from it. I was a rebel and luckily had an American mother."

Nicoletta would spend the next couple of years entrenched in spaghetti westerns. The genre was born in the early sixties. Its nickname came from the fact that these lower-budgeted movies were directed and produced by Italians but filmed in other European countries such as Spain, particularly the Almeria section that looks just like the American Southwest, with Italian and Spanish crews and usually with an American actor or two. The genre took off with Sergio Leone's *A Fistful of Dollars* starring Clint Eastwood as The Man With No Name. The actor's next with Leone *For a Few Dollars More* sent the spaghetti westerns into orbit with many copycats and rip-offs released to cash in on this new popular genre.

Recalling the genre and how she became immersed in it, Nicoletta recounted, "When spaghetti westerns started to become fashionable, I would fly to Spain three times a year and sometimes for a little part with like two minutes of screen time in some cases. We never recorded sound during filming. It was always dubbed in post-production. I was cast in these spaghetti westerns because I spoke English. The main actors I worked with, like Thomas Hunter and Henry Silva, were American so to have a leading lady that spoke their language was good for them and the film as a whole. Many of the American actors took the time and went into the dubbing room. I would only loop my dialog if the producer or director insisted and I had the time. With the spaghetti westerns I was doing one after the other so I was unavailable. I did dub a few of the movies that I really wanted to. Later they started to record with sound while filming."

The dubbing industry is huge in Italy and a bit too powerful for Nicoletta who called it "terrible. A lot of Italians were illiterate in the forties and fifties so instead of subtitles they dubbed all the foreign movies even though the population had progressed by the sixties. The union became so strong that even now they are still dubbing. I really hate to bad mouth a whole group of professionals, but the voices that they do for German, French, and American movies that you see in Italy are always the same! The intonation never changes and you never hear anything new. Even today the voices sound exactly like when I was going to the movies in Italy when I was a little girl. It drives me nuts. I think the Italian public has this habit of hearing this type of woman has this type of voice and that type of woman has that type of voice. I can't stand it. The art of dubbing, though, I found fun. It was its own little world. The actual director of the movie was usually never present though there was a "director" who gave you instructions on the dialog."

Most of Nicoletta Machiavelli's westerns were shot in Almeria. She exclaimed, "It was fabulous to work in Spain. When I went back to the Almeria Film Festival in 2011, I realized from the smell in the air and the beautiful outdoors how wonderful it was that I had the opportunity to shoot there and not to have been in a studio forced to wear petticoats. The Spanish crews brought their incredible expertise with horses. The Italians of course had their own way of doing things and then the Americans I worked with like Arthur Kennedy, Robert Ryan, Henry Silva, and even Burt Reynolds brought this professionalism from another continent. It was a really fascinating experience. After a day's work I'd notice who sat with whom at dinner or who went off on their own."

The actress' spaghetti western debut was in *Un fiumi di dollari* aka *The Hills Run Red* (1966). It was directed by Carlo Lizzani and released in the U.S. on the bottom of a double bill with *Matchless*. Nicoletta played Marianne, sister of sinister Ken Seagull (Nando Gazzolo). This role didn't give her much to do but look regal and bewildered to all that was happening around her. Her brother framed Confederate soldier Jerry Brewster (Thomas Hunter) for a robbery. Not only did Seagull get the loot, but he killed Brewster's wife and left their son motherless. With the help of a Texas Ranger (Dan Duryea), Brewster vows revenge. Keeping his identity a secret, Brewster gets himself hired onto Seagull's ranch crew headed by psychotic Mendez (played by wild-eyed Henry Silva, who chews up the scenery and out villains Seagull) who wants Marianne. He threatens that one day she will fall in love with him. She reviles him and has feelings for the new man on the crew, Brewster. After the big gunfight in the town of Austin, Marianne rushes to Mendez to find out what happened. He pulls her onto his horse and tells her they are running off to Mexico together. Jealous saloon girl Hattie (Gianna Serra) steps out of the shadows and vows she will be the only one going off with Mendez and shoots Marianne. Mendez plugs Hattie with lead before being shot by Brewster. As she lay dying, Marianne vows to Brewster that she knew nothing of her brother's crimes against him. Come fadeout, as Brewster is reunited with his son and named the new sheriff of Austin, an incredulously recovered Marianne (raised from the dead?) looks on.

Nicoletta loved doing this film because she was able to work with Henry Silva again. "He was so magnificent to work with," she exclaimed. "He was an incredible character in his own right and we became such friends."

The film's ending not only confounds moviegoers, but it totally confused Nicoletta, and the crew, even during filming. She said laughing, "*The Hills Run Red* was the one where I die, but I don't die. We did these scenes during the same period when I was on the set so it wasn't added on later. But I didn't know what the hell they were doing. When you do small parts they are filmed out of context even if you read the script. The crew was half Italian and half Spanish. The Italians were laughing that my character dies and then comes back to life. They too didn't understand it."

The Hills Run Red was mostly ignored by the critics in the U.S. but author and film historian Howard Hughes writing in his book *Spaghetti Westerns* found it to be an undiscovered gem that takes "themes from *A Fistful of Dollars* (the warring-clans scenario), *For a Few Dollars More* (the younger Brewster joining forces with seasoned veteran Getz), and *Django* (the death of the hero's wife...)." His verdict, "An imaginative action movie and a cracking take of fifties westerns with a sixties twist, this is one largely overlooked movie that thoroughly deserves a cult following."

Burt Reynolds and Nicoletta Machiavelli in *Navajo Joe* (United Artists, 1967).

Navajo Joe though is more remembered. It is the standout western for Machiavelli, not only because it starred Burt Reynolds, but it has one of the actress' most prominent and interesting roles. The excellent production values, gorgeous cinematography, and rousing theme music by Ennio Morricone with Native American-type choral chants of "Navajo Joe" help overcome the simplistic plot and, for some, the intense dislike for Reynolds in this.

Marlon Brando was producer Dino De Laurentiis first choice to star but when things did not work out with the actor, he traveled to Hollywood to find a leading man for his newest spaghetti western. The working title (and title used in Italy and abroad) was *A Dollar a Head*, an obvious try to cash in on Sergio Leone's hit westerns *A Fistful of Dollars* and *For a Few Dollars More*. Clint Eastwood, who had just returned after making those westerns, encouraged his friend Reynolds, who was a quarter American Indian and could ride a horse better than most, to meet with the producer. Writing in his memoir, Reynolds said that De Laurentiis gushed all of over him. He promised that the film was going to be a bigger hit than *A Fistful of Dollars* and that Reynolds' character would kill more bad guys than Eastwood did. At the same time, Burt landed the TV series *Hawk* playing a full-blooded American Indian police lieutenant working in New York City. He had to report to the set in three months and De Laurentiis assured him that the movie would be completed by then.

Reynolds spent the first five weeks in Italy doing nothing but drinking wine as De Laurentiis rejected script after script. Finally, the movie was to begin shooting and the producer hosted a star-studded party at his enormous home. All this time, Reynolds was under the presumption that Sergio Leone was directing. Reynolds got a big shock that night to learn that a Sergio was directing— a Sergio Corbucci. He had just directed Franco Nero in what was to become a classic in spaghetti western circles, *Django*.

Wanting to make this movie as realistic as possible since he found the final draft to be "the worst script I'd ever read, other than *Operation CIA*," Reynolds not only chose his costume but his horse as well. After rejecting every black and white horse brought to him by a gypsy who was in charge of the horses to be used in the movie, Reynolds asked if he could ride his horse named Destaphanado. Problem was the horse was old and not camera ready. Burt asked the makeup men to work on him and the next day when shooting was to begin Reynolds wrote, "Destaphanado had been transformed from a twenty-three-year-old plug-ugly horse into Ricardo Montalban." The Spanish gypsies who trained the horses was so impressed with Reynold's' riding skills that they invited him to spend the night with them in the camp they stayed in.

Nicoletta had only a professional and cordial relationship with her leading man. She remarked, "He was friendly towards me, but we didn't have lunch or dinner together. While working, Burt would coach me and say things like, 'Keep your head a little bit this way so I can pull your hair without tugging your wig off' or something like that. When I moved to America in the seventies, I saw Burt in *Smokey and the Bandit*. I found him hilarious and really good. More than ten years had passed since we worked together so I didn't even think of contacting him to tell him." When asked what she thought of Burt's jet black wig he wore in the movie, Nicoletta would not comment and just laughed.

Though Burt Reynolds seem to be dedicated to make *Navajo Joe* the best it could be and that the gypsies took favor with him, he did not impress the Italian crew in the least per Nicoletta. "Burt Reynolds was so snooty that the whole crew couldn't stand him. He didn't have any background for us Italians. He had done a few things but we had never heard of him. He came with this attitude so he wasn't very well liked. If things weren't done according to him, he would make it known."

Speaking of the Italian crews who were crazy in their own way, Nicoletta praised them as compared to their Hollywood counterparts and said, "The Italian crews were never silent even after the director yelled action. They were still drinking wine in the background. But there is another side to that. When I did the movie *Those Daring Young Men in Their Jaunty Jalopies* for director Ken Annakin most of it was shot inside the studio. In Italy, if a light went out the director or assistant director would say it needs to be changed and in five minutes we would be working again. Forget it in Hollywood. All these crew members would just stand there and only the guy in charge of the lights could come in and make the switch. It would be like thirty minutes off the clock. This is a perfect example of the differences between the Italian and Hollywood crews."

Though Reynolds was initially disappointed to be working with Sergio Corbucci, he wrote in his memoir they grew to like each other a lot. Nicoletta admired him too and thought her director to be such a character. "Sergio Corbucci was round and was the usual kind of easy going Italian director with quirky ideas. He was surely good as a director— very spontaneous. His scenes were very well concocted. He handled the action scenes with horses, fights, and shootings very admirably. But half the time he waited in the chapel with his new wife. They played poker until we were ready to shoot. I thought that was very funny. Not all the directors were like that."

As most early spaghetti westerns began, the ultra violent *Navajo Joe* too opens with a horrific murder and is a revenge tale with nonstop killings. An Indian squaw is washing clothes by a river bank when bandit Vee Duncan (Aldo Sambrell), a half-breed tired of being disrespected by both races, rides up. Pulling his gun, she screams and flees only to be shot in the back and then scalped while his gang ransacks the Indian village. The dead woman is the wife of Navajo Joe (Burt Reynolds), the sole survivor of the slaughter. He trails the gang from a distance but makes his presence known by watching the men from high above on the mountain ridge. Machiavelli's Estella, the maid to bank heiress and doctor's wife Hannah Lynne (Valerie Sabel), enters the picture when Navajo Joe arrives in the town of Esperanza engineering a train with $500,000 (a state grant earmarked for the town) locked in a safe after thwarting a robbery orchestrated by resident Dr. Chester Lynne (Pierre Cressoy) with Duncan's gang. Also turning up are three saloon girls and their manager Chuck (Nino Imperato) who were fleeing the bandits after they shot up and burned the town where they were performing. They too were saved by Navajo Joe. One of the girls named Geraldine (Lucia Modugno) has been shot and when Dr. Lynne is called to save her, she realizes it is the same man she saw plotting with Duncan. Distracting his helper Estella, Lynne snuffs the life out of the girl and says she succumbed to her bullet injury.

Joe offers to help protect the town that has no guns for a price, but dastardly Dr. Lynne convinces the townspeople not to trust him. Before Joe rides off, he warns that they have a traitor amongst them and that Duncan's gang is on their way. Lynne plays hero and rides off to the town of Wellington for help from the rangers but actually rendezvous with Duncan and his boys. With the doctor gone, the town has a change of heart and sends Estella to convince Joe to come back to help them. She tells him that her mistress Mrs. Lynne practically runs the town and will meet his price. After revealing to Joe that she is Indian on her mother's side, she asks his name. After he responds, she says, "I've never known an Indian named Joe. And I've never seen a Navajo so far south before." He replies, "And me an Indian girl that asks so many questions."

Estella tells the townspeople that Joe will come to help, but they still are nervous in trusting him and have pinned their hopes on Lynne. Joe arrives to tell them that the good doctor took the wrong route and not to expect the rangers. They agree to pay Joe his price, but he adds one more condition and wants to be named sheriff. When they object because he is not American, he points out that his father and grandfather were born in America. The sheriff's father was born in Scotland. This was one of the movie's most insightful moments amongst the slaughter. Vindicated, Joe takes the badge, demands some dynamite, and tells the folks to barricade themselves in their homes so as not to get in his way. Duncan, Lynne and the gang arrive and head straight to the bank. When discovering the money is not in the safe, a mistrusting Duncan shoots the doctor who stumbles outside. Despite Estella's warning, Hannah comes running out to her husband's rescue and is gunned down. As they lay wounded, she reveals that the Indian hid the money. Duncan finishes them both off just as Joe begins his assault by throwing dynamite off the roof from where he has been perched in watch. The assault ends when Duncan drags Estella out by the hair from her hiding place and threatens to kill her. Joe throws down his rifle and surrenders to spare her life.

Duncan strings Joe upside down while Estella goes to Chuck and the girls for help. Though scared, all are indebted to Joe for saving their lives, so they agree to try to free him. Chuck shoots an arrow piercing one of the ropes binding his hands. Joe breaks free and is able to set himself loose from the other binds and escape. Furious that the townsfolk set the Indian free and that he cannot find the money, Duncan rounds them up to execute all one by one.

A grateful Joe, hiding out with Chuck and the girls, exchanges a flirtatious smile with Estella. She says, "I want you to live. Why don't you go before it is too late?" He says that he needs to finish what he started and, annoyed with her questioning, refuses to answer her on why he detests Duncan. Joe then sets Chuck's girls to lure the men away from the corral. The plan works and Joe is able to get to his horse while releasing all the rest belonging to Duncan's men. He then gets the gang to head for the train after delivering a note sent via a flaming arrow telling them that is where the money is. Of course it is a trap, and Joe escapes on foot with the loot in a saddle bag with Duncan and his men in close pursuit. Joe picks off all them until only Duncan is left. They meet face to face in the Indian burial ground Joe hid out before. Confirming for sure that Duncan killed his woman after ripping her necklace off from around his neck, Joe beats up Duncan almost to death. As he goes over to grab a tomahawk, Duncan reaches for a gun and shoots Joe who is able to get and throw the tomahawk killing his adversary instantly. We last see Joe sitting there holding his side. His horse rides into town with the money to the shock of the townspeople. The mayor wants to corral the horse, but Estella insists that he be set free to return to Joe. The horse gallops away and the movie ends with Joe's fate left unresolved.

Lucia Modugno, Pierre Crossoy, and Nicoletta Machiavelli in *Navajo Joe* (United Artists, 1967).

When first released in the States in late November 1967, *Navajo Joe* did not make much of an impression even coming on the heels of Burt Reynolds' TV series *Hawk*. In most locations, it was even released on the bottom of a double bill with the adventure film *Kill a Dragon* starring Jack Palance. To draw audiences, the tag line proclaimed, "Restless in His Vengeance! Deadly in His Violence! There's No Explaining His One Man Navajo Vendetta... For Money—for Pleasure—for Revenge—He Doesn't Care Why He Kills or How."

Navajo Joe received wildly mixed reviews from the mainstream critics. For example, the reviewer in *Box Office* found the movie to be "equal in realism and excitement to the two 'Dollars' westerns." He called Reynolds "ruggedly handsome and extremely convincing" and even praised Nicoletta, remarking that she "makes a beautiful and sympathetic Indian girl." On the other hand, Kathy Orloff writing in *The Hollywood Reporter* called the movie "consistently awful" After trashing the direction, the sound, the dubbing, and the musical score, Orloff surprisingly wrapped up her review commenting that the "only lovely note in the film is the appearance of Nicoletta Machiavelli..." A middle of the road review came from Whit in *Variety*, who commented that the movie "comes out okay for minor action situations which to not demand either top quality or any particular novelty of them" and that "Burt Reynolds makes the most of his role..."

Today with some spaghetti western film historians and fans, it has grown a bit in stature. The Spaghetti Western Database calls it an "Action packed and rather violent western, which unusually presents an Indian as the revenging hero. The film has its ill-conceived moments and scenes, but benefits from Corbucci's skillful directing of tough action scenes and a rousing score by Ennio Morricone." Howard Hughes also praised the movie in his book *Spaghetti Westerns* and singled out "the stunning Italian actress Nicoletta Machiavelli" and "the incredible screaming, clanging score by Ennio Morricone." Though considered one of Sergio Corbucci's lesser western efforts—compared to his masterpieces *Django* and *The Great Silence*—*Navajo Joe* is a rousing, violent, non-stop action film beautifully photographed and scored that is highly recommended. Nicoletta and Reynolds are paired well together and the ambiguous ending has you hoping for a sequel. Alas, it never came to be.

Nicoletta Machiavelli's next spaghetti western received much more attention in the States. *A Minute to Pray, a Second to Die* (1968) was directed by Franco Giraldi and starred American actor Alex Cord who was known around Hollywood for being the fastest gun in the film world, so skilled he instructed other celebrities on how to shoot.

In an unusual twist, Cord's outlaw Clay McCord, who has a $10,000 bounty on his head, suffers from a nerve disorder that causes seizures just like his father experienced (from flashbacks to when Clay was a boy). The movie featured Nicoletta as Laurinda one of the Escondida townspeople bullied by Krant (Mario Brega) and his outlaw gang. Clay draws their ire when he shoots dead one of Krant's men who shot an unarmed woman whose husband was killed because of Krant. The bandits control the "grub" that comes into the town and decides who gets to eat. Clay falls for Laurinda and promises her a better life and says, "Some day I'm gonna take you where people eat until they bust." By ordinance of the governor (Robert Ryan), every town must offer all wanted men amnesty but Escondida won't abide. When Clay goes to the nearby town of Toscosa he is ambushed by the Marshall (Arthur Kennedy) and bounty hunters wanting to collect the reward on his head before he can turn himself in. Wounded, Clay returns to Laurinda's where she hides him as he recovers from a gunshot. Laurinda waits in line to receive food from the governor's representative and when she pulls out a wad of cash to pay for it, Krant becomes suspicious. He and his men follow her and when an unconscious Clay comes to he is surrounded. Laurinda has a gun hidden behind her back, unaware that one gang member is watching her. When she goes to pull the gun on Krant, she is shot and killed. Nicoletta's quick exit from the movie is a surprising jolt.

Unfortunately, Nicoletta doesn't have much to share about this movie and commented, "I was always drawn to hanging out with the American actors, and here it was Robert Ryan and Arthur Kennedy. They were so much older than me but not Alex Cord. If I remember correctly I had a fling with him. I don't recall anything else about *A Minute to Pray, A Second to Die*."

The movie received a national release in the U.S. during late spring of 1968, most likely to capitalize on the star power of Alex Cord who was gaining popularity due to his performances in *Synanon* (1965) and the remake of *Stagecoach* (1966). As a gimmick, the movie had three endings (a tragic one; a happy one where the hero rides off into the sunset; and then a cynical one where the lesson is a man can't change his ways) any of which would be released randomly to theaters. However, the version released in the U.S. is missing about fifteen minutes of film and only has the happy ending.

As expected with this genre, reviews were mixed. One particularly negative one in the *Chicago Tribune* described Cord as being "an underfed Troy Donahue" and that "Nicoletta Machiavelli, cast as an impoverished peasant, but given a dubbed voice that sounds more like Ava Gardner playing Lady Brett." Kevin Thomas of the *Los Angeles Times* called it "lousy" and quipped, "Had the title *The Shakiest Gun in the West* not already been used, it would have been perfect for this trite tale."

Today, spaghetti western aficionados consider *A Minute to Pray, a Second to Die* a bit above average due to the quality production values; a solid performance from the handsome and often shirtless Alex Cord as an atypical vulnerable gunfighter; and a good supporting cast including Brega, Nicoletta, Robert Ryan as the understated governor, and Arthur Kennedy as the double-dealing Marshal of Tuscosa. The Spaghetti Western Database opined, "The film is surprisingly good. It boasts an excellent score by Carlo Rustichelli, some really gritty action, a good story and some solid acting... It's a shame Nicoletta Machiavelli has such a short part though. The cinematography is standard and makes the film look very American, but the action makes up for it. A really gripping tale, an enjoyable Spaghetti Western and definitely underrated."

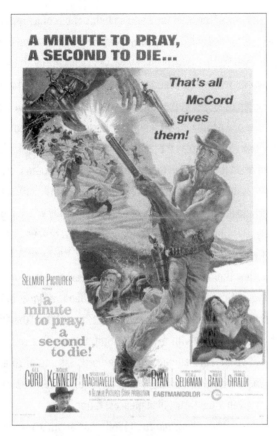

Promotional poster art for *A Minute to Pray, a Second to Die*
(Cinerama Releasing, 1968).

The remainder of Nicoletta's spaghetti westerns never made it to the U.S. *Face to Face/Faccia a faccia* from spaghetti western maestro Sergio Sollima starred Tomas Milian and Gian Maria Volonte and is considered one of the classics of the genre. According to several sources, the actress makes an uncredited appearance though it cannot be substantiated even by Nicoletta, who has no memory of this, or Tomas Milian. Of Cuban descent, Milian became a very popular action hero in Italy and a heartthrob for many a female. Though she did appear in Milian's crime movie *Free Hand for a Tough Cop/Il trucido e lo sbirro* in 1976, their paths never crossed. She said, "Everybody in Italy loves Tomas Milian. I don't think we ever had a scene together, so I don't recall ever meeting him."

Garter Colt/Giarrettiera Colt (1968) was a very rare spaghetti western to feature a female lead. It was also one of the least successful in terms of box office grosses perhaps because of it. Nicoletta is topped billed as a gunslinger (she hides her pistol in her garter belt) and poker player named Lulu newly arrived in town who joins the locals to battle a gang of Mexican revolutionaries led by Red (Claudio Camaso). A very disjointed movie, it features many shots from different angles of the stunning Nicoletta clad in various low-cut outfits. "*Garter Colt* was more of a parody than a serious western," remarked Nicoletta. "It was very low budget. When I was asked to play the lead, Piero Gherardi offered to make my costumes for free so I agreed to do it. We filmed this in Sardinia with a reduced crew rather than in Spain. On paper it was funny and possible to do, but it was more literary than movie if you know what I mean. I do not think it was ever released." It actually was in regions of Italy.

Unfortunately, the film was severely panned by the very few who saw it in May 1968. It still is not well-liked. Writing in his book *Spaghetti Westerns—the Good, the Bad and the Violent*, author Thomas Weisser called it "hopelessly inept; laughable; not even worthwhile for voyeuristic reasons." Roberto Curti described the film as being "downright bizarre, little-seen but highly influential." He went on to reveal that "the film was initially passed by the board of censors with a v.m.18 rating. In appeal, a couple of cuts were demanded, namely two lines of dialogue where the words 'ass' and 'bitch' are uttered, and a dancing scene where the heroine's belly is uncovered for a total of about four seconds. Finally the film was given a 'per tutti' (all audiences) rating."

Hate Thy Neighbor/Odia il prossimo tuo (1968) was another revenge western. Directed by Ferdinando Baldi, it starred the stoic Spiros Focás (though billed with the Americanized name of Clyde Garner) as cowboy Ken Dakota seeking vengeance for the murder of his brother and sister-in-law at the hands of bandit Gary Stevens (smoldering charismatic George Eastman) on orders from evil land baron Chris Malone (Horst Frank). Seems Dakota's brother was in possession of a map with directions to a goldmine. Nicoletta played Peggy Savalas, the dutiful girlfriend of Ken Drake. Dressed and coiffured like a schoolmarm, the actress appears too sultry for this part and seems miscast. Peggy agrees to watch his orphaned nephew Pat while he tracks his sibling's killers. A warped villain, Malone and his blonde mannequin wife get their kicks watching their captured Mexican slaves, complete with long razor-sharp claws on their hands, fight to the death gladiator-style in a makeshift arena that they have on their estate. The equally vile Stevens, after being sentenced to hanging—which he escapes—beats up Peggy, who brought star witness Pat to his trial, and kidnaps the boy. During the finale, after shooting Stevens down in cold blood for revealing his part in the Drake's murder, Malone commandeers Peggy's buggy but he is shot and wounded by Ken, who lets him live.

"George Eastman was quite a name in the westerns in those days and he is another I don't remember working with," deadpanned Nicoletta who seems to have had no interest in the heartthrobs of the day. "But I do remember Spiros Focás because he was the lover of Irene Pappas, who accompanied him. I loved her. She told me, 'Never let them take away your eyebrows from your face.' She was wonderful and traveled with a little entourage. She only ate tomatoes and feta cheese."

Nicoletta's last spaghetti western was *Una lunga fila di croci/No Room to Die/A Hanging for Django* (1969) directed by Sergio Garrone. The movie featured two of the biggest stars of spaghetti westerns, Anthony Steffen and William Berger, though neither were well-known in the U.S. Steffen, channeling Clint Eastwood, played a bounty hunter named Brandon on the trail of illegal immigrant smugglers who partners with an amiable no-named brute (Mario Brega in a rare good guy role) and Berger was Murdock a scripture-reciting, big gun packing treacherous preacher. They join forces (or do they?) to bring the smuggling ring down. Nicoletta had one of her best roles as Maya. Though a strong, opinionated woman in Mexico, she is involved with the film's refined and devious villain Fargo (Riccardo Garrone) who wants to marry her. A wealthy landowner, he uses illegal immigrants as cheap labor (a situation still prevalent to this day, keeping the movie quite relevant) and has no qualms about eliminating them when the authorities snoop around. Maya pays for locals wanting to go to the U.S. unaware of the treatment they receive from Fargo once across the border if they make it alive. She learns the truth from Brandon when one young man escapes and returns to town. He guns down the men sent to retrieve the illegal. Though she despises Brandon for being a murdering bounty hunter, her new-found distaste for Fargo is stronger. He saves her a second time after being kidnapped by Fargo. The film is nonstop action and ranks high in the pantheon of the spaghetti western genre.

Though Machiavelli has pleasant memories about working in spaghetti westerns, she is haunted to this day by an incident that happened on one of them, though she doesn't recall which film. She recounts, "There was a big scandal during a scene with these galloping horses. The trainers and riders were all Spaniards. They usually did an incredible job and had all these tricks when a horse was supposed to fall down. This particular scene was shot in this wide open space with the horses running and running. The horses then were supposed to fall off this cliff and they really did! You are not supposed to actually do it and kill the horses. The American actors and I were horrified. Even for the Italian crew it was a big shock. I can't remember the director. It was a terrible mishap that somebody let happen."

At this time Nicoletta felt she had exhausted working in westerns. Actually she used the genre as a way to escape the fame game in Italy but after a while she decided it was time to branch out. "I had enough with these types of movies and broke off with them," Nicoletta revealed. "I didn't have the ambition to be something else other than an actress. I got into acting too early. You are pulled in different ways and told what to do. I thought 'I can do it. I am half American and independent.' But it is not really true, especially in Italy. There you had to play the game—attending these endless cocktail parties, getting all dressed up. I hated that whole part of the business. My producer or agent telling me you have to go to this event because blah blah blah will be there. Filming westerns in Spain was such a nice respite from all this."

Still under contract to Dino De Laurentiis, he then began loaning out Nicoletta to American and British film companies due to her fluency in English. She had a small role in *Candy* (1968) based on Terry Southern's extremely popular novel and then turned up in the lavish adventure comedy *Those Daring Young Men in Their Jaunty Jalopies* (1969) directed by Ken Annakin. Set in the 1920s, Tony Curtis, Lando Buzzanca, Terry-Thomas, Dudley Moore, Peter Cook, Gert Frobe, and others enter an international car rally in Monte Carlo. Nicoletta played Dominique, who enters the competition with her two friends Marie-Claude (Mireille Darc) and Pascale (Marie Dubois) as the only all-girl racing team.

Recalling the movie, Nicoletta comments, "I really didn't have much contact with Lando Buzzanca, whose bad reputation with women preceded him. Tony Curtis was so far above us and considered us the little people so I don't even think we ever spoke. Ken Annakin the director though was really nice. I basically hung around with the other two girls I was paired with. Mireille Darc and I did another movie together in France [*Les seins de glace*, 1974] since I spoke French as well. Her character was involved with Alain Delon and I played his wife. I did a three-part series in France afterwards so I wound up living there for awhile."

Nicoletta then went through a terrible time trying to break her contract with De Laurentiis so she could do films that she was interested in and not just assigned to do.

However, the producer was not going to let her go without a fight and sued her. Luckily for her, he was distracted due to money issues and eventually let it go. Though now free, the harsh realities of being a freelancer immediately set in for the actress. "When I broke my contract with De Laurentiis I was almost penniless," she confessed. "I was paid something like $500 per month and not per picture. Now I had to look for my own work. In those days we were doing a lot of alternative movies. I remember doing a little part standing on the corner of the Coliseum dressed as a gypsy flinging post cards with everybody around me stoned. I was paid very little. Sometimes I was asked to do a role in a film that was very ideological and do it pro bono. The only movies where you could make some decent money were the westerns."

Nicoletta Machiavelli, Mireille Darc, Marie Dubois, Tony Curtis, and
Susan Hampshire in *Those Daring Young Men in Their Jaunty Jalopies* (Paramount, 1969).

Describing Nicoletta's career at this time after her run of spaghetti westerns, Roberto Curti remarked, "Machiavelli then became some sort of a *cinéma d'essai* muse, taking part in experimental oddities which reflected the most daring side of Italian and European cinema of the period. Her versatility—and bravery in the choice of films—led to the participation to such works as *La coppia* (1968, the only film directed by renowned writer and literary critic Enzo Siciliano); Hans-Jürgen Syberberg's *Scarabea* (1969); Franco Brocani's obscure (in all senses of the word) *Necropolis* (1970); Jacques Doniol-Valcroze's *L'Homme au cerveau greffé* (1971); and Franco Rossi's *Policeman* (1969, released in 1971). It was a dramatic turn which had generated from Machiavelli's break of the seven-year contract with De Laurentiis, which she was very unsatisfied with, as well as from Machiavelli's embracing of the politically committed, somewhat utopian climate of post-1968 cinema."

Of these type movies the standout (and her favorite) was the WWII set *La cattura* (1969) directed by Paolo Cavara and co-starring David McCallum of *The Man from U.N.C.L.E.* fame. He played a German special agent who captures Machiavelli's Yugoslavian resistance fighter. During a blizzard, they are trapped together in a cabin for days and become attracted to each other. When the storm lets up, the agent has to decide to bring her in as a prisoner or set her free. The film was one of eight Italian entries in the 1969 Venice Film Festival. Roberto Curti called it "a philosophical war movie centered on two characters, perhaps inspired by John Boorman's *Duel in the Pacific* (1968), with almost surreal moments and a very strong 1968 feel."

"David McCallum was fabulous to work it," exclaimed Nicoletta. "He was very patient with me since I was such an ignorant actress at that time. Not there was much talking in this, but more gestures. We shot this with sound in English and later I dubbed myself into Italian.

"This film has always been hard to see because there was a dispute between the producers and the distributor," continued Nicoletta. "In 2009, I went to a special screening of this movie and met Pietro, the son of Paolo Cavara. He wants to bring overdue recognition to his father. Before Paolo did *La caturra*, he made documentaries filmed around the world, the most famous being *Mondo cane*. A lot of animal lovers and humanists really put Cavara and his movies down. They really have not been shown since their release. Paolo died quite young and Pietro is trying to revive interest in his career. Whenever I go to Rome, I meet him and we go for coffee."

During this time, Nicoletta ventured into American television with an appearance on *It Takes a Thief* starring Robert Wagner. She thought it would soon be forgotten but years later learned it was not. "I so remember doing *It Takes a Thief* because we filmed on the seaside [in Porto Ercole] where I always went to swim when living in Rome. I knew the costume designer. I had a scene with Robert Wagner in a boat where we kiss. Years later when I came to America with my son who was eight years old we were staying with a friend in Marin County. One day we were talking and my friend exclaimed, 'You did a TV show with Robert Wagner!?! And you kissed him!?!' All my American girlfriends wanted to know about Wagner. In Italy, all my Italian girlfriends wanted to hear stories about Alain Delon."

Also around this time in films, screen nudity became an issue and one that Nicoletta had to face. "I was already in the hippie phase so when they asked me to take my clothes off it wasn't a big deal for me at all. I used to go to the nudist beaches in Italy and Greece. Nudity did not equate sex. If somebody put their hands on me, then I would make a big deal over it.

"I had a nude scene in *Storie scellerate* [aka *Bawdy Tales*]," continues the actress. "This was directed by Sergio Citti the boyfriend of Pier Paolo Pasolini [who co-wrote the screenplay with Citti]. I played this perverted countess who wanted to go to bed with all the young stable men who took care of her horses. They wanted me to enter the stable wearing a shawl only and take it off. Even with all the crew standing around and the bright lights I didn't feel ashamed. Remember back when I was trying out to play Eve in John Huston's *The Bible,* we were on the beach and I was always naked. For me, going nude was not a sin. I think for American actresses like Pamela Tiffin, who had trouble doing nude scenes, there was more of a stigma."

The two post-De Laurentiis movies that Nicoletta is most proud of are the Dino Risi-directed comedy *Dirty Weekend* with Marcello Mastroianni and Oliver Reed, and *Holy Year* (1976) with iconic French actor Jean Gabin. In the former, she is part of a trio of Communist bank robbers led by bullying Reed who kidnap rich businessman Mastroianni, who was trying to sneak away for three days with his free-spirited mistress Carol André.

"*Dirty Weekend* was a really good movie," opined Machiavelli. "It was a film commenting on the times, but it was a comedy. I found out I was pregnant while we were shooting. I had short hair then and it was such a wild part. I liked working with Oliver the best. He was so crazy and so much fun to be around, unlike Dino Risi and Marcello Mastroianni who were so boring. The cast and crew were put up in this lavish hotel where royalty would stay. It was on the coast of Florence and I knew that area really well because I would go there as a child. The hotel was art deco and had a private beach. Sometimes I would wind up at the dinner table with Dino and Marcello. All they would talk about were their ex-wives and the alimony they had to pay. I was young and on the verge of becoming a hippie with all the idealism going on at that time. I would just eat my meal and think 'Do I really have to listen to these two old fogies?'"

Nicoletta's spirits would perk up when Oliver Reed would make his grand entrance. She says laughing, "You would see Oliver Reed cross the dining room with a drunken gaze, not responding to anyone who greeted him. He'd go through the open door out onto the beach and walk right into the sea while in his clothes. The tide was low so by the time he would get where the water was at his waist, his bodyguard would rush out and lead him back to shore. I would always laugh like crazy. I just thought he was wonderful. One time he invited everybody for cocktails in his suite. Without us knowing, he locked all the doors and turned off the lights. He then announced he was going to read a poem. He was so wild. However, on the set he was totally professional. We spoke our lines in English. Mastroianni spoke very little English, so he did his lines in Italian and so did Carol André. I am sure this was dubbed, especially since we did a lot of exterior scenes with all the outside noises that go with it."

In *Holy Year*, Jean Gabin and Jean-Claude Brialy are prison escapees who disguise themselves as priests and board a flight to Italy to retrieve gold Gabin hid before being incarcerated. Nicoletta is part of a terrorist group who hijacks the plane and must contend with the two convicts who are determined to make their destination. "Working with Jean Gabin for me was like oh-my-goodness," exclaimed Nicoletta. "He was always treating me like a little girl. He didn't play the big movie star or put on airs. Neither did Jean-Claude Brialy who was a very funny guy." Sadly, Gabin passed away a few months after filming wrapped.

Nicoletta continued acting in films until the early eighties. Reflecting on her place in Italian cinema, Roberto Curti commented, "One has the sense of a star in the making who never fully blossomed as such. Perhaps part of her appeal is given by the very anticonformist nature of her acting trajectory—the pleasure of spotting her high cheekbones and unmistakable eyes in a dusty and sweaty Western, and then in an avant-garde production destined to the most marginal art circuits. Nicoletta Machiavelli was never a diva, but she had one thing her most famous peers lacked—freedom."

Nicoletta relocated to Seattle, Washington to be closer to her son. Half the year she worked as an interpreter and Italian language teacher at the University of Washington.

The other half found her in Italy where she hosted guided tours, mostly of Sicily. And though for years she dismissed her acting career (because as she told writer Ann Bauer, "I wasn't a good actress. I was just pretty."), she began taking pride in it appearing at screenings of her movies and on discussion panels. Sadly, the actress who was so full of life passed away in November 2015.

10. LARA LINDSAY: THIS FOX GIRL TOOK THE SWEET RIDE

IN 1966, NEW STUDIO HEAD Richard Zanuck revived the 20th Century-Fox talent school. One contract player who studied there was a dark-haired beauty named Lara Lindsay. Compared to other Fox girls at the time, she never reached the heights of Raquel Welch or Jacqueline Bisset, but she has one very memorable drive-in movie *The Sweet Ride* (1968) to her credit. While the Frankie Avalon-Annette Funicello beach movies took a light-hearted look at the denizens of Malibu, *The Sweet Ride* is much more serious and melodramatic in its treatment of the aimless youths who could be found living in that part of Southern California. The last gasp in the sixties' surfing sagas, it realistically (well at least as compared to the Beach Party movies) captures a certain lifestyle from that time in history of aimless surfer boys, tennis bums, and bikini girls who want to keep the beach party going forever and never grow up.

Resembling Jean Simmons, sultry Lara Lindsay was born Gladys Irene Jacobs in Chicago. She was a competitive figure skater, which led to a stint doing ice shows when she got older. A short-lived marriage in the early sixties produced a son in 1963. While living in Tucson, Arizona, she became a local celebrity of sorts. "I appeared in local commercials for the banks there and for Coca-Cola and Pepsi-Cola. I was known there in Tucson because it was a really small town in those days. They told me a movie was coming to town and suggested I try out for something. I said, 'I don't try out for something.'"

That movie was *El Dorado* starring John Wayne and Robert Mitchum and directed by Howard Hawks ("I was so young and didn't even know who he was."). Lara, then still Gladys, without trying out was hired to be Charlene Holt's stand-in. Her beauty won her lots of attention to the chagrin of one of the female co-stars. Lindsay divulged, "I was getting a lot of press because I was the Tucson girl even though I was nothing but a stand-in. Michele Carey didn't like it and made a fuss about it. I was embarrassed and started to leave the set, which was thirty miles into the desert. Somebody told John Wayne and he wanted to see me. I went to him and he said, 'First, this is *my* picture and *nobody* else's. No one walks off my set," He coaxed her to stay. "Wayne then said to me, 'If you ever want to come to Hollywood I think you can do something. Here's my assistant's name. Contact him.' It was that simple."

Publicity photo of Lara Lindsay in *The Sweet Ride* (20th Century-Fox, 1968).

It is surprising to hear that Michele Carey was the one who played diva when Lara was not even her stand-in but Charlene Holt's. As for Holt, Lindsay described her as being "elegant, remote, and lovely. We did not have much interaction." When asked how did Wayne deal with the ornery Carey, Lindsay said, "I don't know how the incident was handled. I believe she was told to settle down." Obviously you don't mess with the Duke on his picture, and he most likely put the Diva starlet in her place. Lara finished her time on the movie without further incident.

Afterwards, with John Wayne's encouraging words ringing in her ears, she took off for Hollywood. "I took Wayne up on his offer and called his associate. I began doing commercials and stand-in work. I then met the Number Three guy at the APA talent agency and he took me on as a client. He brought me over to 20th Century-Fox. I was given a personality test, then soon after they signed me to a contract."

20th Century-Fox was in transition in 1966 and was finally coming out of the financial doldrums due to the overblown $40 million disaster *Cleopatra* that almost sunk the company. Darryl Zanuck had returned as Chairman and tapped his son, producer Richard Zanuck, to be president. The huge blockbuster *The Sound of Music* in 1965 had reignited the studio. Zanuck then reinstated the Fox talent school and began signing contract players.

"I was only at the studio for about a week when Richard Zanuck called me into his office," recalled the actress. "I thought, 'Well this is the end of this after only a few days.' He said, 'Young lady that name of yours has got to go.' I said, 'Yes, sir!' He asked, 'What do you want to be? Who do you think you look like?' I said, 'People sometimes say I look like a Laura.' He said, 'That's it. You'll be Lara from *Doctor Zhivago*.' For my last name he let me pick whatever I wanted, so I chose my brother's first name Lindsay." Hence, Lara Lindsay was born.

The Fox talent school's resident acting coach was Curt Conway, a former member of the Group Theatre and the Actor's Studio. Among Lindsay's classmates were Tom Selleck, Jacqueline Bisset ("She was English, charming, and gorgeous. She was not always at the school because she had an acting background but we partied together."), Christina Ferrare, and Corinna Tsopei. Lindsay exclaimed, "We didn't know how wonderful we had it. There were acting lessons, dancing lessons, personality lessons. How to work with a publicist. It was five days a week and really a nine to five job.

"Of course, there are so many memories of that talent school and those of us fortunate enough to be a part of it," continued the actress. "Tom Selleck was a doll...genuine, gentle, funny, and kind. I do remember once when some of us took a poll and we decided that if only one of us could 'make it' it should be Tom because he was the nicest."

Another classmate was Linda Harrison (later Nova in *Planet of the Apes*) who began dating the married Richard Zanuck. When asked if that caused any problems with the talent school players, Lara replied, "Not many of them knew it, but I did." Despite his philandering, the actress found Zanuck to be "a fabulous guy. He was full of life and acted like a kid himself even though he was older and more experienced than most of us. He was just wonderful and a really fun guy."

When asked if Fox contract player Raquel Welch was part of the talent school, Lara said, "Raquel was already established and had nothing to do with the school. But we would always see her around the lot."

The talent school was there to help prepare the actors and had no input with casting TV shows or movies at the studio. "We would have to go interview with the director and producer," said Lara. "It was then up to them to give you the part or not." One minor bit that Lindsay got was in the title sequence of *In Like Flint* (1967). In the red tinted opening montage, Lara Lindsay is the first face you see as the gal who looks like she is in ecstasy from lovemaking but she is actually being massaged. Jean Hale next appears and the camera follows her as she strolls through the women's spa while the credits start to roll. It is here that Lindsay met producer Saul David who would become more influential in her life a few years later.

The Sweet Ride, produced by Joe Pasternak and directed by Harvey Hart, was Lindsay's official film debut. This was Pasternak's third trip to the beach during the sixties. Prior, he produced the lighthearted Spring Break hits *Where the Boys Are* (1960) and *Girl Happy* (1965) for MGM. *The Sweet Ride* however was a more serious and melodramatic take on aimless youths and thirty-somethings who refused to grow up while enjoying the carefree life in Southern California.

Recalling how she was cast, Lara said, "Truly, like with everything else, I just interviewed. Joe Pasternak then said he wanted to hire me as one of the girls." Lindsay was cast as dim-witted beachcomber Martha. However, there was one caveat—she had to dye her hair. "I had to lighten my hair because Jackie Bisset's was dark. I did not like the process and at first thought I looked like an albino carrot! But after that it was fine."

Promotional poster art for *The Sweet Ride*
(20th Century-Fox, 1968).

Though they wanted hair contrasts between her and Jacqueline Bisset and Michele Carey, Lindsay's Martha does not share any screen time with them. It is a good thing, considering her past with Carey. Lara said, "I saw her but we really didn't interact and I don't think she realized who I was anyway. It had been about two years since *El Dorado*."

Lara Lindsay was excited to be making her official film debut, but noted that "When you are first starting out, you are just so taken with it all that you are not even nervous or take in these little sides that you should be taking in. You just want to get the job done right. Also being under contract, when we weren't on the movie set we were back in class prepping for stage shows that we would be in for the studio. For instance, if I was working on the movie Tuesday and Thursday, the other three days I was back in the school."

Though new to the ways of making motion pictures, the novice did notice immediately that Joe Pasternak was a daily presence, but did not interfere with his director to pick up the pace unlike some other producers such as Sam Katzman. Lindsay remarked, "When we began filming Mr. Pasternak was always on the set, but he was very low-key. He was a very quiet, charming man whose reputation preceded him. He was so nice to me. The movie moved along well enough under Harvey Hart's direction. Pasternak left him alone and it was really Harvey's movie more than anything. For me, Hart was a little bit more getting me to hit my marks and say my lines than trying to help with my performance."

Lindsay's character was just one of the many women in the life of an aging tennis pro played by Tony Franciosa. When asked how she liked working with him, she exclaimed, "Are you kidding, he was as charming as can be and a very sexy man. But he was also helpful and we would rehearse our scenes together. For me it amounted to coming out from under the covers, but there were a couple of other scenes we did together. We had to dance too. He was an easy going guy."

Lindsay also got to work with Michael Sarrazin and Bob Denver during a flashback scene set in a smoky bar invaded by a biker gang. What stands out for her is working with Franciosa and Sarrazin. "I certainly remember this scene being in the middle of those two cute guys. Michael was going together with Jackie Bisset. He was a bit of a hippie and a really nice guy. Bob Denver was so good and he was *funny*! He was that guy in the movie. You'd laugh every time you looked at him or he spoke. He was just a cutie."

In his autobiography, Bob Denver described his experience working on *The Sweet Ride* as being "a treat." According to the actor, the only problem that occurred while making the movie was that the actors hired to play members of the motorcycle gang looked too real and scary for their own good. The cast would sometimes eat lunch at a Mexican restaurant near the studio. As Denver pulled out of the studio's gates, a bunch of police cars whizzed by him. When he arrived at the Mexican joint, "The 'motorcycle gang' was lined up on the sidewalk surrounded by very nervous policemen. No guns were drawn, but hands were hovering. One by one the gang showed their SAG cards and were allowed to go into the restaurant."

Based on the amount of publicity photos that she did to promote *The Sweet Ride*, you would have thought Lara was the female lead and not just a supporting player. Though doing cheesecake photos perturbed some actresses, it did not bother Lindsay in the least. She commented, "Being under contract to Richard Zanuck was like having a father and a home. You felt protected and you knew that the studio's reputation was at stake so they wouldn't let you do anything that was not in good taste."

The Sweet Ride, featuring a great title tune sung by Dusty Springfield, opens with the nearly dead body of a brutally beaten and molested young woman being dumped on a highway in the Malibu Beach area peopled by surfers, drifters, and bikers. A police investigation reveals that the victim is an actress named Vickie Cartwright (Jacqueline Bissett). She was dating surfer Denny McGuire (Michael Sarrazin), who shares a beach pad with Collie Ransom (Tony Franciosa), an aging tennis hustler who won the use of the house for eight months by winning a bet, and Choo-Choo Burns (Bob Denver), a temperamental jazz pianist. Choo-Choo's porn star girlfriend Thumper (Michele Carey) telephones and wakes up a hung over Collie with the news after reading it in the morning paper. He sneaks over to his neighbor's place and steals his paper. Rushing back into the house, he immediately rouses his paramour Martha (Lara Lindsay). The sexy disheveled naked girl pops up from under the covers unaware where she is. ("This being my first movie when I saw this I thought, 'Oh, God my mother will hate this,'" laughed Lara.) Collie then rudely tosses her out, despite her indignation, so he can find Denny who is surfing the early morning waves.

Collie finds Denny and the two race to the hospital only to be met by Vickie's hostile father and her acerbic stepmother. While questioned by Lt. Atkins, Denny explains how he first met Vickie on the beach and how their love affair was rocky from the start. In one of the flashbacks, Lindsay's Martha is seen accompanying Collie and Denny to hear Choo-

Choo perform at a seedy bar that is invaded by a motorcycle gang. After some bikers make rude comments about Martha, Collie's quick wit enables him and his friends to exit without getting hurt. Unfortunately, Martha is last glimpsed dancing at a discothèque before Collie replaces her in his bed with one of his tennis students (Corinna Tsopei).

The rest of the movie has Collie and Denny trying to figure out who beat up Vickie and left her for dead after they are released from the police station while Choo-Choo deals with a marriage-minded Thumper who claims to be pregnant. Their main suspect is the leader of the biker gang. He at first lies that he never saw her again after the time on Denny's deck. But after being jumped by Collie and Denny, he confesses that he saw her on the beach one night after she had an argument with some older guy. After she had slipped out of her dress and offered herself to him, he wrapped her in a blanket and split without touching her. Her producer turns out to be the culprit. In revenge, Denny attacks him at his home, leaving him bloody and unconscious. Denny tries to reconcile with a recuperating Vickie but she sends him away. At last recognizing that there must be more to life than the endless 'sweet ride' that he has been on, Denny abandons Collie, the still-single Choo-Choo (Thumper lied about being pregnant), Martha, and the rest of the aging beach denizens to take a job at a Santa Monica hardware store.

While the prior year's *Don't Make Waves* took a light-hearted look at the denizens of Malibu, *The Sweet Ride* is much more serious and melodramatic in its treatment of the aimless youths who could be found living in that part of Southern California. The film is interesting and realistically tries to capture a certain lifestyle from that time in history. What weakens the film is the head-scratching motivation of the two lead characters. The surfing scenes are expertly filmed and feature impressive small wave riding. The producers smartly left this footage to surf filmmakers Greg MacGillivray and Jim Freeman who expertly captured the crowded surfing scene at Malibu, which top wave rider Mickey Dora was constantly riling about in interviews. As the last gasp in the sixties' surfing sagas, *The Sweet Ride* offers an interesting glimpse into the world of restless youths and aging beach bums living a carefree Southern California lifestyle who are forced to face reality.

The movie's standout is the tall, tan, and muscular Tony Franciosa who puts a lot of the younger guys on the beach to shame. He is excellent as an arrogant and flippant tennis hustler who refuses to mature and treats the women in his life, most notably Lindsay's vapid Martha, horribly. His last scene where he desperately pleads with Sarrazin's Denny to stick around instead of moving to Santa Monica for a job is both sad and pathetic. Franciosa truly captures a man who wants to stay carefree and single for the rest of his life.

Lara Lindsay and Tony Franciosa in *The Sweet Ride* (20th Century-Fox, 1968).

By 1968 the Hollywood surf movie had run its course, though *The Sweet Ride* pulled in $1.5 million at the box office. Reviews were mixed, with the critic in *Variety* most amusingly remarking, "*The Sweet Ride* could sum up as 'Hell's Angels' Bikini Beach Party in Valley of the Dolls near Peyton Place.' Though well mounted and interesting...the overall result is a flat programmer."

Lara Lindsay made an impression in her film debut and it is mind boggling why Fox didn't give her more movie roles. She deserved better than what came next—a small part in the failed TV pilot *Braddock* about a private eye of the future starring Tom Simcox and a few more episodes of TV's *Peyton Place*. She liked doing the latter and said, "I wished I was given a bigger role on it."

Lindsay then landed a small part with her natural dark hair in *The Boston Strangler* (1968) directed by Richard Fleischer and starring Tony Curtis as the notorious killer. Based on a true story, she played victim number eight who met her end by the hands of the maniac between 1962 and 1964 in the Boston area. Clad in an orange coat, Lindsay steps into her apartment after kissing her date goodnight and hearing the door buzzer she opens it thinking it is her beau, only to be greeted with a sharp knife held to her throat by the Strangler. Though Lara doesn't have many lines, that image was used in a number of promotional materials.

"This was a fabulous experience," remarked Lindsay. "Tony Curtis was nuts. In your ECU [Extreme Close-Up] when the camera was only on my face, you saw only the back of him. I had to act surprised and release all the emotion you would thinking your boyfriend is at the door and it turns out to be a murderer. All those reactions are finite. I'm trying to concentrate and he is mouthing, 'I love you.' You can't keep a straight face. Tony really worked for that part and it was amazing that they gave it to him. He did a great job.

"Richard Fleisher was a wonderful man," continued Lara. "He was a hands on director and very gentle. He would take you aside and say, 'Why don't you try it this way.' I loved working with him."

Lara reveals that she was never considered for any roles in Fox's big "starlet" movies of the time, including *Valley of the Dolls*; *Myra Breckinridge*; or *Beyond the Valley of the Dolls*. But she did come close to appearing in Fox's big budget musical *Hello Dolly* starring Barbra Streisand. "I wish I would have pushed for this and wish my agent would have pushed for it as well," sighed the actress. "The studio asked me to do the test scenes with the actors they were auditioning [for Cornelius and Barnaby]. Gene Kelly was the director. One day he came over to me and said, 'You know I think I would like you to try out for Molly.' She was the number two girl. I was doing *The Boston Strangler* at the time and had to come back to do my own test. I know they also tested Ann-Margret and a girl from Broadway [E.J. Peaker] who got the role. That was it and I did not appear in the movie at all."

After making two guest appearances on the TV detective series *Felony Squad* in "A Fashion for Dying" as a model and "Matched for Murder" as yet another murder victim – this time of a psychotic killer whom she was matched with from a computer dating service—Lara Lindsay's time at Fox ended because "father and son had a fight. The school was closed down. They kept me and a few others under contract for another six months and then that fizzled out. We were on our own after that."

Now thrown to the unpredictable world of freelance acting and having a child to support, Lindsay decided to make a career change to sustain her family. "I needed a steady income," said Lara matter-of-factly. "When you are under contract and then no longer under contract, it is a little difficult. I went behind the camera and worked for various producers on movie sets."

Movies did beckon one more time for her in the Academy Award winning sci-fi classic *Logan's Run* (1976) starring Michael York and Jenny Agutter. She played a small role of an anonymous Woman Runner fleeing from the Sandmen after reaching her thirtieth birthday.

Explaining how this came to be, Lindsay explained, "One of the men I worked for was Saul David, who produced *Our Man Flint* and *Fantastic Voyage*. He had hired me to be in the opening scene of *In Like Flint*. I would see him on the lot and when I decided I needed a steady job I asked him if he needed an assistant. That's how I started working with him. He was producing *Logan's Run*. One day he sent someone from the set over to me and said that Saul wanted me to play this role, so I did. I also voiced the computer [at Sandman headquarters] and did other things like voices of the city and even some of Farrah Fawcett's lines but I did not take the credit for it. Farrah became popular right about this time due to the *Charlie's Angels* TV series and we couldn't get her back to loop. I didn't dub all her lines just some."

"It was so great to be working on this movie," continued Lara. "It was the first time that they got all the special effects guys out in a long time to work their magic. It was really exciting for everybody to watch. I think it was under-credited really. If you look at it these guys were working on little films and then this wonderful movie comes along that required miniature sets and elaborate special effects. They couldn't wait to start working."

Not only did the special effects crew impress Lindsay, so did the cast. She remarked, "Michael York was a darling guy and such a gentleman. Jenny Agutter was a sweet fun-loving girl. Stars stay a little bit to themselves but because I worked with Saul we would have dinners together and they were very nice. Michael Anderson was the director—another Englishman. He was very soft-spoken but he didn't give me much direction. I did my scene and that was it. I am not sure if he was that way with others but I am only talking for me."

Logan's Run was Lindsay's acting swan song. She began working at MGM in television development and worked her way up to head the department. When asked if she liked working in front or behind the camera more, Lara replied laughing, "My ego liked in front, but my pocketbook liked in back of the camera. I think the true answer is that the itch of performing never goes away. As a result I am now competing in ballroom, salsa, and tango dancing (sometimes even in front of a camera)."

11. MAGGIE THRETT AND SCREENWRITER STEPHEN YAFA REMEMBER THREE IN THE ATTIC

AMERICAN INTERNATIONAL PICTURES WAS PLEASANTLY surprised when its college campus exploitation film *Three in the Attic*, released in late 1968, became the studio's biggest box office hit of 1969 and of the entire decade. The story of a campus lothario held prisoner in a sorority's attic by three comely coeds vowing to drain him of his potency for his cheating ways struck a chord with young audiences at the time. The fact that the movie starred the then-very popular Yvette Mimieux and Christopher Jones, and up-and-comers Judy Pace and Maggie Thrett also helped boost its box office take.

Movies begin with ideas from writers and *Three in the Attic* was no different. Stephen Yafa had just graduated from Dartmouth and received a playwriting fellowship at Carnegie Mellon in 1963. "I was really more interested in screenwriting and I saw this notice posted that the Writers Guild was sponsoring a contest for original screenplays," recalled Yafa. "This is before everybody on Earth was writing screenplays. My idea for *Three in the Attic* began as a novel, but I put that aside to write the screenplay. I was actually living in an attic apartment while writing this and it took about four weeks. I then sent it off.

"The inspiration for the story was nothing specific," continued Yafa. "It was just something that popped into my head. The plot has three girls screwing a guy to death because he has betrayed them. It is their idea of revenge. That never really happened. I had a girlfriend attending Bennington so I used that as the setting, but changed the name for the movie. When I wrote Paxton Quigley I was torn between being envious of this guy and being more moralistic then I should have been. I didn't set out to make him an evil character who deserves punishment. He was both fortunate and doomed by what happened. It was suppose to be ambiguous. That was the essence of it—a goofy fantasy but I worked hard at it. About two months later I learned that I won and they flew me out to Hollywood. I was about twenty-four years old at the time."

As happens in Hollywood, Yafa received nothing but praise from producers regarding his script but no offers because "they thought the idea was too salacious to pursue. Everybody liked it but nobody was ready to step up and do it." Disappointed, the novice screenwriter accepted an offer to work at a TV station in Seattle. After settling down in his new gig, he received a phone call from producer Harold Hecht, who was partners with Burt Lancaster. Hecht was working on a novel set in a college. Impressed with Yafa's *Three in the Attic* script, Hecht offered Yafa a job to help write his screenplay. The young man quickly accepted the job and hightailed it back to Southern California.

"Harold Hecht worked out of the Columbia Studios lot then on Gower Street in Hollywood," said Yafa fondly "It was like a fantasy for me. I was using Steve McQueen's old dressing room to write. People would knock on the door and say, 'Hey Steve' and their faces would drop to see me there. I'd be riding up and down the elevator with people like Cary Grant. It was quite funny. Out of this experience, I wound up writing a piece, which was called 'My How Fast They Learn.' It was Harold Hecht talking to his associate producer about me and my experience as a first time screenwriter in Hollywood. *Playboy* published it and it got a lot of notice. Directors like Stanley Kubrick contacted me and wanted to read my [*Three in the Attic*] screenplay."

Promotional poster art for *Three in the Attic* (AIP, 1968). Billy Rose Theatre Division, The New York Public Library for the Performing Arts

Though a hot commodity once again in Hollywood, Stephen Yafa could not take advantage. When all the top producers originally turned down his screenplay for *Three in the Attic*, the frustrated writer allowed his agent Hal Landers to sell the option to one of his clients, director Richard Wilson. He seemed an odd choice to be interested in this youth-oriented drama since his last directed film was the western *Invitation to a Gunfighter* (1964) starring Yul Brynner. Wilson began as an actor working with Orson Welles on his radio show *Mercury Theatre*. He remained a fierce ally of the director and produced a few of his movies including *The Lady from Shanghai* (1947) and *MacBeth* (1948). He branched out into directing in the late fifties with *The Big Boodle* (1957) starring Errol Flynn and shot entirely in Cuba: *Raw Wind in Eden* (1958); the well-received *Al Capone* (1959) starring Rod Steiger in the title role; and the horse race track drama *Wall of Noise* (1963).

Things got complicated for Yafa when Richard Wilson refused to give up his option on *Three in the Attic* despite the pressure. Stephen said, "I have no idea what drew Richard Wilson to my screenplay and can't to this day tell you what it was. None of his previous movies were like this. He worked with Orson Welles but even so it was an odd film for him to want to do. Not only would he not let his option go with all the renewed interest in it, but he insisted on directing it himself. It became a bit of a struggle for me because it was clear I had other opportunities. But like everybody else, I suppose I did not find my way through it very comfortably or strategically. The only company willing to let Wilson direct the movie was Sam Arkoff's American International Pictures."

Yafa was initially disappointed with AIP getting the film rights to his movie. They were not MGM or Paramount. The studio was known for their drive-in fare such as Edgar Allan Poe horror movies with Vincent Price; beach movies with Frankie Avalon and Annette Funicello; and now a wave of biker flicks begun with the success of *The Wild Angels*. However, Yafa quickly learned that working with AIP was going to be a fantastic learning experience. "I didn't realize it but one of the great things about doing this at American International was that there really were no boundaries between what is the director's decision and the writer's. It was a fluid environment."

Stephen Yafa, ca. 1967. *Courtesy of Stephen Yafa*

One of those areas that Yafa took advantage of where most writers had no say with the major studios was in the casting process. He sat in with Richard Wilson on a daily basis as they auditioned actresses for all three female leads. At this point their relationship was working quite well as Yafa reflected. "Looking back, I was basically Wilson's assistant director without having that title. He was quite open to have me get really involved, which was a great learning experience." Perhaps because Wilson had collaborated with Orson Welles on projects and he too was a screenwriter, he had no issues getting Yafa's input. He may have respected Yafa's vision on what his characters should look and act like. Wilson even allowed Yafa to invite some of his friends from Carnegie Mellon to come in to read for various roles.

Wilson and Yafa, though, had no say in the leading man. AIP cast hot newcomer Christopher Jones as the college playboy, Paxton Quigley, who though in love with Tobey Clinton can't control his cheating ways. He had just starred for AIP in the hit movie *Wild in the Streets* and the studio wanted to capitalize on that film's success. "At that time they were trying to push Jones as the next James Dean. In some ways, he had a certain similarity to Dean. So that was the studio's decision entirely."

A number of well known actresses came in to read for the character of Tobey, the mastermind of locking Paxton in the attic to drain him sexually after discovering he was making it with two other coeds. The actress had to have the right combination of fortitude but a softness so the audience would forgive her thirst for vengeance. Regarding how Yvette Mimieux came to be cast, Yafa stated, "Yvette and I didn't know each other initially. She came in and talked to us. She is an extraordinary person and so beguiling in so many ways. We were all happy she came on board. There were some other names floated for the role but she was by far the best. Yvette had a certain amount of star power and was willing to do the movie so I agreed to casting her without a problem. It really had little to do in terms of what I physically envisioned when I wrote this. Granted, she was a bit old for the role [she was 26]. It was 1968 and the world was falling apart and she had a social consciousness for that time."

There were many actresses who came through to audition for the other two roles. Yafa was fine with Judy Pace being cast as Eulice but was initially disappointed that Maggie Thrett won the role of Jan but more due to her physical appearance than her acting talent. "I pictured the character with a more ethnic Jewish look than what Maggie had," confessed Yafa. "She was very WASPy but very pretty and lively. I remember bringing in a very good actress and friend of mine named Iris Ratner to audition for Jan. She later [as Iris Rainer] became a successful TV writer and novelist [*Beaches*]. I wanted Iris for the part because she had the quality I envisioned. American International wanted Maggie Thrett and she was their final choice but I do not know why." Maggie Thrett had no knowledge of this at the time and did not choose to comment.

AIP undoubtedly wanted Maggie Thrett to play Jan due to her stunning beauty, long dark hair, and the quirkiness she brought to the role. Thrett was born Diane Pine in New York City. She had a natural gift for singing and in junior high school was chosen to be part of the All City Glee Club. She then attended the High School for the Performing Arts and began working as a model after accompanying a tall beautiful Israeli classmate to her modeling agency Plaza Five. One look at the attractive gal with long luxurious dark hair and they signed her as a client. Her first appearance in *Harper's Bazaar* had her modeling street clothes accompanied by actor Michael J. Pollard. Soon after, she was gracing their cover and then signed with the more prestigious agency Eileen Ford but they wanted to change her look. "Eileen kept telling me I had to cut my hair," said Thrett. "She explained they don't want to hide the collar of the clothes. I really didn't care because I was sing-ing during the day. I had a record out called "Your Love Is Mine" when I was thirteen. The B-side was 'Lucky Girl.' I had met Al Cooper, later of Blood, Sweat, and Tears, who played piano at this summertime country club where I was hired for one night to sing. He brought me to 1650 Broadway [where Carole King, Neil Sedaka, and other young pop composers toiled] and I got a manager. Everybody thought I was black because of the way I sang." She had a very soulful voice and was more R&B than rock 'n' roll.

She performed with Vito and the Salutations as their opening act at local joints around Manhattan. "This all was happening while I was still in high school. I sang on the weekends and they paid me fifty dollars a show—I was very happy with that. I was still modeling as well. I came from a non-show business family. I was raised Catholic and my father was an electrician. I was doing pretty well for somebody who didn't know anything about the business."

Bob Crewe (most famous for writing a number of hits for The Four Seasons) was taken with the aspiring singer when she was dancing at the Greenwich Village discothèque Trude Heller's the year she graduated high school. "This was a summer job. It was *the* hot place to be and I saw some very famous people there like Salvador Dali. I danced on the wall wearing a leotard and opera hose. Your legs itched like crazy by the end of the night. The shift lasted eight hours with a couple of breaks. I was doing anything I could to pay the bills."

Crewe produced her next single called "Soupy" for his label DynoVoice Records, but he changed her name to Maggie Thrett because "he thought it sounded British and more with it for the time. He threw a party for me when the single was released and people like Mick Jagger and Brian Epstein came." The song rose to #36 on MCA's Fabulous 57 in June of 1965 and in some parts of the South hit #1. However, it never took off nationally. Thrett played at a few clubs to promote the song, including the Basin Street East where she appeared with Lesley Gore and Bo Diddley ("He just loved to perform and wouldn't get off the stage.").

During this period Maggie revealed that she was ensconced in an unhappy abusive marriage. "My boyfriend wanted to marry. I didn't, but relented. He spent all the money I earned and dated other girls. He fancied himself an actor and had an audition with Universal Studios. The gal who was working with him on his scene was Dorothy Kilgallen's daughter and she cancelled. I volunteered to go with him and I learned the lines the day before. We read and they told him to forget acting and gave me a contract. It was after this that my husband beat the hell out of me in the street, probably from jealousy. I flew out to Hollywood to get away from him. Universal also signed Robert Wolders, who was involved later with Audrey Hepburn, and we traveled to the Coast together." Though she was an accomplished singer, Thrett also studied drama at the High School for the Performing Arts and was focused on being an actress only. She had no inclinations to sing on film.

Thrett initially stayed at the Montecito Hotel where a lot of newcomers trying to break into show business stayed. She met future husband actor Donnelly Rhodes there. Her wacko husband followed and climbed to the hotel's roof. Maggie recalled, "He is yelling down to me, 'You gotta come home. I love you.' I am wearing a bikini sitting poolside with Donnelly and I yell back, 'Jump, you motherfucker, jump!'" Thrett then lost a husband, via divorce, and landed a manager named Ruth Aarons "who also represented

Shirley Jones and George Chakiris. I went to the Academy Awards with George during my first year in Hollywood. Julie Christie was sitting in front of me and won the Best Actress that year. My picture was in *Life Magazine* but they blurred out my face and you just see my gown."

Maggie Thrett in *Out of Sight* (Universal, 1966). *Billy Rose Theatre Division, The New York Public Library for the Performing Arts*

Life in Hollywood was not going as smooth as Maggie hoped, especially at Universal Studios. She recounted, "I had trouble with a casting director who literally chased me around the desk. I wouldn't let him catch me. He made it so Universal was going to drop my option so I had to write a letter of apology to save my job. Today, they would never get away with that crap."

Her first film for the studio was the beach/spy spoof *Out of Sight* (1966) starring Jonathan Daly, Karen Jensen, and *Shindig* dancer Carole Shelyne. Maggie played the karate-chopping F.L.U.S.H. assassin Wipeout who arrives in Malibu on a surfboard from Hawaii. She (along with Wende Wagner as Scuba and Deanna Lund as Tuff Bod) are hired by Big D

(John Lawrence) to terminate secret agent John Stamp (Daly). Thrett plays her goofy role amusingly. When Big D's henchmen Mousie (Jimmy Murphy) asks her, "Wipeout, did you come all the way from Hawaii on that board?" She replies drolly, "Sure. I caught a good wave." Despite her martial arts talents, Wipeout fails in her mission to stamp out Stamp.

Maggie Thrett doesn't have many memories of the *Out of Sight* cast but said, "I became really good friends with Wende Wagner a bit later through Ann [the wife of a big shot TV and film producer]. He was a real bastard and something else. He would withhold his alimony and child support to the last second before it was due, leaving her strapped for money all the time. Wende was married to Jim Mitchum and he was the spitting image of his father Robert Mitchum who I met at Del Mar. He had a box seat and a horse running. It didn't win and I lost my two dollar bet."

Television kept the actress busy between films with guest stints *The Wild Wild West*, *Cimarron Strip*, and most notably *Star Trek* in the classic early episode "Mudd's Women." She had small roles in two completely opposite type movies. *Dimension 5* (1966) was a low-budget spy adventure starring a slumming Jeffrey Hunter and France Nuyen. "It was only a day's work," said Thrett. "I never met France, but Jeffrey was very nice. The only lead actor I didn't like was Robert Conrad from *The Wild Wild West*. I did two episodes. He was a little louse. On the second show when I wouldn't go back to his trailer with him, he had me replaced in a love scene we were supposed to do."

Trett's other film from this time was the big budget WWII adventure epic *The Devil's Brigade* (1968). This was directed by Andrew V. McLaglen and starred William Holden and Cliff Robertson. A ragtag bunch of American GIs are assigned to Holden's outfit at Fort William Henry Harrison in Montana to train, along with their Canadian counterparts, to become 1st Special Forces assigned for a dangerous commando mission in Norway, but then switched to Italy. Thrett played a stunningly beautiful local girl named Millie, who clad in a tight form fitting blue and purple patterned dress, accompanies Canadian soldier Richard Dawson to a bar when the GIs are given a break from training. At the tavern, the antagonistic American and Canadian troops join forces to fight the nearby town's bullying lumberjacks. Millie inadvertently starts the brawl when she tells main troublemaker Paul Hornung to "Shut your big ugly face" when he tries to take her away from her date.

"I had to go for a number of readings to get *The Devil's Brigade*," recalled Thrett. "They picked three girls and then we were sent to Salt Lake City where the movie was being filmed. Andrew McLaglen was a gregarious guy. I knew Andrew Prine. When I had a house on the beach, he and his girlfriend Brenda Scott would come over. Richard Dawson was very easy going and really sweet. He was married to Diana Dors. After filming, he wrote me a funny letter, which I still have."

Unhappy with the way her career was going at Universal and prodded by her manager Ruth Aarons, Thrett severed her contract with the studio. "Most of this had to do with the trouble I had with that casting director and the studio forcing me to write that apology. I was very easy to work with and did what I was supposed to do. I always knew my lines and came to the set prepared. I went to the High School for the Performing Arts and you don't fool around there or they kick you out. Ruth also got me out of my contract with Bob Crewe. I never should have listened to her, but I had no one to guide me. My parents didn't know a damn thing about show business and my mother just wanted me to marry and have kids. Ruth promised to do this and that but forget it. She was a good manager but not right for me."

Now freelance, Maggie was able to audition for the role of flower child Jan in *Three in the Attic*. "Because of my look, I played Mexicans and Native Americans. Here I was cast as Jewish girl. Whatever part was offered I took. I just wanted to work and you just take the jobs that come along. The whole interview process is hard. I didn't even have a car for a while and got around town on a Honda 90 motorcycle. I bought it from my neighbor who was the niece of the guy who produced *Perry Mason*. I lived on Larrabee Street around the corner from the Whiskey a-Go-Go and my roommate was Playboy Playmate Hedy Scott [Miss June 1965]."

Soon after Thrett signed for the role, another movie came her way that she had to turn down. She revealed, "I was offered *Easy Rider*, but I already committed to *Three in the Attic*. A friend of mine recommended me to Dennis Hopper and Peter Fonda. They wanted me to play the part that went to Karen Black. I had to pass. But it didn't pay as much so at the time I didn't care. Also I don't think I would have been very happy on that set working with those guys. Dennis Hopper was very raunchy. A girlfriend of mine had dated him in the fifties and shared some stories about him."

With casting now complete, Stephen Yafa thought his involvement with *Three in the Attic* was over. AIP received permission to shoot the movie on location at the University of North Carolina at Chapel Hill. This was an unusual move by AIP since they usually shot their movies in the surrounding areas to save money. Yafa does not know what possessed them to film on the other side of the country.

Christopher Jones and Yvette Mimieux in *Three in the Attic* (AIP, 1968).

Just before cast and crew were to depart for North Carolina, the screenwriter received an unexpected offer. "Richard Wilson really wanted me to come to Chapel Hill but he wanted me to be the one to ask Sam Arkoff if I could go," said Yafa incredulously. "What the hell that was all about—I don't know! I remember going up to Arkoff who was wonderful and an interesting character. He would walk around with this big fat cigar in his mouth like right out of Central Casting. I said, 'Sam, I would really like to go to Chapel Hill.' He snapped, 'Yeah? How much money do you want?' I said something like $500. He said, '$500? Is that a day, a week, or what?' I replied, 'No, for the entire time.' He was like 'Sure go do it, do it, do it.' What a deal he got and that is how I wound up on location. It was pretty funny. It turned out to be a good location and the weather was great. It was a beautiful campus."

As filming began, Yafa found that his relationship with director Richard Wilson soured a bit and that Christopher Jones took a disliking to him. Sensing that Wilson's direction was off, Yafa said, "Richard and I got to know each other pretty darn well on location filming in Chapel Hill. To be honest, it was a very uncomfortable situation after it was all said and done. It was probably not the strongest material for him in terms of what his strengths were. It was one of those situations where it also had to do with the way I had written the screenplay.

"Christopher Jones was a moody, introverted character," continued Yafa. "Looking back on it, he was pretty troubled. He and I didn't get along particularly well. There were some good reasons for that. But he was a talented actor. Chris was one of these guys, who when you are standing next to the camera watching the scene, you just don't see him in the role. However, later watching the dailies you see something that he is doing and you know this guy is exactly right as a film actor. Jones had that certain something that transmitted on screen that you didn't notice in real life. He was very much the method actor and I think took cues from guys like James Dean. I think he was the only actor in the film that was having a hard time. He got through the shoot but as I recall he was going though a difficult period in his life and it spilled over a bit into work."

Maggie Thrett agreed with Yafa's assessment of Christopher Jones and opined, "He was weird and a pain in the ass. He was married to Susan Strasberg at the time, who was another weirdo. I am not sure if he intentionally was aping James Dean but that is who he came across as. I thought, 'Why does anyone want to be James Dean? He's dead.' He was fine though while shooting our scenes."

Stephen Yafa thinks perhaps the main reason Christopher Jones disliked him because he and Yvette Mimieux were having an on-set romance to the actor's chagrin. For all the disappointment the shoot was bringing him, Mimieux seemed to be the brightest spot. "Yvette Mimieux was wonderful to work with," exclaimed Yafa. "We became intimate. She was my real friend throughout the whole shoot. She is a terrific, remarkable person and a great deal of fun. Yvette was very smart and very enthusiastic. We got along great, which frankly is what pissed off Christopher Jones." When hearing this, Maggie Thrett stated matter-of-factly, "Chris Jones was definitely not her type.

"Yvette was so sweet," Maggie continued. "She gave big bouquets of flowers to Judy Pace and me on the first day of filming. Judy was very nice as well."

One of the most complex characters was African American coed Eulice. Smart and poised around other people of color, she used a phony Southern accent and would say some outrageous things on campus. She also turns out to be the most level-headed one in the bunch when it comes to romance. Yafa based the character on a black girlfriend he had at the time. "I envisioned her to be very smart, very funny, and very ironic," he said. "I wanted her to always be putting people on. She was mocking the stereotyped Southern African American woman. That was the concept and that was what Judy Pace picked up as an actress. Judy was great to work with. She was dating baseball player Curt Flood, who came to visit, and I got to meet him."

As for his opinions on others in the cast, even though Maggie Thrett was not his first choice for Jan, Yafa found working with her to be "great and she did fine with the role. Her character became somewhat of a Flower Child because there was four years between when I wrote it and when the movie was made. Flower Children came up during that time and I made it more prominent as a theme. John Beck [who played Paxton's best friend] was a really good guy. He and I became buddies. I was much closer with him than with Chris Jones. We'd hang out. We were in Chapel Hill and there was so much you could do. We had dinner usually every night when I wasn't with Yvette Mimieux. He was a good guy and went on to have a very successful career."

The nights that Stephen spent time with Yvette, John Beck got together with Maggie Thrett. "We hung out after shooting a few times," she remembered. "John was a very nice guy. It was kind of boring there at Chapel Hill. I didn't spend much time with Yvette or Judy. At the end of the day you are tired from working. Also, Judy was dating baseball player Curt Flood and he came to visit her a few times."

Another surprise guest who popped up on location was Chad Stuart of the singing duo Chad and Jeremy. They were tapped to compose songs for the movie, the standout being "Paxton Quigley's Had the Course," which was the title of Stephen Yafa's 1967 novel. It is played throughout the movie. It is quite rare to have a songwriter on set and usually songs are composed in post-production after filming has been completed. "I don't know why or how Chad wound up in Chapel Hill, but he did," said Yafa laughing. "We became buddies and even played music together. He wasn't there for a long time—maybe a week. Chad liked being there because now he had something to write about. Usually you are just sitting around writing songs from your head with no story. Now he had a certain amount of content that he could compose the song around. I thought his songs were okay." Fans were not excited either and the song never charted in the U.S.

Christopher Jones and Maggie Thrett in *Three in the Attic* (AIP, 1968).

Three in the Attic stretched the boundaries regarding free love and on screen nudity with Chris Jones baring his backside and the actresses all topless though filmed from the back. Per Stephen Yafa and Maggie Thrett, the cast was all game and there were no issues doing the scenes naked or half-naked. "There was actually a lot more nudity in the rough cut," Yafa revealed. "But AIP was an extremely conservative production company and you didn't find much nudity in their movies at the time. It was more titillation than nudity.

"There was never talk about any of the actresses doing a frontal topless scene," he added. "All of them were pretty cool about doing these scenes. We only had the people who actually had to be there on the set when shooting. We tried to be discreet and I do not remember any of them having any issues at all."

Maggie Thrett concurred with Yafa and said, "I remember Richard Wilson getting pressure because the movie wasn't racy enough. The nude scenes were not an issue for me and I cannot remember if I was even topless. They never asked us to be filmed naked from the front. AIP was aiming for a certain market and they couldn't reach that with too much nudity. It would have bumped the movie to a more mature rating." That would have lost AIP the teenage audience—its bread and butter at the box office.

Making this movie for Stephen Yafa was not all socializing and watching the cast undress. He was kept very busy working. As shooting progressed, Yafa was called on to do some minor rewriting and says, "The odd thing for me as a writer was that it went from being a film that was going into new territory from when I wrote it in 1964. It was essentially written as an antidote to all those stupid college romances that were put out in the world that pissed me off. These had no connection to my experiences. That was the genesis for writing it. Let's get down to what's really going on here. I marginally rewrote scenes [to give it a 1968 feel] but there were no wholesale changes. I was actually pretty good about sitting down and working on the spot. I screwed around with some dialog and so forth, which you typically do. By and large that wasn't a major issue for me."

Maggie Thrett doesn't recall any of the over-the-top lines Yafa gave her to say, such as, "Do you think it's possible for a woman to be both Jewish and psychedelic at the same time?" Or "My Id does not realize that I am the product of a conservative lox and bagel upbringing." Now reminded, she laughed and stated, "I got away with it apparently."

One character change did not come from Yafa but from Richard Wilson, with the addition of a simple prop. Actress Nan Martin's college professor was given a pipe to smoke in her scenes by the director, making some audience members suspect she was a lesbian. The writer surmised, "I think it was probably to show she was tough-talking and straight-forward. She was no fan of this guy screwing these girls. That may be my master stroke in this thing, having her a co-conspirator. As I recall, when writing the script I had no interest in portraying anyone as a lesbian."

The most pressing change came when circumstance forced Yafa to redo his entire ending. "What happened was that *The Graduate* had come out and there was an ending on a bus. I had written something similar that looked like it was a knockoff, though I obviously had not seen this movie when I wrote the screenplay initially. Oddly enough, reality had caught up to us, so I had to go back and rewrite the ending a few times." The bus was kept as a big part of the ending, but there is no similarity to *The Graduate*.

While Yafa expected to do some additional writing during the shoot, he had no idea he would soon step into the director's chair when Richard Wilson took ill. "He got laryngitis and was worn down from it," divulged the screenwriter. "There were a couple of scenes that took place in a house where Paxton and Tobey run off together to Provincetown and her parents show up. I directed those scenes. Ironically, AIP went back and re-shot them in Hollywood with another actor as the father. They didn't like the actor originally hired. There were some other scenes they re-shot as well. As with a lot of movies, what you wind up shooting the first time doesn't wind up making the final cut."

Three in the Attic opens with campus coeds coming and going on a beautiful fall day. The atmosphere turns darker when the camera peers into the attic of a sorority house. The narrator states, "You heard of the sexual revolution. Well I am probably one of its first causalities—Paxton Quigley that's me." He goes on to explain that he is being held prisoner by three chicks who are trying to torture him to death. The screen flashes images of him having sex with all three coeds as he appears weaker and weaker. He ends the narration by saying, "Go with me—Paxton Quigley—and I will take you on a tour of a groovy little subculture—today's female." After the credits role, we learn that Paxton Quigley is his campus' reigning Casanova who beds all the chicks (one frat brother remarks, "See that guy over there? He scored fifty times before he was a sophomore."). After leaving a party, Paxton notices a beautiful coed at his local hangout. He introduces himself and learns that she is Tobey Clinton (Yvette Mimieux a bit too long-in-the-tooth to make a convincing 19 year old) who attends a nearby women's college called Fulton. His intellect and self-assuredness beguiles her (he recites Kierkegaard) and her beauty turns him on. The couple spends a joyous summer in Provincetown but their idyllic life living together is interrupted by her disapproving parents, who whisk her back to New Jersey.

Reunited at the start of the fall semester, Tobey is living in a girls' residence and Paxton is at the boy's college nearby, staying in a frat house. One weekend they take a motorcycle trip to a country house and Tobey announces she found an apartment for them to share. Paxton is not ready for this, especially without being consulted, and an argument ensues. Tobey's possessiveness drives Paxton back to his old promiscuous ways and he beds African American art major Eulice (Judy Pace) whom he recently encountered. She is on the search for the best guy in bed. Naturally, Paxton steps up to the plate. Eulice has him pose nude for her (she just wanted a gander of his oh-so-cute backside and we thank her for that), but paints a collage of his face before they hit the sheets.

While sneaking over to Eulice's for another tryst, Paxton literally stumbles onto a dippy gal (Maggie Thrett) in the woods. Tripping over a small plot of artificial flowers, Jan says, "Did you have to land just there sir? My flower collage unsalvageable." After picking up the smashed flowers named after planets around him, Jan bemoans, "Frankly, I didn't expect the apocalypse so soon." Paxton thinks she is a hippie with her poncho, long dark hair, and love beads around her neck. She introduces herself as Janet Sarah Weingarten and asks, "Do you think it possible for a woman to be both Jewish and psychedelic at the same time?" Agreeing with her that she scares men away, Paxton is about to flee when Jan says in a deep voice, "It might be better if you stick around a bit Mr. Quigley." Taken aback, Paxton stops in his tracks and Jan explains that sometimes her inner Id takes over. She explains, "My Id does not realize that I am the product of a conservative lox and bagel upbringing." She asks if he wishes to discuss her Id more and Paxton says he only confers with women in bed afterwards.

At his frequent hotel where the elderly manager is amazed with the stud's stamina, he calls Eulice to break their date. High on Jan's "magic brownies," the stoned Paxton allows her to paint marigolds on his back. She then asks to be taken home. Paxton tries to stop her by kissing her, and she pleads, "Please you'll traumatize me. Leave while we'll still friends?" He then falsely confesses that he is "queer as a three dollar bill." Playing on Jan's desire to set him straight, so to speak, Paxton gets her into bed.

Later back at his frat house, Paxton shares the story about Jan. His friend Jake (John Beck) thinks she is a nut, but helps him devise a schedule where he can be with each girl twice a week, leaving Sunday for him to recuperate with a night at the frat watching *Bonanza*. They even draw a map on where the girls live on campus so Paxton can plan his escape route without running into any of them. It works for a time but he is almost caught when attending a movie with Tobey. She says his name loudly and Eulice and Jan—who are also in attendance—quickly turn around. Paxton is able to avoid them by ducking below the seats and then feigns illness as he sneaks off.

Soon after, he is lured up to the attic at Tobey's sorority house. His luck runs out as Tobey informs him that she saw Eulice's painting of him at an art show. They compared notes and Eulice realized there must be a third girl Paxton was sleeping with on the two remaining nights of the week when neither of them were with the cad. They then found Jan. Infuriated and wanting revenge, Tobey convinced the two girls to go along with her scheme to lock Paxton in the attic and give him all the sex he can handle since that was his game plan.

Judy Pace, Maggie Thrett, and Yvette Mimieux in *Three in the Attic* (AIP, 1968).

Paxton is in disbelief especially when Eulice and Jan emerge from the shadows. At first he goes along but as time goes by he is literally drained. A distressed Tobey will only let him leave if he confesses why he cheated on her. The desperate girl needs to know what she did wrong. Paxton really doesn't know why he cheated on her with Jan and Eulice. He then goes on a hunger strike but the girls continue to force sex on him. Montage after montage show the gals entering the attic and disrobing while mounting a shirtless

Paxton. Jan is the first to worry about his health ("Can he have a heart attack at twenty? With no fresh air...") and wants to stop after about the second week. Eulice agrees, but Tobey is a deranged woman obsessed (hell hath no fury like a coed scorned) and pressures them to continue. Eventually the pipe smoking female dean (Nan Martin) learns of what the girls are doing after being tipped off by a nerdy sorority gal (Reva Rose) and unbelievably is willing to turn a blind eye after Tobey explains her reasoning.

Eulice and Jan finally have had enough and Tobey unlocks the door for Paxton to leave. Weak and delirious, he stumbles into the sorority where the coeds think he is an intruder and beat him unconscious. He is rushed to the hospital. Not wanting to bring shame on their college, the administration brushes the incident under the rug and releases a statement that the girls had no idea Paxton was in the attic despite Tobey's willing to take full blame. She decides to leave school and take the bus back to New Jersey. Eulice gets word and springs Paxton from the hospital knowing that deep down these two twisted young people love each other. He stops Tobey from departing and they are reunited in the luggage compartment of the Jersey bound bus.

Tacked onto the film is an unnecessary animated segment with two blobs representing a married middle-aged couple discussing *Three in the Attic*. They talk about how sexy it was and as they undress and get into bed. Despite the lady blob in curlers, it doesn't stop the man blob from making the moves on her. As expected, Stephen Yafa had nothing to do with this. It was most likely added by the AIP producers who probably got cold feet about the film's subject matter and wanted to make light of it. Yafa had no reaction then or now to this add-on.

Three in the Attic received mixed notices from the critics. Comparisons were made to *The Graduate* and *Portnoy's Complaint* in a few reviews. Some of critics, who disliked it, seem to go out of their way to pan the film with colorful language such as "a tasteless, perfervid, steam-heated study of sexually perverted nonsense" (*N.Y. Morning Telegraph*); "sexploitation masquerading as an art film is the only possible way to describe this tasteless little endeavor" (Jerry O'Connell, *The Villager*); and "nauseating, though occasionally diverting" (*New Leader*). The latter's critic also remarked that "it was directed by Richard

Wilson with a tape measure and a stop watch. The moment a zipper reaches a danger area, we cut to something else."

Promotional poster art for *Three in the Attic* (AIP, 1968).
Billy Rose Theatre Division, The New York Public Library for the Performing Arts

More positive responses came from *Time* magazine that thought the film's "unabashed vulgarity has a certain sleazy charm, and producer-director Richard Wilson manages an occasional telling glimpse of current campus life styles" and Bob Geurink of *The Atlanta Constitution* who, comparing it to *The Graduate*, found the film "gives your credibility a workout and your imagination a rest, but sheer energy...can do a lot for a movie, and makes *3 in the Attic* fairly enjoyable." Writing in *The Globe and Mail*, Megan McCracken described it as "an under-25 type film with a flavor much like *The Graduate* and just as good...*Three in the Attic* is a pleasure." The review went on to extol how open and liberating the movie was in terms of its relaxed treatment of sex and race.

As for the performances, none of the four leads received overt praise. Chris Jones received the best reviews for making Paxton likable, while his three leading ladies for the most part were found to be adequate in their roles with Judy Pace usually singled out as best.

Two major industry magazines had polar opposite reactions to the movie and its box office chances. *Variety* called it a "crudely made sexploitationer" and predicted that "there is some inherent hard-sell b.o. [box office] potential, but probably not the broad market response that apparently was anticipated." The *Film Bulletin* however thought "the story is provocative—and not just because of its interracial sex angles. Teenagers and young adults are certain to be buzzing about the reasons for the young man's imprisonment, its justification (if any) and his refusal to submit to the demands of his beautiful captors, while the oldsters will be set to pondering the ethics and moral values of today's younger citizens. Audience predisposition figures to be high at all levels, from teenyboppers to curious oldsters, from the ballyhoo trade to, most especially, the college crowd."

The *Film Bulletin* was proven correct. Despite the tepid reviews, young people flocked to see *Three in the Attic*. It had a box office take of $5.5 million making it the fifteenth highest grossing movie of 1969. "I had no clue," exclaimed Maggie Thrett. When asked if he was surprised how much money the movie made, Yafa replied with a laugh, "No, I was surprised how *little* money I made! I remember Yvette Mimieux saying to me, 'Stephen this movie is making a lot of money and I am making a lot of money from it.' She should because she was the star. Everybody wound up happy. AIP wanted me to write other screenplays for them. The guy who was the location manager on *Three in the Attic* particularly wanted me to write a script that was to be set in Hawaii but I didn't want to do it."

The movie's appeal to audiences may have been that it broke the boundaries on the sexual revolution that drew in the young people. It featured one of the first nude scenes done by a famous actor. Christopher Jones' backside is exposed as he posed for Judy Pace's character who sketches him for her art class. The women in the movie (shown naked from the back with brief flashes of derriere) stand up to the Casanova and give him all the lovemaking he thinks he wants making a statement on physical sex versus love. It was done with a feminist's viewpoint a few years before the women's movement took off. These coeds were having sex before marriage (something unthinkable on screen just a few years prior during the days of Gidget, Tammy, and beach party movies) and none were demanding a wedding ring.

Three in the Attic was also a leader in regards to race. It was still taboo for interracial marriages, and Paxton and Eulice were having an affair with abandon. Eulice was treated just as another coed and this was highly commendable on the part of screenwriter Stephen Yafa and AIP for not forcing her skin color to be an issue. This was very important and radical per Judy Pace who commented in *Fantasy Femmes of Sixties Cinema*, "There was also never mention of race in regards to my characters in their [AIP] movies [*Three in the Attic, Up in the Cellar,* and *Frogs*]. It was the time of the Civil Rights Movement and my color was never an issue. It was a very forward move for AIP.

"I enjoyed playing Eulice immensely," continued Pace in *Fantasy Femmes*. "This was *the* first time where a black female was being romanced by a white male and they were equals. My character was neither a slave nor a maid. *She* was a college student and *he* was a college student. Eulice was an artist and a volunteer schoolteacher. Those kinds of characters were not on the screen at that time. They didn't exist. Eulice was in cahoots with the other two women as equals in their plot against Chris Jones' character."

Maggie Thrett also gave American International props and said, "Everybody always looked their nose down at AIP because at that time they were considered the real B-movie makers. But AIP allowed Judy's character to be just another college girl. Her race was not an issue. Good for AIP."

Stephen Yafa was unhappy with the final cut and made it clear in the media. He practically disavowed the movie despite all the time and effort he put into it and said regretfully, "It was a mistake and an impetuous act. I had cut a version of the film myself. But AIP took the movie away from Richard Wilson. I think in the great scheme of things what they did was relatively minor in terms of re-cutting the movie. What ticked me off was that I thought they made it trashier than what it needed to be, oddly enough. It was cheesy in the way it was edited. All those montages and quick cuts were all AIP. At the time I really did not like it. Looking back, I would not have acted as I did."

Watching the film though from a 2017 perspective, the ease in which the characters jump into an interracial romance without backlash is still quite satisfying. It is the revenge taken on Paxton that is not. Much has to do with Chris Jones who plays Paxton quite sympathetically. He is perplexed and terrified about his true feelings for Tobey and you feel empathy towards him. Not being able to comprehend that he may truly be in love, he falls back into his old patterns bedding other chicks. At first you do feel badly for the marriage-minded Tobey, but Eulice and Jan seem only out for kicks.

Any sympathy for them is erased once their behavior turns downright criminal. Literally kidnapping Paxton and locking him up in the attic to drain his potency, almost killing him in the process, is a very extreme and over the top reaction from Tobey. Her obsessive desire to know why Paxton cheated is bordering on the psychotic. Having Paxton forgive the nutcase and reunite at the end may have satisfied the audiences of 1969 pre-Women's Liberation, but from today's viewpoint that ending may not be as lauded. Instead of a walk down the aisle, a trip to the Big Doll House may be more appropriate for Tobey.

After filming *Three in the Attic*, Maggie Thrett continued working on television. Her last film was 1970's *Cover Me Babe* (originally titled *Run Shadow Run*) directed by Noel Black, the then-hot director who scored with *Pretty Poison* (1968) starring Tuesday Weld. Unfortunately, this movie was an ambitious failure but foreshadowed today's reality television. It starred Robert Forster as an arrogant student filmmaker who wants only realism in his movie no matter how much it may hurt or degrade the participants. "This was silly," remarked Thrett. "I played a prostitute and Robert Forster's character just wants to talk to me. I'm topless in it. I saw it recently and thought it was crap.

"It was hard to get work after *Three in the Attic* because I wasn't with my agent, Elliot Birnbaum, any longer," she added. "What a character! He worked with Elizabeth Taylor and had a thing for Frank Sinatra. He got me a lot of jobs. I remember years later he came after me for his share of my residuals. Can you believe it!?! My career has gaps also because I was involved in two motorcycle accidents. The first was when I was still with Elliot. My leg was in a cast because I tore my knee cartilage. We were in Beverly Hills and he introduced me to Oleg Cassini and Omar Sharif, whom I began dating. He wanted me to live with him but I think he was still married with a wife and child in Egypt. I never went after the bucks. Some might think that was foolish, but I was never like that. I threw Warren Beatty out of my apartment several times. He was very nice but all he wanted was to have sex."

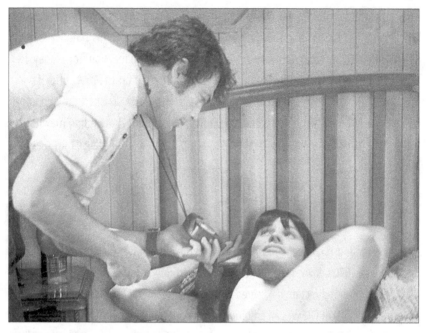

Robert Forster and Maggie Thrett in *Cover Me Babe* (20th Century-Fox, 1970).

Maggie's second motorcycle accident occurred when she was riding on the back of Gram Parson's bike. She met him through John Phillips of the Mamas and the Papas when she sang background on some of their albums. She remembered, "We went about a block and then landed in the road. I scrapped my knees, but Gram was hurt badly and was in the hospital. The only thing he said to me afterwards was 'Are you going to sue me?' I didn't." Though she didn't give up her acting career, singing kept Maggie busy through most of the seventies as she toured the country. One of her gigs had her singing backup for Wayne Newton. She made a record "Fly by Night" with Lamont Dozier—the noted Motown songwriter—but it was never released. "It would have been a hit," stated the confident actress. "Lamont said it was one of the best songs he ever produced. But I had a falling out with the guy who put us together. I got possession of the tapes."

After doing a small bit in the movie *Scarface* (1983) as the girl running on the beach watched by Al Pacino and Steven Bauer, Thrett called it quits in 1985. "My mother got very ill and I was sick of Hollywood at that point. The town changed a lot since I first got there. I was tired of the transients and wanted to be around people I knew."

Stephen Yafa's next and last produced screenplay was *Summertree* (1971) based on a play by Ron Cowen. It starred Michael Douglas as the All-American college student dealing with the Vietnam War and the threat of being drafted. In between, he worked on other scripts and was teaching in the Watts area. ("That whole social consciousness kept creeping in much more.") He had one screenplay in particular that went unproduced to his disappointment. He recalled, "I got a call from my agent that director Robert Mulligan wanted to shoot a movie for MGM in the Bay area written by a guy from there. It was called *Piano Sport* to star Elliot Gould who, with his then wife Barbra Streisand, was already renting a houseboat in Sausalito. I met with Mulligan and we hit it off. It was really a great experience rewriting that screenplay. I pretty much started from scratch and re-wrote the whole script. Unfortunately, the studio was sold days before we were going to begin shooting and the deal fell apart."

As with Maggie Thrett, Yafa too needed to get away from Los Angeles and his time working in Watts helped him realize that. The writer relocated to the San Francisco Bay area. "Being there was good for me because I was not surrounded by Hollywood types in all directions." Since then Yafa has had a varied career. He was a video producer for a long period; has written about wine for various publications as well as producing his own Pinot Noir in the Russian River region of West Sonoma; and is the author of the recent books *Grain of Truth* and *Cotton*.

Asked if he has seen *Three in the Attic* recently, Stephen Yafa replied, "A buddy of mine sent me a copy of this a few years ago. I looked at it and I thought the weakest part of it was the writing. Some of the dialog was just okay but some of it was really embarrassing. I am not ashamed of the movie by any means but it was from such a particular time and place that really represents a part of my past that is long gone in some ways. I am glad it's there, though."

12. MOTORCYCLE MAMA! VALERIE STARRETT IN RUN, ANGEL, RUN

PRETTY VALERIE STARRETT HAS THE distinction of being the only sixties starlet who ever wrote a biker chick role for herself, though she never intended in starring in her own script. The film was the big drive-in hit *Run, Angel, Run* (1969) about a biker and his gal who go on the lam after selling a story about his gang to a major magazine. Despite its success at the box office, Starrett disappeared into the world of daytime television shortly thereafter.

Valerie Starrett's first official acting credit was playing a small role on the TV series *Dan Raven* in 1960. Skip Homier played the title character of a detective who worked the Sunset Strip beat. She followed this up in 1961 with a guest appearance on the western *Death Valley Days* working with future *General Hospital* co-star Peter Hansen. She played a woman engaged to a man who is secretly smuggling guns to the Sioux Indians. Hansen was a doctor in love with her who uncovers her intended's dirty deeds. Shortly after, Starrett's brief TV career was sidelined due to her marriage to actor Jack Starrett and birth of their daughter.

The idea for *Run, Angel, Run* came to Valerie while on location with her husband, who was appearing in the biker movie *Hells Angels on Wheels* starring Jack Nicholson. "It was rather a coincidence that I did this," Starrett explained. "I wrote it for a specific purpose as opposed to thinking I would be part of another biker film. Jack was working on *Hells Angels on Wheels*. We were also friends with Tom Laughlin who was making his own biker film, *The Born Losers*. We knew a lot of actors and actors who wanted to be directors who were part of this new genre. It was just part of our consciousness. I was looking for a vehicle for Jack to switch from acting to directing because that's where his strengths and interests laid. In the era before the Al Pacino's and Dustin Hoffman's, Jack was too atypical in looks to get work as an actor. I thought, 'Why struggle to be an actor when he could be a great director?'

"My daughter and I accompanied Jack on location to Bakersfield, California where they were filming the movie," continued the actress. "We were friends with Jack Nicholson and Adam Roarke who were starring in it. While observing the making of the movie, I thought the biker genre hadn't peaked yet and decided I could write one with Jack directing keeping the budget lower than all the others. Rather than having Sonny Barger and the real Hells Angels in it like they were in *Hells Angels on Wheels*, I started recording Sonny and his biker buddies. They enthralled me especially the women. I taped them talking about what they did and it was a subculture that seemed amazing and fascinating to me. The director had a hard time because some of the Hells Angels would go out at night and get drunk. They would then ride their bikes and crash. They were absolutely fearless and would show up the next day all beaten with their faces all torn up."

Based on a story called *Angel's Flight* by Richard Compton, Valerie Starrett produced a tight screenplay with a strong male and female lead character on the run with the biker gang in hot pursuit. "The only way I could conceive of getting the movie made on the cheap was to remove the two lead characters from the pack so that way we didn't have to hire a whole contingency of bikers," Valerie revealed. "It was a plot device. Plus I realized it would be a stretch for me and it would be easier as an actress to have a strong yearning for something different that would make it more interesting as a character. Some of the ladies I interviewed weren't terribly bright or interesting so I thought I'd make my character more remarkable."

Starrett now had the enviable task to sell her script. She felt her *Run, Angel, Run* was different and novel from the biker movies that had come before it, but still commercially viable that would attract the exploitation film backers. As luck would have it, she was friendly with one—Joe Solomon who was the executive producer on *Hells Angels on Wheels*. He was now running the Fanfare Corporation. "Joe was very interested in producing it," said Valerie. "The deal though was he had to accept Jack as director." Problem was Jack Starrett had never directed a movie before and Solomon was hesitant. Valerie pitched her husband to him. "Jack previously appeared in this low budget movie called *The Girls from Thunder Strip* with Jody McCrea that was filmed in the Lake Isabella region. The frustrated director walked off the picture. Jack stepped forward and said, 'I could do that.' He finished the film. He was a brilliant man and could do anything. There were no dollies for the cameras so he used wheel barrels. It was a horrible shoot but he did remarkable things to compensate for having no budget. He was one of the most original thinkers and did whatever needed to be done to get the shot."

Publicity photo of William Smith and Valerie Starrett in *Run, Angel, Run* (Fanfare Films, 1969).

Joe Solomon then took a leap of faith and green lighted the movie with Jack as director. He placed announcements in all the trade magazines and even boasted that *Run, Angel, Run* would be the first independent movie to employ the multi-screen effect that had become popular recently in such movies as *Grand Prix*, *The Boston Strangler*, and *The Thomas Crown Affair*.

The movie now needed actors. Just as the casting process began, the Starrett marriage was ending. This inspired Valerie to test for the female lead even though her estranged spouse would be directing. "I traded full writing credit [she is listed on screen as V.A. Furlong—her maiden name- along with co-writer Jerome Wish] for a chance to screen test for the female lead," Valerie divulged. "Jack was absolutely wonderful, but terrible with money. Knowing that I would may have to go back to work to support my daughter, I thought I better protect myself by having some current film. Joe was testing two other actresses whose names escape me. I hadn't acted in a number of years and was extremely nervous due to the strange marital situation. I think by default I was the best at the time. It wasn't the right vehicle for me and certainly doing every scene in one take was not going to be the best format for me since I hadn't acted in awhile. Anyway, I agreed to do it."

With Valerie Starrett set, a leading man was still needed. Joe Solomon asked her to read with a bunch of different actors. The one she liked best for Angel was Tom Skerritt. "He gave an absolutely wonderful audition," Starrett exclaimed. "However, Joe felt Tom wasn't really physically marquee-type for a biker film. Then Bill Smith came in and he was marquee biker ready and could ride a motorcycle quite well. It was one of those decisions in retrospect I regretted. I would have gone with Tom, who was my first choice, but I am not sure how much weight that would have had with the producer. Perhaps the film would have been a lot more interesting. Not that I have anything against Bill Smith, who was fascinating and I really, really liked him, but Tom was so appealing against type. For a formula film it was a reach to put me in it and if Tom was cast it would have been a different movie."

Though Valerie did not get her choice of leading man, she did get most of the other roles cast with people she had in mind while writing the screenplay. The biker named Space, for example, was played by her friend Gene Cornelius whom she knew when living in Carmel where she started in theatre. They did *Caesar and Cleopatra* together. The only role other than Angel not pre-cast was the young girl who gets raped by the biker gang. That role was played by Margaret Markov. "She had to test for it and was an inspired choice," remarked Starrett. "Margaret was just marvelous in it and I saw her in 2009 at an art show she hosted at her Hollywood Hills home. We talked for a long time. She retired from acting years ago and has a great life."

A different take on the genre, *Run, Angel, Run* features William Smith as Angel, a former member of the Devil's Advocates who not only left the gang but sold his story to *Like* magazine infuriating his former biker buddies ("Our Angel baby burned us real bad!"). Angel is roaring down the highway (as Tammy Wynette sings the title song) to pick up is $10,000 payment from the publisher in San Francisco when he is jailed for speeding in a school zone. He phones his flame Laurie (Starrett) a part-time go-go dancer and hooker. She picks up a few tricks and is able to spring the biker with some cash left over, causing Angel to sarcastically ask, "What'd you do? Form an assembly line?" They travel a ways when he realizes that his former gang—the Devil's Advocates—are in hot pursuit. Thinking of her safety, he drops Laurie off in a small town only for the biker gang to spot her and begin terrorizing her in the film's most exciting sequence shot in split screen with sometimes as many as five on-screen panels. This montage sequence is truly impressive. Having a change of heart, Angel returns to pick up Laurie and saves her in the nick of time as the duo makes their escape by hopping onto a freight train where they are confronted by three hobos one of whom tries to rape Laurie.

Despite jumping on Angel's bike in a mini-dress, Laurie has a number of costume changes during the trek north. Perhaps her tiny purse doubled as a suitcase? The pair winds up in a small town where they decide to lie low after Angel retrieves his money, which he takes in cash stuffed into a bag. They rent a small house from Dan (Daniel Kemp), a motorcycle riding rancher, and Angel takes a job as a handyman. Fighting his uncontrollable urge to be free, which results in a few arguments with Laurie, Dan shows the former gang member the benefits of traditional family living. Realizing he loves Laurie and wants a more tranquil life, Angel asks Laurie to settle down with him. Unfortunately, the Devil's Advocates have picked up Angel's trail again when they find one of the hobos wearing Angel's jacket. At a drive-in frequented by teenagers, biker Ron (Gene Shaw) meets Dan's naïve teenage daughter Meg (Margaret Markov) admiring his hog. She stupidly goes on a joy ride with the bikers and reveals that Angel is staying on her parent's land. The hoods then viciously gang rape her, leaving the poor girl for dead. The Devil's Advocates find Laurie and brutally beat her. Angel takes them on and is about to be killed by Duke when Dan appears with a shot gun and blows the gang leader away, leaving unanswered whether Laurie decides to remain with Angel or not.

He Squealed On His Gang...And The Word Was Out... WASTE HIM!

JOE SOLOMON presents RUN, ANGEL, RUN! COLOR

WILLIAM SMITH
VALERIE STARRETT

Promotional lobby card for *Run, Angel, Run* (Fanfare Films, 1969).

For a low-budget biker movie, *Run, Angel, Run* opened with a lot of fanfare living up to the new production company's name. It was due to Joe Solomon's determination to make the movie a hit so Fanfare would succeed. "We had the premiere in a big theater in New York City," remembered Valerie. "Joe Solomon paid to fly the Hells Angels to New York and we had a parade down Fifth Avenue. Bill Smith and I rode in a limo. We then went to three or four other cities to open and promote the movie. It became a financial hit [earning a reported $13 million on a $100,000 budget making it one of the highest grossing movies of 1969] and made a lot of money for Joe who piggy-backed three films on all the money earned from *Run, Angel, Run*."

Since *Run, Angel, Run* did not glorify sex and violence, as a number of biker films did at the time, reviews were better than average. The critic in the *Boston Globe* commented that "there's a good deal of fascination to this seamy scene" and that it was "a cut above most in the genre...because it is somewhat more sophisticated and restrained in its handling of the theme." *Los Angeles Times* critic Kevin Thomas, who seems to have had a warm spot for the biker genre, remarked, "Smith... and Miss Starrett are able, attractive performers of considerable promise" and he found the film to be "a good low-budget picture." The critic in *Variety* remarked that "Valerie Starrett is talented but a bit too pretty to ride the back of a bike." The actress also recalled a wonderful review that came out in *Time Magazine*. "It was absolutely mind-blowing to me that *Time* would even cover a biker film. The critic said the movie was 'curiously better than it should have been.'"

Valerie attributed the film's success to her estranged husband Jack Starrett, though the casting of William Smith is a major factor as well. "Jack was quite amazing and had to be innovative working with such a low budget," she commented. "Everything was one take and then he'd say, 'Move on, move on.' It was shot so cheaply that though there are references to the Russian River of Northern California it was all shot in Malibu Canyon. Those endless shots of us on the Pacific Coast Highway were all in Malibu.

"The actual filming was extremely painful and I hated all of it," continued the actress. "It is one thing to envision a rape and another to be the active person in it. Gene Cornelius is bursting through a window and it was so laughable to me. That scene was hard to do. There was another scene at the railroad station—which was actually a great action piece—where as I am running I accidentally fell and banged up my knee. For most of the rest of the filming I was in excruciating pain."

Run, Angel, Run to this day is considered a biker film well worth watching because it provides something a bit different in the genre though not wholly successful. Authors John Wooley and Michael H. Price writing in *The Big Book of Biker Films* agreed with some critics back in 1969 that the scenes of Angel and Laurie experimenting with a settled life slowed the film down and didn't ring true. However, they summarized their feelings and remarked, "*Run, Angel, Run* might be best described as an interesting failure, given its ambitious agenda and the hit-and-miss quality of the exploration. But the emphasis, definitely, should be more on the interesting than on the failure." As for Valerie Starrett, the authors agreed with the critic in *Variety* who praised her performance, but felt she lacked the physicality to make a truly believable biker chick. Author David Stidworthy had more praise for Valerie and wrote in his book *High on the Hogs: A Biker Filmography*, "The pairing of Smith and Starrett was a superlative matchup. Though they sometimes stumbled in their tender moments, Angel and Laurie each had a physical counterpoint to some conditions. Big brawny Angel was like a confused kid at times while Laurie's good grooming couldn't conceal the fact she was getting a bit old for whoring or gypsy travel on a hog."

Despite the box office success of *Run, Angel, Run*, Valerie Starrett did not appear in another movie. Shortly after, she began her long run playing scrappy waitress-turned-nurse Diana Maynard Taylor on the popular soap opera *General Hospital*. "I was in my early thirties when I did *Run, Angel, Run*," admitted Starrett. "The only place—at least in my thinking—for me to work again and support a daughter was something steady. I had film offers but when I was offered the soap I thought, 'Okay, regular life. I can go back to the PTA.' I would be able to raise my daughter and not have to deal with the film world again."

Valerie Starrett quickly became one of the most popular actresses on *General Hospital* and in all of daytime television. Fans were enthralled by the trials of tribulations of her character, who has an affair with married man Phil Brewer, becomes pregnant, and then enters into a marriage of convenience with another, Peter Taylor. After losing the baby to pneumonia she is raped by Phil, becomes pregnant again, and tries to pass the kid off as Peter's but he leaves her when the truth comes out. In 1975, Starrett's Diana Taylor was one of five people suspected of killing that cad Phil Brewer in one of the series' most suspenseful mysteries up to that point. For weeks the audience was kept guessing who was the killer. Trying to keep the culprit's identify hidden, each actor filmed a scene revealing that their character murdered Brewer.

Knowing she could be facing unemployment, Starrett remarked in the *Los Angeles Times* during this period, "A few years ago [Diana] had Hodgkin's disease and at that time it was almost incurable. Well, when I read that in the script, I made all my preparations for leaving and finding a new job. Then we found out that that the diagnosis had been a mistake. The writers can work marvels; so I've been very fatalistic about my career here ever since."

Starrett recalled that doing the show was hard. Low budget, it was shot like a live TV show and you couldn't break tape. If there was a miscue or someone flubbed their lines you had to keep going. "I had one scene where Diana was being raped in the kitchen and I had to reach for a frying pan to hit the attacker over the head, "she recalled. "The prop guy situated the pan incorrectly so the handle was not sticking out for me to grab. I was able to reach for the rim of the pan and beat him with the handle. Blood then ran down his face as planned. It was absurd." Of course, they could not reshoot, so that is what the audience watched.

In 1977, fans were outraged when Starrett was let go and replaced by actress Brooke Bundy. "I left—I love this term—because of creative differences," laughed Valerie. "Tom Donovan replaced the producer I had always worked with and who I'd been the darling of. I was the antithesis of that with Donovan. It was amazingly volatile and bloody. I didn't fall into the mix nor would I. I didn't like the lines now being written for me. I remember being called to his office right before I was let go and he screamed at me, 'You're Marilyn Monroe!' I yelled back, 'You're worse!' It was not a happy relationship."

Donovan did not last long at *General Hospital* when ABC quickly replaced him with Gloria Monty, the former producer of *The Secret Storm,* to shake up the show and boy did she deliver. To be fair, she had full support of the network along with a much bigger budget than what was previously allocated. Her pairing of characters Luke and Laura would change the dynamic of daytime television forever.

As for the character of Diana Taylor, she went from the show's heroine to a grasping, desperate woman who would do anything to keep her adopted son from his biological parents. Valerie quipped, "I didn't watch the show when I was on it, so I surely wasn't going to watch it with someone else playing Diana." Four years after Starrett left the role, Diana Taylor was part of another popular murder whodunit on the show. However, this time Diana was the victim instead of one of the suspects as she was found murdered lying in a pool of blood in her kitchen. Valerie had a happier ending and after retiring from acting she became co-owner of a successful bookstore in Malibu, California and concluded by saying, "This was one of the greatest experiences of my life."

13. WE'LL ASK, HE'LL TELL: CHRISTOPHER RIORDAN ON THE GAY DECEIVERS AND HIS TEENAGE MOVIES

ACTOR/DANCER CHRISTOPHER RIORDAN WAS ONE of the sixties' busiest, most hardworking performers who never received the recognition he deserved. Though he had acting talent, it was eclipsed by his dancing prowess. Hollywood back then had a horrible practice of not giving dancers the billing they deserved and regulated them as background extras without screen credit. Riordan was a true victim of this as he danced in everything from Academy Award winning musicals, to Elvis movies, to beach parties, to teenage exploitation films, rarely seeing his name on screen. It was a truly insulting practice that has rightly been corrected. By the end of the decade, he had let the dancing drift and had turned up in small roles in two cult classics *The Gay Deceivers* (1969) and *Beyond the Valley of the Dolls* (1970).

Christopher Riordan (sometimes billed with his real name, Ronnie Riordan) arrived in Hollywood after leaving home at eighteen due to personal family strife. Discovered by MGM in 1955 and given small roles in *Somebody Up There Likes Me* (1956) and *Raintree County* (1957), Riordan began getting work dancing in nightclubs and in stage productions, which in turn led to dramatic stage work in Los Angeles during this time. Though he won some awards for his acting, his big break came as a dancer when the renowned Fred Astaire and choreographer Hermes Pan chose him to be Astaire's replacement partner for Barrie Chase's nightclub act in Las Vegas.

After a long run, he returned to Hollywood. A short-lived marriage left him as a single father. He worked constantly acting and dancing his way through a myriad of TV shows and movies, from big budget Grade A-productions to quickie Sam Katzman-produced teenage movies, to provide for his son, who was born in 1964. One of Riordan's first movies at this time was dancing in the hit Elvis Presley film *Viva Las Vegas* (1964). With his talent and professionalism, Riordan made such an impression on Elvis, who liked to surround himself with people he felt comfortable with, that he was brought back to work in six more of his movies.

In *Roustabout* (1964), Riordan was a carnie at Barbara Stanwyck's ailing carnival where Elvis' motorcycle-riding, guitar-playing drifter becomes a roustabout to help out and to be closer to her niece, Joan Freeman. He next danced in the background on *Tickle Me* (1965) where Elvis played a singing rodeo cowboy who gets a job on a health spa catering to gorgeous models and starlets, but he is attracted to aloof fitness instructor Jocelyn Lane. This was followed by *Spinout* (1966), *Double Trouble* (1967), and *Clambake* (1967). The latter was supposed to be Christopher's last Elvis movie—that is until the King personally requested that he be part of the live concert movie *Elvis* (1968).

Riordan's work in drive-in movies was not just relegated to Elvis musicals. Producer Sam Katzman, nicknamed "King of the B's," had been catering to teenagers since the mid-fifties with rock 'n' roll and juvenile delinquent movies. By 1964, he was delivering more wholesome fare but in a few years he too would begin producing more alienated youth movies. Despite a dust up with the frugal producer on his first movie for him *Get Yourself a College Girl* (1964) starring Mary Ann Mobley and Joan O'Brien, Christopher would work for the producer again in *Hot Rods to Hell* (1967) starring Mimsy Farmer.

After working for Katzman and then with Connie Francis in the minor musical *Looking for Love* (1964), Riordan was cast in the big budget musical *My Fair Lady* (1964) thanks to choreographer Hermes Pan. It would become one of his fondest working experiences, mostly due to the graciousness of its star Audrey Hepburn. He was also so liked by the director George Cukor that he was used in three different segments of the movie with the makeup, hair, and costume designers changing his look for each so he would not be recognized. After this type of royal treatment, it is no wonder that soon afterwards he felt it was a real letdown—though he appreciated the work—to shake his swimsuit clad booty in a myriad of quickly-filmed beach party movies. In rapid succession, he played surfers or beach boys in the 1965 releases *The Girls on the Beach* , *Wild on the Beach*, and *A Swingin' Summer* before working at AIP where he popped up in and helped choreograph *Ski Party*, *How to Stuff a Wild Bikini*, and *Wild Weird World of Dr. Goldfoot*. After doing the same in AIP's last beach party movie, *The Ghost in the Invisible Bikini* (1966), Riordan was officially named choreographer on *Fireball 500* (1966) and *Thunder Alley* (1967).

Christopher Riordan, ca. 1964. *Courtesy of Christopher Riordan*

In between all his fun teenage drive-in movies, Riordan somehow found the time to appear on numerous TV shows, including a recurring role in the failed 1964-65 sitcom *Many Happy Returns* starring John McGiver, and on the big screen in such lauded motion pictures as *Von Ryan's Express*, *The Great Race*, *The Glory Guys*, *The Loved One*, *The Cincinnati Kid* (all released in 1965), and *Fantastic Voyage* (1966). He even landed dancing gigs in such prestige musicals as *Camelot* (1967) and *Thoroughly Modern Millie* (1967). By the end of the decade he let the dancing lapse, passing up a number of musicals including *Finian's Rainbow,* and instead focused on only acting. This culminated with a featured supporting role in the notorious *The Gay Deceivers,* quickly followed by a smaller role in the camp classic *Beyond the Valley of the Dolls*.

Though *Beyond the Valley of the Dolls* is better known to the masses and where Riordan is a bitchy party guest, *The Gay Deceivers* gave him his most memorable role. This was a daring-for-its time comedy produced by Joe Solomon (who defended the movie back in 1969 remarking, "The subject of homosexualism is treated with utmost finesse.") and directed by Bruce Kessler. It starred boyish Kevin Coughlin as Danny Devlin, a preppy 22 year-old with a steady girlfriend named Karen (Brooke Bundy) and handsome blonde Larry Casey as Elliot Crane, a ladies man and lifeguard who get drafted. To avoid being sent to Vietnam, they indicate on their draft forms that they might be homosexual. When questioned by army officer Dixon (Jack Starrett), the friends pretend to be lovers who desperately want to serve their country together. Their ruse works and they are denied entry. Danny lies to his parents that an old sports injury kept him out, but when celebrating with some nubile lovelies at Elliot's pad they notice Dixon watching from the street. Realizing they will have to give up women for awhile, the duo shack up in a one bedroom apartment in a swinging gay complex and try to convince their friendly flamboyant landlord Malcolm (Michael Greer who told *Gay Scene* magazine in 1974, "I made the audience like me, like the character. Parents went out of that theatre saying I like him. It was only after they got home that they asked how can I like him—he's a fairy?"), his partner (Sebastian Brook), and the resident stud Duane (Christopher Riordan) that they are homosexuals while keeping Danny's family and Elliot's paramours, who all seem to pop over unannounced at the wrong time, in the dark.

Things get thorny especially when at a gay bar Elliot slugs a guy named Freddie (Ron Gans) coming on to him and it is witnessed by Danny and Karen. Outside Elliot plays up the gay routine and Karen flees into the night thinking her fiancé prefers his friend. The next day a black Speedo-clad Elliot runs into Danny's sister Leslie (Jo Ann Harris) on the beach. Coming on to him, he takes her back to his place to prove he likes girls, though she is skeptical after previously being to their apartment and meeting their neighbors. Elliot gets cold feet after spotting a military officer outside, but he is there for a liaison with

Duane. When the blonde stud can't get it up, Leslie believes the rumors about him and her brother and storms out. Later at their landlords' costume party, Elliot—after rejecting the advances of Freddie and Duane—takes a blonde woman to bed to prove his virility. He freaks out when he discovers it's a guy in drag. This is all witnessed by Dixon. After Karen leaves him, Danny goes to Dixon to try to set the record straight, so to speak, but is still rejected. The surprise ending reveals that Dixon is the real homosexual (don't ask, don't tell) and purposely kept "their kind" out of the Army.

Christopher Riordan makes his entrance in *The Gay Deceivers* (Fanfare Films, 1969). *Courtesy of Christopher Riordan*

Christopher Riordan as Duane makes a grand entrance without speaking a word. As the boys' real estate agent tries to divert them to another complex, Duane emerges from his apartment in very tight jeans walking his dog. He catches the eye of Elliot and gives him the once over. When Elliot winks back, the agent knows this is the place for them. At the costume party, he is shirtless, wearing tight red pants and beads around his neck. He and Gans as Freddie trade bitchy barbs about who has the better chance to get Elliot into bed. They both lose out. A short while later Duane tries to impress Elliot by protecting him from a big brute, only to have the guy's boyfriend in drag knock the guy out instead.

The Gay Deceivers (whose taglines included "They had to keep their hands *off girls* in order to keep the Army's hands *off them*" and "Is he or isn't he? Only his draft board knows for sure") was released in the late spring of 1969. The critics of the day did not take too kindly to it. A. H. Weiler of the *New York Times* said *The Gay Deceivers* "is, unfortunately neither gay or deceptive." Some reviewers used derogatory language such as Gene Siskel of the *Chicago Tribune* who remarked, "I wouldn't recommend this limp-wristed comedy to my worst enemy" and placed it seventh on his list of the Worst Movies of 1969. Even cruder was critic Marjory Adams of the *Boston Globe* whose review included such terms as "homos," "a colony of weirdies," and "faggoty landlady."

Some in the gay community did not take to the movie either. It was reported by Jerry Parker in *Newsday* that at the San Francisco opening members of the Committee for the Freedom of Homosexuals picketed the theater with signs condemning the movie for "flaunting every sickening prejudice and bigoted misconception which supposes we homosexuals are both lacking in manliness and patriotism."

One very positive review came from Kevin Thomas of the *Los Angeles Times* who exclaimed, "*The Gay Deceivers* is a hilarious yet surprisingly inoffensive comedy…" Critics aside, the movie was a big draw for homosexuals craving to see themselves portrayed on the screen, and more adventurous filmgoers. Also the Stonewall riots happened shortly after it was released, making the topic even more relevant. The movie was a hit and grossed an estimated $5 million at the box office.

Viewing *The Gay Deceivers* nowadays, it is a bit dated with stereotypical gay characters and plays like an elongated episode of *Love, American Style*. Offensive it is not, as some folks deemed it back then—quite the contrary. This was very daring and trail blazing for the time. Kessler, whose previous credits included *Angels from Hell* and *Killers 3*, takes a surprisingly sincere approach and knows his audience, even cladding Larry Casey in a Speedo and giving them glimpses of his fine naked behind. With the controversy today about gay marriage, it is quite surprising that for a movie made in the late sixties, Greer and Brook's relationship is treated respectfully and not poked fun at. They come off as the typical wacky married next-door-neighbors ala Fred and Ethel Mertz found on any TV sitcom at the time. Greer's effeminate Malcolm is countered by neighbor Riordan's swaggering stud, but no dummy he. Even the gay bar scene is toned down with normal looking guys and not played over-the-top.

Some of the scenes are truly funny like the opening split screen montage where an army psychologist questions Danny and Elliot to see if they are truly homosexual and when Danny's parents pop into the "couple's" new apartment to find Malcolm making breakfast, nude male statues throughout the home, and a pink bedroom with only one bed. While Danny talks about painting it dark brown to his bewildered father, Malcolm fawns over his mother's designer outfit. Later scenes with the straight characters are played much too seriously and it becomes more a hand-wringing drama (is the duo gay or not?).

What even makes the film campier today is not Michael Greer's flamboyant character but how the womanizing gigolo character of Elliot comes off as perhaps the real queen. First, though he is a male hustler with legions of ladies young and old lusting after him, it is a profession more associated with male customers than women. Secondly, with his handsome features, groomed hair, and buff suntanned muscles, the always shirtless Elliot has the body most gay men crave and loves to show it off in Speedos or a fig-leaf bikini brief. And finally, the way actor Larry Casey enthusiastically throws himself into impersonating a gay man, compared to Kevin Coughlin's projected uneasiness, you cannot look at Elliot and go *hmmmmmm*. Having him remain at the gay complex instead of moving to Miami to hustle rich old broads would have made for a surprise ending and kept the audience guessing.

The Gay Deceivers should have led to bigger film roles for Christopher Riordan but it didn't. He continued, though, to get work due to his talent and professionalism. He followed *The Gay Deceivers* with the cult classic *Beyond the Valley of the Dolls* (1970) playing a catty homosexual at music promoter Ronnie 'Z-Man' Barzell's Hollywood bash. The long forgotten but interesting sci-fi sexploitation curio *The Curious Female* (1970) directed by Paul Rapp featured Riordan again as a partier. This time he has much more screen time as shirtless Troy, one of the toga-wearing guests who defy the Master Computer who controls their lives and views an old sex film from 1969 called "The Three Virgins"—one of whom is sixties starlet Angelique Pettyjohn. The audience watches entranced and bewildered by foreign terms such as "virgin" and "marriage" and sexual customs. He then was cast again by director Bruce Kessler to play a warlock in *Simon, King of the Witches* (1971) starring Andrew Prine as a sewer-living warlock masquerading as a "magician" who falls for a district attorney's hippie daughter.

A few more small roles on TV and in film plus some stage work followed during the seventies before Riordan went behind the camera into production. He lived in Mexico for a time and when he moved back to LA in the mid-2000s he resided at Falcon Lair, the former home of silent movie star Rudolph Valentino. Since 2006 he has returned to acting and keeping quite busy with appearances in a number of TV sitcoms, including *Ugly Betty*; *Outsourced*; *Black-ish*; and *Superstore*.

How did you get cast in *The Gay Deceivers*?

Bruce Kessler originally considered me for Larry Casey's part. In those days, I was very buff. I shocked everyone when I opted to try for the part of Duane.

Why did you choose the smaller supporting role over the lead?

After my agent described the part of the lifeguard, I thought it was boring; and that was before even being able to read any of the 'sides'. I had spent so many years in a bathing suit, in all those AIP beach party movies, that I just didn't see any fulfillment in playing that part. I also knew that there were many actors in consideration for it [including Kent McCord of *Adam-12* fame]. That is, until it became known what the movie was about. Indeed, a lot of actors shied away from this script.

Also, I had *always* considered myself to be a 'character actor.' I didn't enjoy playing the 'handsome leading man.' For one thing, I never considered myself that handsome. Now, when I look at old pictures, or films, I say to myself, 'Oh, that kid was pretty good looking.' Now, I understand why they were always trying to put me into that 'boring' category.

Christopher Riordan (*far left*) looks on at the party melee in *The Gay Deceivers* (Fanfare Films, 1969). *Courtesy of Christopher Riordan*

What was Bruce Kessler's reaction?

He was shocked and I don't think he was going for me as Duane. So I went home, did some shopping, and returned to his office the next day or so. Bruce took one look at me, and seemed astonished at the transformation. He then said, 'If you really want it, then that part [of Duane] is yours.' My thinking was, and I was right; that this role would be a stand out—Duane and Malcolm would be the parts that one remembers.

Do you think the producer and director treated the material respectfully?

Joe Solomon was a real character—typical producer. I'm sure he was exploiting the whole idea. Bruce Kessler, on the other hand, took all of this very seriously and really wanted to do a good film. He ended up as one of my favorite directors.

Why did Bruce Kessler impress you so?

Because it was how well Bruce, the crew, etc. were treating me. They seemed to respect the years of experience that I brought to the table. I recall Bruce applauding when I made my entrance. It was my first shot. I told him, 'I have an idea....' He said, 'Good, do it. Don't tell me, I'll go along.' Obviously, I brought a lot more to the part than what was written on the page. But I also wanted to be very careful [with my performance], as I knew, one day, my son would see this movie. Bruce was so thrilled at my delivery that he called my agent and told her, 'I'm giving Christopher single card billing along with the leads.' She was excited at that, and frankly, so was I.

Did Kevin Coughlin or Larry Casey show any reservations about taking the lead roles?

Kevin was a really lovely guy. He too, took it all very seriously, and wanted to do a good film. I'll never understand why Larry took the part. He was truly *spooked* the entire time.

How so?

I'm sure Larry Casey is/was a very nice man. I know he was a husband and a father, and that he had been a regular on *The Rat Patrol*. In his defense, as I mentioned, I thought his part was very dull and I don't think he had the charisma, or the understanding, to pull it off. Throughout the entire shoot he seemed to be drowning. I felt that nothing he did actually connected. I know that Kevin was always trying to work on their scenes together, but Casey *never* picked up the subtle hints. I hate to say it, but I don't think I ever worked with an actor that I got less from, than Larry Casey. A life-size photo might have been more affective. It was painful, during the party scene. So much more could have been done with that. [On a side note, actor Larry Casey began being billed as Lawrence Casey or Lawrence P. Casey after this movie was released. Was he trying to run away from it?]

What do you recall about Michael Greer who played the one of the landlords?

This was the second of three films I did with Michael who was openly gay. The first was a film called *What Am I Bid?* It was really an awful film—the things I did to put my son Sean through diapers. Michael loved what I was doing with my role, and stole my adlib of "Miss Thing" for his act—and, ever after, I think. We were encouraged to add things if we thought they might work. However, Michael tended to 'take over' the directing of some scenes, especially the party scene moving people around and giving them bits of business.

In regards to Casey, I recall him rolling his eyes and muttering, '*Where* did they find this guy?' He even said to me, 'you poor thing—you have to act like you're attracted to him.' Michael was *very* direct. I don't think he and Bruce Kessler ended up on the best of terms. Michael was definitely trying to make his mark and he did offend some people. Not me, until about five years later, during one of his live performances. He introduced every one of his actor friends in the audience except me. He went right around me and never mentioned my name. I kept thinking, 'Oh, he's saving me for last.' He wasn't. Everybody looked at me thinking, 'What happened here?' I thought, 'Wasn't that a bitchy thing to do?' But I just shrugged his slight off.

Do you recall the reaction of the fans when the movie was released? It was a box office hit.

Indeed, I was at the premiere. Somewhere, I have a shot of the huge line, going all around the block, lining up to see this film. My entrance got a huge hand, with much shouting and foot stomping. I think it let the audience know it was all OK to laugh at all of this. I was then only offered the same kind of roles for ages. In fact, Dominick Dunne and I had a bit of a fight over my turning down a part of a hustler in his movie, *Play It as It Lays*.

They brought the movie back every summer for a few years. Then, it seemed to disappear. It was ages before it became available on video. By the way, I was also told that the rental prints (16mm) often came back with my entrance, and my billing, missing—sort of 'early days of rewind', no? It got so that they had to run the film when it was returned. If those scenes were excised, the customer was told to either return the missing footage, or pay.

Ron Gans and Christopher Riordan in *The Gay Deceivers*
(Fanfare Films, 1969). *Courtesy of Christopher Riordan*

Looking at some of your other drive-in movies, you worked a number of times for producer Sam Katzman.

I had a huge fight with him while I was working on *Get Yourself a College Girl* in 1964. It was my day off and someone called me to report to the set. I said, 'I'm not scheduled to work today and I am feeling ill.' They were insistent so I obliged. When I got there, Sam Katzman wanted me to dance on this platform the size of a shoebox about forty-five feet in the air. I said to him, 'You've got to be out of your mind! That's insane.' He demanded that I do it and wouldn't take no for an answer. I then asked how much additional compensation I would get. Again he ranted and raved not wanting to pay me anything extra. I started to walk away with Katzman bellowing at me, 'You'll never work in this town again! Somebody with your experience should be able to climb up there and do this with no trouble.' I turned to him and said, 'If it's so fucking easy, get your fat ass up there and do it yourself!' Even his wife Hortense Petra laughed hysterically. Ultimately, I did it and got about four times of what I normally would have been paid. And after all this I believe it was cut from the final print.

You got to appear in one of Elvis' best sixties musicals *Roustabout* for Paramount co-starring the legendary Barbara Stanwyck that same year.

Barbara Stanwyck was terribly professional, very kind, and very nice to everybody no matter whom it was. She especially got along well with the crew. She was very sweet towards Elvis. They were both very respectful of each other. She realized what type of film she was doing and why she was doing so she acquiesced to it, and he bowed and scraped to her, which of course he should but he was such a gentleman to everybody, so it was no surprise.

Joan Freeman [Elvis' main love interest] on the other hand was just so quiet and distant. She did not seem to me to be the type of person who should be an actress. While watching her scenes with Elvis, I thought there was no chemistry at all between them. Her husband coincidentally is director Bruce Kessler from *The Gay Deceivers*.

You also worked three times with Raquel Welch before and after she became a star. Did her attitude change?

Yes, yes, and yes—boy did her attitude change. She was the Billboard Girl on *The Hollywood Palace* where I danced with Barrie Chase. Raquel still had a terrible complexion on this. Then we did the film *A Swingin' Summer*. Her husband Patrick Curtis was on the set constantly. He remolded her and all of a sudden there was this whole different girl. I didn't even recognize her. She wouldn't talk to anybody and you could tell she knew where she was going. I think her attitude was part of Curtis' influence to behave that way. But my feeling was, do you think you are going to get there on this dreadful film? From what I'm told, Curtis bought up every print to keep it off the market. And finally we worked on *Fantastic Voyage* where she never talked to me *but Stephen Boyd talked to me*!

You say that with a leer in your voice.

Stephen Boyd was gay. They brought me in and I remember we were all sitting around when Boyd said pointing at me, 'Those are the legs I want.' Somebody quipped, 'Well yes but where do you want them?' It was kind of an embarrassing moment. But I became his leg double in the film where you see the scientists in their rubber suits swimming through veins and arteries. I said to him, 'Well, you finally got my legs.' He just looked at me askew.

How did you progress from dancing in the AIP beach movies to becoming a choreographer on them?

Jack Baker was the choreographer for the AIP beach movies. He was impressed with my dancing and asked if I would assist him on the next film. I said fine, and we did a couple together. We also worked on *The Wild Weird World of Dr. Goldfoot* TV special. It was a fun job and I was being paid good money, so I had no reason to complain. I was raising my son and had no family to speak of at that time, so I had to work a lot to support him. Eventually I am the one doing all the choreography and Jack is off at Paramount working on another movie. The AIP executives caught him and they were furious. Annette Funicello spoke up for me and said to them, 'I don't know why you don't just give the job to Christopher. He's the one who has been doing it anyway.' With that, I was called into a meeting and asked if I would be the full-time choreographer. I negotiated an outrageous amount of money for just telling people to shake their fanny. How many different ways can you do that? It wasn't dancing as far as I was concerned.

You worked with a number of popular young actors of the sixties trying to get them to dance—any failures?

Yes, Yvonne Craig on *Ski Party*. She had a hard time and I fought for her because I liked her and we got along very well. Yvonne was so talented and such a sweet person. Because of her ballet training, she felt very uncomfortable doing those dances. I kept saying, 'But honey it's nothing.' She was too self-conscious about it, so we had her sit on the sidelines and clap.

Which film was your first as official choreographer?

It was *Fireball 500* with Frankie Avalon, Annette Funicello, and Fabian. Guy Hemric, who wrote a lot of the songs for the AIP movies, put me up to play a trick on Frankie. Annette went along with it because she enjoyed a good joke, too. He had a number to do with Annette and we arranged for him to do these awful, terrible dance moves. Well, he threw a fit. Annette, Guy and all these people are laughing and I got scared because I thought he was going to have me fired. He didn't think it was humorous at all. This was surprising because I thought Fabian would be the pain in the behind and Frankie would be easy to work with but it was just the opposite.

How did you get along with William Asher who directed *Fireball 500* and *Thunder Alley*?

William Asher directed a lot of the early beach party films and some *I Love Lucy* shows. In his day, he was considered quite the director. When I first worked for him I was just one of the beach boys—like number 99 on the list. When I started to assist Jack Baker as choreographer for whatever reasons Asher had taken some time off from AIP. So the next time we met again I had been hired as choreographer on *Fireball 500*. For whatever reason, he just took an instant delight in hating me. I had no idea where this was coming from. Somebody told him that I choreographed this particular number wonderfully. It really was good and funny. So he said quite nastily, 'Well let me see it!' The dancers did the number. He looked at me and I could tell he didn't know what to say to find some fault with it. Finally, he said, 'I really think that at the end of the number, the girls should say 'oomp' when they do the bump. I think that makes more sense.' I said, 'Are you sure?' He confirmed it and I informed my dancers to do it as their director instructed. We shot it perfectly in just one take. Immediately after Asher yelled, 'Cut and print.'

The production manager then came running over screaming and hollering. Asher asked what the problem was and he said, "Do you realize they just said 'oomp'?" Asher explained it was his idea and thought it worked well. The production manager then exclaimed, "Do you realize you just bumped the girls up to SAG and now we have to pay them a hell of a lot more money?" [Dancers at that time were part of Screen Extras Guild.] With that Asher turned and glared at me. I said, 'I like it the way you suggested.'

Choreographer Christopher Riordan (*far right*) demonstrates some dance moves to Salli Sachse (*2nd from right*) and unidentified dancers during rehearsal for *Thunder Alley* (AIP, 1967). *Courtesy of Christopher Riordan*

Were you still getting dancing offers at this point?

Yes, one in particular that I worked on but did not want to was *The Cool Ones*. Director Gene Nelson was a good friend of mine so I agreed. Sometime after Hermes Pan, whom I worked with on *My Fair Lady*, asked me to dance in *Finian's Rainbow*. I said, 'Hermes, I just don't want to dance on film anymore.' It was a kind of a falling out between us and we weren't as close for several months after that. Sometimes you have to pass on work in this business if you don't want to continually do the same thing.

You went from dancing in Elvis and beach movies to *Hot Rods to Hell*.

They wanted somebody who could say lines convincingly and dance a little bit. It was hard in those days, even though we were doing some dreadful dancing, to get people who looked good to do both. The sad thing about this was Dana Andrews. He was a lovely man but a drinker. He finally admitted that he was an alcoholic but he was one of those people that when he announced this he then had to make the entire world sober, which bores you to tears. He would say to me on the set, 'I am so ashamed I'm doing this.' I'd reply, 'How do you think I feel? I'm not happy about this either.' Poor Dana Andrews and Jeanne Crain were sort of rolling in their early graves.

You appeared in a number of major films but the cult classic is *The Loved One*.

My scene was shot at the old Doheny Estate where they were already filming when I got a casting call. In those days you could not drive to a film location due to insurance reasons. We had to report to the studio and they bussed a bunch of us actors up there. As soon as I stepped off the bus I heard Tony Richardson [the film's director] bellow, 'That one! I want that one!' He was looking directly at me and that was that. I didn't even say a word and felt very lucky to work on this movie.

What was it like to work with that colorful cast?

Sometime before filming *The Loved One* I was invited to this fabulous black-tie cocktail party up in the Hollywood Hills over looking Lake Hollywood. I was talking with one of the hosts, Julio Alvarez, and John Gielgud—who was in town to do a play—entered. Julio turned to him and said, 'John, I want you to meet our friend Christopher.' Gielgud takes my hand, steps back and gives me a long up and down look before saying, 'Ah, one of the true male beauties.' That's something you don't forget. Of course, when we worked together a short time later he never brought it up.

I remember Terry Southern was always on the set and always taking notes of what Jonathan Winters would say. Talk about somebody who has a quick wit. Years later Jonathan signed his book to me, 'To Christopher, Wasn't it fun playing with the stiffs?' I liked Robert Morse but Anjanette Comer acted very grand during the shoot. Consequently, she sat alone most of the time. She did not partake in any of the merriment. Can you imagine with that cast? God, what fun we had. In my scene I am playing this best man at a wedding and we are quickly shoved out the door for a funeral. It was done with great hilarity. Tony Richardson was just wonderful to work with.

You played another gay character in *Beyond the Valley of the Dolls*. How did you get cast in that?

I was taken over to 20th Century Fox by my agent at the time, Leon Lance, who signed me to do a picture there. At this particular time there were two films that were about to be made—*Beyond the Valley of the Dolls* and *Myra Breckenridge*. The original script they sent me for *Beyond the Valley of the Dolls* was a true sequel to *Valley of the Dolls*. I then went to meet with Michael Sarne, who was directing *Myra Breckenridge*. He was so stoned and so out of it that I did not want to work with him. I next came in contact with Mae West who wouldn't talk directly to you. She turned to her assistant and said, 'Ask him if he'll cut his hair.' I said, 'What do you mean *ask him*? I'm standing right here.' I felt very uncomfortable so I told my agent that I'd do *Beyond the Valley of the Dolls*.

When did they switch scripts for *Beyond the Valley of the Dolls*?

I was told we had two weeks before filming began and to go home to study our scripts. In the interim the Manson murders took place. That is when they brought Roger Ebert in [to work with Russ Meyer] and they decided to reject the original draft screenplay given to us. [A lawsuit filed by *Valley of the Dolls* author Jacqueline Susann was also a factor.] I thought the original script was good, Ebert's was horrible. I was contracted to do it so I did. Surprisingly, I had fun and really enjoyed Russ Meyer. He was wonderful

It must have taken a lot of time to fill that party scene with all the different players and all those extras?

Yes, it took over two weeks. Even that little interaction between me and the hippie blonde girl took time with all the different camera angles and lighting set-ups. It was a good thing I enjoyed saying the line or I would have gotten very bored. We're dancing and I am not paying any attention to her at all. She tries to break the ice and says to me, 'And you're a Moon Child.' And I reply, 'And you're a bitch!' Russ loved it and asked me how I could deliver the line the same every time. I said to him, 'It is real easy when it comes from the heart.'

Do any of the "Dolls" stand out for you?

Dolly Read really was a doll. I loved her and thought she would become a star. But she was smart and married Dick Martin. I worked with Phyllis Davis [who played Susan Lake] several times before this. She was such a hard worker and did everything to get into the business from being an extra, a stand-in, and a dancer in all those awful beach movies, some of which I choreographed. Years later when she hit with that series *Vega$* I thought, 'Good for her! Now she is on her way.' But after it ended she seemed to have disappeared. The weirdest girl on this was Erica Gavin [Roxanne in the film] who worked with Russ before [on *Vixen*]. She really gave me the creeps.

What about the actors?

I had worked with Michael Blodgett [who played Lance Rock] several times before this and he was a really nice guy. We'd look at each other and role our eyes while filming this knowing it was not going to be received well. He got hit on all the time by men *and* women, and really burned out on acting. It destroyed him for awhile and he became an alcoholic. Happily, he became a very well-respected novelist and screenwriter. David Gurian [who played Harrison], though, was strange. He was convinced that this movie was going to make him a big star. I thought, 'you poor delusional boy. It is not going to happen with this piece of crap.'

Are you surprised that *Beyond the Valley of the Dolls* has a huge cult following?

You have no idea how many people love that movie when I bring it up. I was living in Mexico and came to LA for a visit when I went to the Samuel French bookstore in Studio City. A boy working there was a huge fan and recognized me. He was so excited because they were having a midnight showing at some theater that night. I was about to leave when he ran into the back and came out with a *Beyond the Valley of the Dolls* movie poster magnet. I couldn't believe they were selling it for $6.00. He gave it to me and I took it home to put on my refrigerator.

One of your last movies at this time was the sci-fi exploitation movie *The Curious Female*. How did you wind up in this?

The director was Paul Rapp, who worked as the production manager on *The Gay Deceivers*. It was his dog that I used in the entrance scene in that movie. I never saw this but the original script was titled *Love, Computer Style*. I got this because they were impressed with my work in *The Gay Deceivers* so Fanfare Films signed me to do two more pictures. Stupidly, I did not ask for script approval as I did with 20ᵗʰ Century-Fox, which gave me a choice of movies to do. I don't recall how the script veered from this take-off on computer dating to the final product about viewing erotic videos.

You appear in the futuristic orgy scenes.

Most of these people involved in this were actual actors who did nudie films at the time. There was this very funny woman who felt this was the big time for her. An actor turned to her and said, 'You really are taking this *far* too seriously.' She had this wonderful kind of Jean Hagen-voice and she said to him, 'Look this may be just another fuck film to you but to *me* this is my *Gone with the Wind*!'

14. LADA EDMUND, JR. IS OUT OF IT

IN 1966, GO-GO DANCER LADA (pronounced Lay-da) Edmund, Jr. was itching to break free from her cage. After appearing on Broadway in two hit musicals, the blonde with the wild mane of hair became famous overnight dancing on TV's newest teenage music show *Hullabaloo*. Fans looked forward to her energetic gyrating to rock and rolling songs performed by the show's guest performers. It was this notoriety that brought her to the attentions of the producers of the teenage coming-of-age movie *Out of It*, one of the undiscovered gems of the sixties, who cast her as every teenage boy's fantasy girl.

Lada Edmund, Jr., her real name, made her Broadway debut originating the role of Penelope Ann, one of drafted pop star Conrad Birdie's many teenage fans, in the hit musical *Bye Bye Birdie* in 1960. She then went on to play the tough-acting tomboy Anybodys in a revival of *West Side Story* before making her film debut as one of Pamela Tiffin's sorority sisters in the beach movie, *For Those Who Think Young* (1964).

Trading dancing onstage to gyrating in a cage, Edmund, Jr. was just one of many talented performers, including future choreographer Michael Bennett, Donna McKechnie, Suzanne Charny, and Patrick Adiarte, plucked from Broadway to go-go dance on NBC-TV's newest pop music variety series *Hullabaloo* in January 1965. It was similar to ABC's primetime music show *Shindig* but *Hullabaloo* featured a different celebrity host each week to introduce the musical performers. The show received most of its press not for the rock groups or vocalists that guest starred but for its choreography by David Winters and its dancers, particularly the cage-dancing Lada—usually clad in a tasseled mini-dress with matching go-go boots, who bumped, grinded and twisted their way into the homes of teenagers every week. It was reported that college boys would watch the program with the sound turned off just to see Lada shake, rattle, and roll. So popular was the curvaceous wiggly blonde (NBC dubbed her "the Mary Poppins of Rock & Roll" and columnist Jack

O'Brian remarked that she "frugs like a mad-maned lioness") that she graced the covers of *TV Guide* and *Life* magazines. However, Edmund soon became known for her outspokenness (she told *The Hartford Courant* she was "*Hullaballoo*'s best dancer") and outrageous comments. For example, she thought men over twenty-five "look ridiculous doing the frug, monkey, and jerk" and thought women over thirty should "stick to the waltz or their knitting." This did earn her detractors who dubbed her "a lamebrain" and "a conceit with no talent."

Lada Edmund, Jr. ca. 1964. *Courtesy Lada Edmund, Jr.*

Lada however was more than just the girl-in-a-cage who could do the Twist or Watusi. The producers let her sing as well, resulting in a few released singles "I Know Something" and "The Larue," and allowed her to perform on other variety shows, such as *The Tonight Show Starring Johnny Carson* and *The Sammy Davis Special*.

Hullabaloo was cancelled in the spring of 1966 and Edmund decided to concentrate on acting, beginning with an unsold TV pilot, *The Flim-Flam Man* based on the movie starring George C. Scott. In 1967 she landed the female lead in the movie *Out of It*, which was produced by Stanford graduate Edward Pressman and directed and written by Paul Williams, a Phi Beta Kappa from Harvard University. Both were twenty-three year old aspiring filmmakers. They crossed paths in London where Williams was an affiliated student at Cambridge University in 1965. He was making his fourth short film when he was introduced to Pressman, working as an accountant on the movie *Casino Royale*, at a party in London. With money he inherited, Pressman invested in Williams' film to help him complete it. Shortly after they formed a production company Pressman-Williams.

Williams got the idea for *Out of It* in the spring of 1966. The script was based on his experiences growing up in the suburbs of Long Island combined with a real-life incident of a bullied kid gunning down a jock in the locker room at the high school Williams attended in Massapequa. The story unfolds easily and slowly as some high school students enjoy their last summer on the beach before they begin their senior year, ending with the locker room incident minus the murder. Williams and Pressman shopped the screenplay to the Young Talent Programs the major studios were offering during the summer of 1966 but it was rejected by all. They then decided to finance the movie themselves. Reportedly, the budget was estimated to be $125,000 to $250,000 with a fair portion contributed by Pressman.

Though Lada Edmund, Jr. was known to TV viewers, she was not a movie star. The only "name" in the cast was Barry Gordon who had just previously co-starred in the Academy Award winning film *A Thousand Clowns* (1965). Per Williams, the actor's managers were against him doing an independent movie despite his love of the role. Purportedly, a sweetening of the pot with a 2% participation offer sealed the deal.

Out of It began filming in the summer of 1967. The shoot was scheduled for approximately six weeks with a lot of it shot at Pressman's family summer home in Atlantic Beach. When completed, the movie came in within budget. However, Edward Pressman commented to Joseph Gelmis in *Newsday*, "But what it took out of Paul was tremendous. I don't think it can be done by the same people that way more than once or twice. It drains them."

Lada Edmund, Jr. dances in her cage on TV's *Hullaballoo*, ca. 1965. *Courtesy Lada Edmund, Jr.*

After nine months of editing, *Out of It* was ready in May 1968. A number of studios wanted to distribute. United Artists was chosen since they offered a three-picture deal.

However, the movie sat on the shelf because the studio could not decide to use it to introduce Jon Voight to the public or to take a wait-and-see approach until the currently filming *Midnight Cowboy* wrapped. They opted for the latter so *Out of It* was not released until late 1969 after *Midnight Cowboy* was in theaters.

Out of It is set during the summer of 1964 on the beaches of Long Island and centers on a bunch of middle-class suburban teenagers. Lada played pretty cheerleader Christine, who was not your typical stuck-up popular high school student. She and her football jock boyfriend Russ (Jon Voight in his film debut)—a laconic blonde-haired Neanderthal—are out on his boat. They are accidentally run into by shy, film-loving, puny Paul (Barry Gordon). He is with Steve (Peter Grad), a user who likes to be out on the water, and was distracted by Steve talking about his disastrous date the night before with a girl named Barbara (Gretchen Corbett) who did not take too kindly with skinny dippy. Russ lashes into Paul for hitting his boat. Christine is annoyed with her boyfriend's bullying ways and comes to Paul's defense. Thinking he has a shot with her, Paul later asks Christine to double date with Steve and Barbara to go see a production of *Romeo and Juliet*. To the nerd's shock and horror, Christine surprisingly agrees, which is the catalyst for the drama ahead. There is a constant tug-of-war in the mind of Christine between the brainy, sensitive Paul and brawny, insensitive Russ.

Christine bails out early on the date feigning illness, but runs into the trio later at a bar where she is back with Russ. Paul is humiliated and the next day at football practice is purposely injured by Russ who blindsides the place-kicker and tackles him to the ground. Miffed again by the antics of Russ, Christine searches Paul out and they go to the beach together. They then wind up in his bedroom. Being subjugated by men due to her stunning looks, Christine is taken aback when alone with Paul he doesn't make a move on her despite his endless gazing at her breasts and her attempts to kiss him. Russ learns that Paul has once again spent time with his girl and embarrasses him in front of his friends by burning holes in his varsity sweater with his cigarette. As the saying goes, nice guys finish last and Christine once again chooses the boorish Russ despite his bad behavior. The jock takes her back and they have a wild make out session in a life guard station while Paul decides to try to make it work with Barbara. Paul gets his revenge on Russ pulling a gun on him in the locker room and watching him quiver while the other players look on. As he backs away, a trembling Russ says, "I *like* you. I've always spoken very highly about your kicking." Pulling the trigger, a flame comes out and Paul lights Steve's cigarette with it. They all wind up back at the beach with Paul lounging with Barbara on the sand while enviously eyeing Christine and the jock.

Shot after Frankie Avalon and Annette Funicello had hung up their surfboards, the serious *Out of It* was mistakenly considered by some to be a late-in-the cycle beach picture. However, there was not a singing surfer or an inept biker to be found. That, coupled with the fact that it was shot in black-and-white and that the teenagers are all clean-cut and a bit naïve as compared to 1969's Vietnam War protesting, drug-taking, free loving teenagers of the moment, hurt its box office chances. Though quite good and intelligently written, it was considered dated. Pressman commented in *Newsday*, "The problem with timing has haunted us. All of our films [their second was 1970's *The Revolutionary*, also starring Jon Voight] have come out third or fourth in a cycle of similar themes. But Paul isn't doing a film because it is a trend. Each film reflects his interests, his personal concerns." Williams agreed about the ill timing of *Out of It* and remarked in the same article that the film "was ten years too late."

Out of It received mixed reviews upon its delayed release in late 1969. *Time* magazine praised the film for its "warmth and wit," Kevin Thomas of the *Los Angeles Times* found it "quite affecting," the reviewer in *Box Office* felt it was "pleasant and entertaining," but Nadine Sabonik in *The Cedar Rapids Gazette* called it "dullsville" and Stanley Kauffmann of the *New Republic* described as being "accurate enough in its social details, but is severely circumscribed in its range." Roger Greenspun of the *New York Times* remarked the movie "does pretty well as a young man's first feature . . . but not well enough for its material." He then went on to describe Lada Edmund, Jr. as "fantastically, overwhelmingly, heartbreakingly sexy" and raved that her performance was "stunning." Lada also received praise from Richard Gertner writing in the *Motion Picture Herald,* who remarked that she played the role "with a skill that matches Voight and Gordon.".

In 1970, director Paul Williams entered the movie in the Berlin Film Festival where it was in competition for the top prize, the Golden Berlin Bear. Though the film was "warmly greeted by a mixed audience of public and film business professionals" per the *Los Angeles Herald Examiner*, it did not win. Actually, no film claimed the top prize that year.

Lada Edmund, Jr. and Jon Voight in *Out of It* (United Artists, 1969). *Courtesy Lada Edmund, Jr.*

Lada followed *Out of It* with a supporting role in the action film *The Devil's 8* (1969), which beat *Out of It* to the screen. From AIP, this was a blatant low-budget rip-off of the hit film *The Dirty Dozen* (1967) less four characters and shifted to moonshine country. Christopher George plays Ray Faulkner, a federal agent who—while undercover on a Southern chain gang—escapes with seven prisoners all serving life sentences including a blondish Fabian as hard-drinking Sonny; Tom Nardini as bigoted mechanic Billy Joe; Ross Hagen as Frank a former moonshine driver; Larry Bishop as bible-reading Chandler; and Robert DoQui as Henry the lone African American. In exchange for parole, they are recruited to help him bring down the state's most notorious moonshiner Burl (Ralph Meeker) wanted for murder, extortion, influence-buying, and more. After a crash course and training in fast driving and using all sorts of firearms, the gang heads to hillbilly country to do damage to Burl's operation. Successful, Burl has no choice to bring in Faulkner and his guys for a cut of the profits. Lada plays hillbilly Inez, first seen taking her bra off and naked from the back, as she and her friend Hailie (Marjorie Dayne) undress to go skinny dipping in a lake. They are seen by Sonny and Chandler. When Hailie notices the guys swimming over, she asks, "What are we going to do now?" and Inez replies smiling, "nothing." They then join the guys for a nude swim. Shortly after, Inez and Hailie head to the local bar where Sonny, Chandler and the rest are drinking. After spurning Billy Joe's advances, they head right over to Chandler and Sonny and begin making out. The gals' burly boyfriends then enter the bar looking for them and a huge barroom brawl breaks out with Inez right in the middle swinging away. Edmund's athletic abilities were surely put to good use here. The movie ends with a bloody gun battle at the mountain location where Burl has his still operation.

The Devil's 8 was released beginning in April 1969 sometimes on a double-bill with the biker flick *Hell's Belles*. Lada was sent out by the studio on a cross-country promotional tour where she visited drive-ins screening the movie. As with most AIP films, most of the mainstream newspapers failed to review it but some did. Kevin Thomas of the *Los Angeles Times* remarked, "As silly as it is...at least moves mercifully fast, has a sense of humor and packs plenty of action." The critic at the trade publication *Box Office* found it to be a "fast-paced action release." Joseph Gelmis of *Newsday* however called it "a hillbilly *Dirty Dozen*, with nothing to recommend it except some well-photographed auto wrecks." However good the camera work of the chases were, they were severely marred by the awkward and phony-looking process studio shots of the actors driving their cars.

Lada Edmund, Jr. could act, had no qualms about doing nudity, and could do her own stunts. If AIP was smart they should have cast her in the biker movies they were producing at the time. Instead she hightailed it back to Broadway (she almost returned in the 1966 Joshua Logan musical *Hot September* but due to his illness it closed out of town) to work in the hit musical *Promises, Promises* directed and choreographed by *Hullaballoo* alumni Michael Bennett. She replaced fellow *Hullaballoo* dancer Donna McKechnie as office worker Vivien Della Hoya who leads the show stopping "Turkey Lurkey Time" number.

Edmund kept acting in the seventies but her real passion was stunt work. The few acting roles that followed were all action related such as the fast-driving Enid in the stock car racing adventure *Jump* (1971) starring Tom Ligon, and as a karate instructor named Tiny in the violent revenge drama *Act of Vengeance* a.k.a. *Rape Squad* (1974) starring Jo Ann Harris and Peter Brown.

Her most notorious film though at this time was the Philippines-lensed blaxploitation film *Savage!* (1973) from New World Pictures co-starring ex-Pittsburgh Pirate center fielder James Iglehart and Carol Speed. It was sort of a part of the genre of tough-acting women in the jungle films popular at the time, such as *The Big Birdcage; Women in Cages; Black Mama, White Mama*, etc. And, like most of these movies to lure young moviegoers, it had an outrageous tag line—"Men call him SAVAGE...Women call him all the time.

He's more than a man, he's a death machine!" Iglehart played a sort of Special Ops agent assigned to help the dictator of a country in Southeast Asia squelch a rebel army. He does and then is charged with the murder of their leader, forcing him to switch sides to oust the dictator. Lada played knife-throwing Vicki and Carol Speed was Amanda two nightclub entertainers Savage meets after his capture of the rebel leader. When the military police raid the club to arrest Savage, the girls hide him and then join his cause.

Though Edmund dropped out of the limelight to become one of the most sought after stunt women working on such films as *Smokey and the Bandit* and TV shows such as *Charlie's Angels* and *Starsky and Hutch*, her brief romance with Henry Kissinger kept her name alive in the gossip columns. And her stunt driving for testing air bags in U.S. automobiles made her one of the highest paid stunt people of the time.

Tiring of the danger that went with stunt work, Lada chose a life of domesticity instead after marrying and giving birth to a daughter. Years later, when she decided to return to work now as Lada St. Edmund (looking better than ever), she became a professionally certified personal trainer, developing her own program called *Minor Miracles* counseling clients on diet, weight and nutritional management. Her celebrity clientele over the years has included Burt Reynolds, Bernadette Peters, Vanessa Williams, Raquel Welch, Chita Rivera, Sally Field, Diana Ross, and many others. But today Lada's main focus is on getting children healthy with *Trim Kids Program*, which she developed.

How did you get the female lead in *Out of It*?

I'm not really sure. I was sort of famous for *Hullabaloo* at the time. The writer/director was Paul Williams. He and the producer Edward Pressman were friends and the movie was about Williams' time in high school. They decided somewhere along the line that I was exactly the girl they had in mind. It was pretty much a done deal and was the easiest job I ever got. I went in to audition and didn't even have to read for it.

What did you think of Jon Voight and Barry Gordon?

Barry Gordon was very professional but standoffish and a different kind of actor. He already had a name and was getting a lot of attention. That made a difference.

Jon Voight however was just focused on being an *actor*. Ordinarily I would find that boring and over-thought. But he really studied his craft and was amazing in the fact that he was so far above us. There was no surprise that he became a movie star right after this with *Midnight Cowboy*. He kept to himself. He was totally into the part and became that character. The rest of the cast was having a great summer going to the beach and having the best time. It was like going to summer camp. Jon however would walk around reciting Shakespeare all day and all night. We would look at him and go, 'What is it with this guy?' He was very serious—an actor's actor right from the beginning. He wouldn't talk to anyone because his part called for him to be away from the rest of us. I was just too dizzy at the time and not as professional as I should have been as an actor to totally get it.

Where was *Out of Sight* shot?
It was filmed on Long Island in either Lido Beach or Long Beach. Edward Pressman came from a wealthy family who owned Pressman Toy Company so they used his parents' house to shoot as well.

Out of Sight was Paul Williams' first film as a director. How was he to work for?
Paul Williams was very kind and patient. He had the scenes very well thought out. Jon Voight sort of directed himself and Paul was smart enough to let him do it. I respected that from him. Paul knew who to train and who not to. We were all disciplined and not a bunch of nuts, but compared to Jon we were just amateurs.

You have a topless scene with your back to the camera. That was daring for 1967. Did you have any problems doing nudity on film?
No, it didn't bother me at all. I began on Broadway when I was twelve years old doing *Bye Bye Birdie* and then *West Side Story*. You learn quickly how to change clothes in the wings with people all around you. It is not that horrifying if someone sees your body. The scene wasn't that big of a deal.

Is it true that scene was improvised for the most part?
Yes, I didn't know Jon was going to take off my shirt. It was our big romantic scene and we fall on the floor, which I didn't know we were going to do either. And then I say to him, 'Are you chewing gum?' And he was! He says, 'Yeah' and takes the gum out of his mouth

and sticks it to the wall. I thought that was one of the film's funniest shots. That was pure Jon. It was brilliant and so in his character to do that. And it was my character to get huffy about it.

Jon Voight and Lada Edmund, Jr. in *Out of It* (United Artists, 1969).

John G. Avildsen was the associate producer and cinematographer. He went on to become an Academy Award winning director—any memories of him?

He was a very cool guy—an original hippie. His wife and child were there on location with us. John was always in control but very laid back. He was never rattled and acted like he had been working all his life but I think this was only his first or second movie.

Was this a rushed production being it was low-budget?

Not that I noticed. I don't think it was at all. We were pretty much all living at the estate [of Edward Pressman's family] so hotel rooms weren't costing anything. The shoot was kind of easy going actually.

For a 1960s youth film, it is very serious and more realistic than the Frankie/Annette beach movies.

There is no comparison to the beach party movies and had nothing to do with that genre. It was a story about Paul growing up on Long Island. He and Pressman were both film students and shot the movie in black-and-white. It was more of a psychological situation about a typical outsider kid versus the WASP football player. It was less about dating and all that, and more about two kids who felt out of it.

Besides, the cabana scene with Jon Voight did any others stand out for you?

There is that one scene where I am with Barry in his room and he is reading. If you notice, there are all these Italian film posters on the wall. I liked that because these little details showed that the movie was really all about Paul and Ed during their teenage years.

Were you disappointed that *Out of It* didn't get released until two years later after Jon Voight hit it big in *Midnight Cowboy*?

No, after working on this I was into so many other things and then began doing stunt work, which interested me more than acting. I didn't even go to see it when it first came out.

Do you know why to this day *Out of It* was never released on video or DVD?

No, I don't. Maybe Jon Voight bought all the rights to keep it under wraps? I don't know how proud he is of it because I never heard him mention *Out of It*. When he reflects on his career, it is from *Midnight Cowboy* on. I know it was on cable television a couple of years ago and that is the first time I really saw it.

What do you remember about your first movie, *For Those Who Think Young*?

I did this before I began dancing on *Hullabaloo*. That show was shot in New York in Studio 8H, which was the studio above where Johnny Carson used to shoot *The Tonight Show*. Johnny would always look up and make fun of me banging on the ceiling with my dancing. I was a guest on his show a number of times.

You have to remember that I was young and excited to be on the show all the time. I thought it was great to be on the Carson show and getting all this attention. So a lot of times I didn't think pretty much about what I was saying, which is why Johnny had me on three or four times a year. He asked me about working with Pamela Tiffin and it was open mouth, insert foot. She was not particularly polite to me on *For Thos Who Think Young*. I wasn't holding a grudge, but I was desperate to come with something to say. I said that Pamela was absolutely stunning and since it was a beach movie she was getting her whole body painted. I didn't realize it and I opened up her trailer door by accident. She was supposed to be this sweet quiet little girl, but you couldn't believe the curse words that came out of her. I had never heard half of them in my whole life. I had worked on Broadway for years and was not a sheltered kid either. I said to Johnny, 'I don't know why she was so upset because it was an accident. And quite frankly Johnny from the waist down she looked like Sophia Loren and from the waist up she looked like Roddy McDowall.' I knew I should never have said it immediately after I did. It came out like toothpaste out of a tube. Johnny laughed and during the break leaned over and said, 'I love you.' Of course it was in every column the next day and for a month afterwards. I am sure to this day if you ever mentioned my name to Pamela Tiffin she'd cringe.

Did you have better luck with co-star Nancy Sinatra?

She was so nice and highly professional. I remember she appeared on *Hullabaloo* and everybody gave her a very hard time because she was the boss's daughter kind of thing. She wasn't a particularly great singer or performer, but was on the show because she had a hit record ["These Boots Are Made for Walking"]. The dancers on *Hullabaloo* doing the Frug were extremely professional coming from the stages of Broadway. We weren't *Shindig* or kids off the street on *American Bandstand* who could dance well. Professional kids get a little resentful when somebody walks in and is famous for no other reason than their dad is. But I have to say, Nancy Sinatra worked her booty off. She won everybody over.

Nancy Sinatra, Lada Edmund, Jr., and Pamela Tiffin on set in *For Those Who Think Young* (United Artists, 1964). *Courtesy Lada Edmund, Jr.*

Any other guests on *Hullabaloo* have a hard time?
George Hamilton was another one the dancers would make fun of. They were ragging on him saying he had no talent and he couldn't dance or sing so why did the show need him. Man, that guy worked hard. He hired extra people to rehearse with him for hours after everybody left for the day. He won everybody's respect.

David Winters choreographed a few beach and Elvis movies. How come you didn't work with him on any of these?
I went out to Hollywood to be *an actress* not a dancer. I then got into stunts by accident and loved it. It was very thrilling.

You danced with Michael Bennett on *Hullabaloo* and he went on to become an outstanding choreographer. What did you think of him?
I loved him and we stayed friends. He chose me to replace Donna McKechnie on Broadway in *Promises, Promises*. He contacted me when he was putting together *A Chorus Line* but I said to him, 'I'm done with dancing for awhile and am doing stunts.' I was involved in a whole different world and not really interested in participating in the round robin talks about being a dancer. It is something I have always regretted and would have liked to been a part of it.

How did your stunt work begin?
I was doing an episode of *Love, American Style* and I met Hal Needham, the best stunt-man in the business and Burt Reynolds' roommate at one time. We became a couple for years—we were like the Lunt and Fontanne of the stunt world. Since I was an athlete and dancer, I was able to keep up with him riding motorcycles and racing cars. I was not afraid of getting hurt. I then decided to become a professional stunt woman.

At that point did you decide to give up acting?
Hal and Burt said to me, 'Lada, if you do this you will never again get a job as an actress." I didn't care because I loved it, but immediately I learned I had to be better than a lot of the guys because I was taking jobs from them who would put on wigs and stand in for ac-tresses. I was really good at it thanks to Hal Needham showing me the ropes. Soon I began

to get noticed for it. I would go to a Hollywood party with some great directors like John Frankenheimer or John Huston. They would practically ignore the starlets in the room and then come up to me to talk about a particular stunt they witnessed. It was a whole different level of respect. I knew I wasn't a particularly good at acting and there were so many beautiful actresses to compete against so I decided to stick to the stunt work. I did it at a time when there weren't many women doing it.

But you did keep getting movie roles intermittently like in *Devil's 8*.
That was only because they were too cheap to hire a stunt woman *and* an actress. With me they got two for one. It was because of my reputation doing stunts and I could talk that I got the part. I really don't remember much about this movie except that Tom Nardini was such a great guy to work with.

Do you remember anything about making the exploitation adventure *Savage!* with Carol Speed?
Yes, it was one of the best times of my life. We shot this on location in the Philippines and it was an exciting time to be there right before Marcos was overthrown. It was kind of like being in the Wild West because you were right in the middle of the making of history. There was one area that was like Miami Beach with all these big luxurious hotels with private clubs where you needed to know someone to get into and right next door people were starving. Every time you went out to dinner you had a bodyguard with a machine gun literally standing there protecting you. I visited this guy's estate where he had his grapes flown in from France. You'd peer out the window and in the distance you could see half-naked people living in shacks. It was ripe for a revolution. It was just wild.

You seem to have done a lot of socializing there.
I met a guy that I became taken with and we had this mad romance. His family had a helicopter and he took me all over the islands. I was young and it was very exciting. I met a lot of interesting people. But then again we'd fly up to their resort town and we'd have to leave in twenty minutes because the revolutionists were coming with their machine guns.

What do you recall about your co-star Carol Speed?
She hated me. I don't know why. I thought I got along well with everybody and I was preoccupied with this guy most of the time off-camera. I don't even remember having words with her, but a few years ago one of my clients told me that Carol Speed wrote on her web site how horrible I was to her during the filming of *Savage!* Trust me when I say I was *very, very busy*. I did not have the time or inclination to be mean to anybody. For some reason I struck her wrong. I came close to contacting her to find out what her problem is. I never said a bad word about her and actually always praised her. Carol was really good in the part and was very professional, but I guess I rubbed her the wrong way.

Why did you leave Hollywood and show business?
There was one close call after another with the stunt work and in that field you are only as good as your last stunt. I was taking too many risks and doing some crazy things. I had been working so hard for so long and I wanted to settle down. I got married and had a child. After I stayed home for about eight or nine years to raise my daughter, I decided to return to work. You'd be surprised to learn how few jobs there are for people who only know how to drive a motorcycle off a cliff. I can't count and I can't cook so I concentrated on what I have been doing all my life—physical training.

What do you think in the renewed interest in your career?
Nostalgia is not my thing. I'm probably in better shape now than when I was thirty years old. I love being at my age now an inspiration and to bring back sexy to the menopause set. It's my second fifty years and I am much more involved with what I am doing now than then. If I was Ann-Margret I could see the interest but I was a marginal name at the time. But it is flattering.

15. SHE'LL STRAP YOU ON: TALKING EDY WILLIAMS IN BEYOND THE VALLEY OF THE DOLLS

IN 1969, 20TH CENTURY-FOX TOOK a chance and hired exploitation film king Russ Meyer to direct *Beyond the Valley of the Dolls*, the studio's follow-up to the enormously popular *Valley of the Dolls* (1967), which was based on the bestselling novel of the same name by Jacqueline Susann. A sequel in name only, none of the characters from the original movie appeared, though "Susan Lake" was a veiled disguise of Barbara Parkins' Anne Welles and "Baxter Wolfe" was supposed to be Anne's love interest Lyon Burke played by Paul Burke.

When a sequel was first announced, Fox tapped Susann's husband Irving Mansfield to produce the movie based on a treatment by his wife. Two scripts were commissioned and were rejected by the studio. Then Mansfield was let go, possibly due to the fact that his wife sold the film rights to her second novel, *The Love Machine*, to Columbia Pictures.

Fox then settled on an original over-the-top spoof of a screenplay by Meyer and film critic Roger Ebert. *Beyond the Valley of the Dolls* was the story of All-American girl rock trio who travel across country to Hollywood where they are re-named the Carrie Nations by music industry impresario Ronnie 'Z-Man' Barzell (John Lazar) and experience fame, fortune, and heartache. Keeping with his casting of big bosomed actresses in lead roles, such as Lorna Maitland in *Mudhoney*, Tura Satana in *Faster, Pussycat! Kill! Kill!*, and Erica Gavin in *Vixen*, it is not surprising that Meyer cast two former Playboy Playmates as the girl rockers. British Dolly Read (Miss May 1966) played Kelly MacNamara, the lead singer and long-lost niece of her dead mother's sister Susan Lake (Phyllis Davis). Success goes straight to Kelly's pretty head as she dumps naive Harris Alsworth (David Gurian) her loyal high school sweetheart and the band's unofficial manager, falls in with the pot-smoking

Hollywood in-crowd, and begins a romance with actor/gigolo Lance Rocke (Michael Blodgett) who cajoles her to go after a bigger share of her grandfather's inheritance held by rich Aunt Susan. Kewpie-face Read projected a sincere naivety with her performance as she spirals down into the valley of the dolls but comes to her senses, ditches the drugs, drops the suit, and reunites with a now paralyzed Harris who accidentally fell from a catwalk during one of her concerts. Read also convincingly lip-synched all her songs including "Come with the Gentle People"—which were actually sung by Lynn Carey—and bared her breasts a number of times.

Cynthia Myers, *Playboy*'s Miss December 1968, clinched the role of Casey the guitar-playing lost soul of the group due to her 39DD cup, which bosom master Russ Meyer flipped over. A powerful senator's daughter who has been used and abused by men, Casey falls in love with lesbian clothes designer Roxanne (Erica Gavin). However, when her jealous lover learns that she is pregnant by Harris after a drunken one night stand, she demands that Casey have an abortion. She goes through with it, but pays for her wanton ways when at the film's climax she and Roxanne have their pretty little heads blown off by the crazed Z-Man, who reveals a set of knockers to rival any Playboy Playmate. He goes off the deep end as Super Woman, also beheading a bound Lance clad only in leopard bikini briefs.

The third member of the group is African-American actress and former high fashion model Marcia McBroom, who played drummer Petronella Danforth. Her adventures in Hollywood were less tawdry as she marries struggling law student Emerson (Harrison Page) but cheats on him with stud boxing champ Randy Black (James Iglehart).

Russ Meyer aimed *Beyond the Valley of the Dolls* to be "the first rock, horror, exploitation film musical." He expertly directed Read and her cast mates to treat it as a serious drama and not a comedy—knowing full well he was aiming for camp, which he achieved. However, none of the female characters was campier then Ashley St. Ives as portrayed by Edy Williams, who undoubtedly got some of the film's best and most memorable lines. Standing 5-foot-7 with dark brown hair and brown-green eyes, Williams had a curvaceous body measuring 39-26-37, breathy voice, and captivating personality that made men drool over. Loving the camera, Edy posed bikini-clad for numerous cheesecake and pin-up photos leading up to her most infamous role.

Edy Williams in *Beyond the Valley of the Dolls* (20th Century-Fox, 1970).

Edy Williams was born Edwina Beth Williams on July 9, 1942 in Salt Lake City, Utah but grew up in California's San Fernando Valley where her next door neighbor was Johnny Carson. After graduating from Van Nuys High School, she attended Valley State College for three semesters. As a teenager she worked as a model and became a local beauty queen, being crowned "Miss California Bikini," "Miss Tarzana," "Miss San Fernando Valley," and "Miss Sherman Oaks" in 1964, the year she began acting. She landed small roles on TV and in a few movies, including *For Love or Money* (1963), before getting noticed playing call girls in *A House Is Not a Home* (1964) and more memorably in Sam Fuller's film noir *The Naked Kiss* (1964) as one of Madam Candy's "Bon-Bons" nicknamed "Hatrack." The ravishing beauty then signed a contract with 20th Century-Fox around the same time as Raquel Welch. But wherein the studio handed Raquel movie leads, Edy toiled on television making appearances on a number of their highly popular series such as *Batman* and *Lost in Space*. Despite being named a Hollywood Deb Star for 1965, Williams was still only able to scrounge up small movie roles in *Nevada Smith* (1965), *Red Line 7000* (1965), and *Paradise, Hawaiian Style* (1966).

Lara Lindsay was also a Fox contract player at the time and a member of their talent program. Regarding Edy, she remarked, "We saw her often. She was someone special—different from the rest of the contract players. She *knew* who she was and what she wanted to present to the screen. We were all looking for our own personas. Edy was (on the inside) a rather shy, sweet girl—believe it or not. That's my perception of her."

Williams first film role of note was as one of playboy James Farentino's delectable girlfriends in *The Pad (and How to Use It)* (1966) produced by Ross Hunter ("I walked into his office and his eyes popped out.") before going blonde to play the "dumb but well-stacked" suburban neighbor of Anne Jackson who imagines Edy as this sexy siren who can seduce any man in *The Secret Life of an American Wife* (1968). Williams told the *Los Angeles Times* that what helped her land these roles was the publicity she generated attending premieres and parties in outrageously sexy outfits that were designed by her mother. "I'm an exhibitionist. I dig reading that my micro-mini stopped traffic on Wilshire. I dig walking into a place in a sheer see-through and shocking the old ladies. I mean, if I didn't look the way I do, they wouldn't be looking at me, would they?"

Actress Melodie Johnson recalled in *Glamour Girls of Sixties Hollywood* doing a photo shoot with Williams. "I refused to straddle an oversized rocket in a Universal Studio publicity shoot. Edy Williams and I were posing in Fourth of July outfits. I told the photographer that it was a phallic symbol and he replied, 'so?' I still wouldn't do it. He looks at Edy—and God love her —she leaps up on it and wraps her legs around the sides straddling away. I watched Edy and thought, '*You know you're just not going to make it in the movies Melodie.*'"

Roger Ebert claimed the he introduced Edy Williams to Russ Meyer at the Fox commissary, though others contend that Fox studio head Richard Zanuck insisted that his contract player be given a role in *Beyond the Valley of the Dolls* (1970). It was first announced in the trades that Williams, now with chestnut brown hair with blonde highlights, would be playing Ashley Famous, a writer of pornography, but when the original script was jettisoned the character morphed into the voracious porn star Ashley St. Ives. Edy felt that Meyer wanted her all along to play Ashley and promised that she would be the star of the movie. Williams remarked in *Interview*, "Russ is really a schemer. He was telling me, "Oh—you're going to be the star. You've got the greatest role in the whole film. Well, he was telling the same story to all the other girls too." This may be true, but Ashley really is the best female part in the movie, made more so due to Williams' expert performance.

We meet wild-haired Ashley St. Ives dancing furiously with an African-American dude to "Incense and Peppermints" sung by the Strawberry Alarm Clock at a wild happening at producer Ronnie Barzell's. He points out a gyrating Ashley to his new friend Kelly and says, "Look there—the infamous Ashley St. Ives, famous indeed for her portrayals in pornographic pictures. See how she gives her body to the ritual—delicious." When the innocent goofy-looking Harris Allsworth shows up, the amorous vixen, clad in what looks like a crocheted brown micro mini-dress with matching bikini bottoms, immediately sets her sights on him and is a like a Black Widow spider honing in on her defenseless prey. As he makes his way through the throng looking for his girlfriend Kelly, Ashley puts her arm out blocking his way and seductively asks, "You don't drink?" He responds, "Later" as he pushes her arm down and moves on his way. Ashley watches and says assuredly, "*Yeah*, later."

Soon after as Ashley is describing the plot of her new porno movie (or as she later describes them, "my controversial box office block busters") to two party guests, Harris sits next to her putting his drink down on a coffee table. Ashley slides it over with her foot while he is looking the other way. When he goes to retrieve it, he grabs her ankle instead and she says, "Well now Harris we meet again. Come into my den said the spider etcetera." After exchanging some barbs back and forth, Ashley finally gets to the point and says, "You're a groovy boy—I'd like to strap you on sometime." Edy Williams is so deliciously over-the-top in this scene as she sticks her tongue in the guy's ear and lasciviously licks her lips as he walks away.

Ronnie Barzell decides to manage Kelly's group and after changing their name to The Carrie Nations they soon become superstars. After a successful live concert performance,

Kelly rejects Harris' plea to be with him and goes off to Ronnie's with matinee idol Lance Rocke for another wild party. Waiting in her Rolls Royce, "the princess of carnality" pulls up to the dejected boy and offers him a ride. It's a ride he'll never forget. After parking in his driveway, Ashley climbs into the backseat and removes her panties while seductively licking her forefinger. She says, "Now it's your move" as the horny youngster joins her and remarks, "It's my first time in a Rolls." The sex is wild and Harris has the porn star squealing in delight, "*There's nothing like a Rolls...nothing...not even a Bentley!*" as the song "In the Long Run" plays in the background.

The more famous Kelly and her band become, the more Harris turns to booze and pills to ease his misery. Ashley takes him to the beach where she does her best to arouse him but he is not interested in having sex on the sand. After Harris won't get it up, a frustrated bikini-clad Ashley standing above him (Russ Meyer filmed with the camera at a low angle facing up giving her an Amazonian look like he did with the gals from *Faster, Pussycat! Kill! Kill!*) mocks him and declares, "Harris you're drunk and you're stoned. And the worst of it is you're a lousy lay. You're never get into one of my films sweetheart—unless as a *hairdresser*." She tells him to find "a nice tender boy" and salutes in farewell before finding another boy-toy right there on the sand to take his place and disappointingly disappears from the rest of the movie.

There was only one scene Edy admitted that she had a problem shooting and that was the seduction of Harris in the back of the Rolls Royce, since she had to remove her panties. She told *Interview* magazine that she "was scared shitless" and commented to Nicholas von Hoffman in the *Washington Post*, "Imagine making love to a guy with thirty other guys watching. I know it's not really making love, but it's a pretty thin line. I hope I don't end up perverted." Trying to accommodate his nervous star, Russ Meyer agreed to set up the camera and have everybody, including him, leave the set and for Edy to yell "Cut!" when it was completed. She didn't mind if Meyer stayed, but did not want actor David Gurian there and would pretend like he was. Even though she was shaking, the scene went excellently and Edy cried after it was completed, as she told *Interview*. "I felt like I'd been disgraced...But, yet, on screen you couldn't see anything, so I don't know why I got so shook up."

David Gurian and Edy Williams in *Beyond the Valley of the Dolls* (20th Century-Fox, 1970).

Christopher Riordan played one of the two elegantly-dressed homosexuals at the Z-Man's party scene that took almost three weeks to film. He found Edy to be "a strange girl. On the set, she was very professional and I didn't expect her to be quite so serious. She was really trying to do her best and I think she realized this could be her big break. This and Russ Meyer's next movie *The Seven Minutes* were her chance for stardom, but unfortunately it didn't pan out for her. For all the seriousness she gave you on the set, she'd go out in public and make a fool of herself like showing up for the Academy Awards when she didn't even have a ticket, wearing a bikini and holding a dog. That is not going to make people respect you. Again on the set she was fine and I did not find her offensive as I did some of the other young girls.

"As for her interaction with Russ Meyer, I could see there was some flirtation going on between them," continued Riordan. "I had to laugh at that, but I compare Russ Meyer to working with George Cukor. He was that much of a gentleman—very sensitive and very kind. I really enjoyed working with him. Though I could see he was flattering to Edy, he was flattering to all the girls. This is a man who really loved women. I don't think he gave her any more attention than anybody else. By the same token when it came to do my scenes, he was very attentive to me. He just wanted the scene to go well."

The credit for making Ashley St. Ives a standout goes all to Edy Williams. She goes all out stealing the film with a truly entertaining performance and gets most of the big laughs. While all the other actors followed the instructions of Russ Meyer to play it straight as if it was a serious drama, you can tell Edy knew it was high camp and went over-the-top but not to the point of ridiculousness (i.e. John Lazar as Z-Man).

Made for less than $1 million dollars, *Beyond the Valley of the Dolls* grossed nine times that, making it one of the studio's most profitable films of 1970 despite some lack-luster reviews. For example, the critic in *Variety* called it a "heavy-handed put-on (many will consider themselves put-upon) with sex and violence." He did go on to praise Edy and said, "the sole good running gag involves Miss Williams and Gurian."

Unfortunately, Edy Williams, once dubbed "the eternal starlet," never got an opportunity to shine like this again on screen despite her now-husband Russ Meyer giving her another big role in his next movie *The Seven Minutes* (1971). Williams instead seemed to focus more on trying to drum up publicity for herself with her outrageous public appearances. It began when she went to the Cannes Film Festival with her Meyer to promote *Beyond the Valley of the Dolls*. She then became a fixture there year after year removing her bikini top and sometimes even more posing on top of cars, in fountains, and even in the middle of traffic for whatever photographer aimed his camera her way. Back in Hollywood, she'd appear at openings and award shows in shockingly skimpy outfits. As she told the *Los Angeles Times*, "This sex thing it's all a put-on, you know. It's what I have to do to get where I want to go. And believe me, I'll get there if I have to walk nude down Hollywood Boulevard." She almost did.

BIBLIOGRAPHY

1. Talking Elvis Presley and His MGM Musicals, 1964-1967 with Arlene Charles, Nancy Czar, Shelley Fabares, Gail Gerber, and Christopher Riordan

"Change Title for Overseas." *New York Amsterdam News*, Oct. 16, 1965.

Craig, Yvonne. *From Ballet to the Batcave and Beyond*. Venice, CA: Kudu Press, 2000.

"Cynthia Pepper Cast" *Los Angeles Times*, Nov. 5, 1963.

"Elvis Going Harem-Scarum." *The Atlanta Constitution*, Mar. 15, 1965.

Graham, Sheila. "Ann-Margret's On Her Own." *The Atlanta Constitution*, Mar. 2, 1964.

McBain, Diane and Michael Gregg Michaud. *Famous Enough: A Hollywood Memoir*. Duncan, OK: Bear Manor Media, 2014.

McGee, Mark Thomas. *Katzman, Nicholson, Corman: Shaping Hollywood's Future*. Albany, GA: Bear Manor Media, 2016.

Scott, John L. "Hollywood Calendar. *Los Angeles Times*, Apr. 4, 1965.

____. "Hollywood Calendar. *Los Angeles Times*, Apr. 18, 1965.

2. Yah! Yah! It's Beach Movie Star Bobbi Shaw

Canby, Vincent. "Young Actors Father a Troupe Without Any Help from Home." *New York Times*, Jul. 29, 1967.

Darling, Julie. "Starlet Bubbles." *The Sun*, Nov. 16, 1964.

Graham, Sheila. "Befriending Newcomers, That Was Buster Keaton." *Boston Globe*, Feb. 6, 1966.

UPI. "Wardrobe for a Starlet: Gold Lame, Mink Bikini." *The Hartford Courant*, Jan. 24, 1965.

Wilson, Earl. "It Happened Last Night" *Newsday*, Dec. 15, 1964.

4. Arlene Charles: The Epitome of the Bikini Clad Starlet

Bare, Richard L. *Confessions of a Hollywood Director.* Duncan, OK: Bear Manor Media, 2014.

McBain, Diane and Michael Gregg Michaud. *Famous Enough: A Hollywood Memoir*. Lanham, MD: Scarecrow Press, 2001.

5. Rediscovering Steven Rogers: Heartthrob of the Sixties Drive-In

Albright, Brian. *Wild Beyond Belief! Interviews with Exploitation Filmmakers of the 1960s and 1970s.* Jefferson, NC: McFarland & Company, 2008.

Davidsmeyer, Jo. *Combat!* http://www.jodavidsmeyer.com/combat/main.html

Lloyd, Jack. "Frenchman Runs, Is Shot; Revives, Repeats." *The Atlanta Journal and the Atlanta Constitution*, Sep. 2, 1962.

Shuff, John. "A Lesson in Coping." *Salt Lake Magazine*, Dec. 26, 2012. http://saltlakemagazine.com/blog/my-turn-a-lesson-in-coping/

6. Slaygirl Jan Watson Celebrates the Matt Helm Spy Spoofs

Altshul, Jack. "Heads and Tales." *Newsday*, Mar. 21, 1966.

Lane, Lydia. "Posture Makes Perfect." *Los Angeles Times*, Dec. 13, 1965.

"Mountain of Mail: 10,000 GIs Like 2 Girls." *Hollywood Citizen News*, May. 17, 1967.

"New Matt Helm Film in Works." *Chicago Daily Defender*, Jul. 26, 1966.

Seidenbaum, Art. "Oh, Pity Them All in Acapulco!" *Los Angeles Times*, Aug. 6, 1967.

7. Irene Tsu Returns to *Paradise, Hawaiian Style*

Hopkins, Jerry. *Aloha Elvis.* Honolulu, Hawaii: Bess Press, Inc., 2007.

Leigh, Suzanna. *Paradise, Hawaiian Style.* London: Pen Press Publishers Ltd., 2000.

Lichter, Paul. *Elvis in Hollywood.* New York: Simon and Schuster, 1975.

Lisanti, Tom. *Drive-in Dream Girls: A Galaxy of B-Movie Starlets of the Sixties.* Jefferson, NC: McFarland & Company, 2003.

____. *Fantasy Femmes of Sixties Cinema: Interviews with 20 Actresses from Biker, Beach and Elvis Movies.* Jefferson, NC: McFarland & Company, 2001.

Moore, Dennis Michael "Mickey." *My Magic Carpet of Films: A Personal Journey in the Motion Picture Industry.* Duncan, Oklahoma: BearManor Media., 2013.

Morse, Edward R. Memo to Eugene H. Frank. July 6, 1965. Hal Wallis Papers, Margaret Herrick Library, Academy of Motion Picture Arts and Sciences

Nathan, Paul. Memo to Hal Wallis. May 19, 1965. Hal Wallis Papers, Margaret Herrick Library, Academy of Motion Picture Arts and Sciences

____. Memo to Hal Wallis. June 17, 1965. Hal Wallis Papers, Margaret Herrick Library, Academy of Motion Picture Arts and Sciences

____. Memo to Max Raskoff. June 24, 1965. Hal Wallis Papers, Margaret Herrick Library, Academy of Motion Picture Arts and Sciences

Robinson, Bill. Memo to Paul Nathan. July 26, 1965. Hal Wallis Papers, Margaret Herrick Library, Academy of Motion Picture Arts and Sciences

Simpson, Paul. *Elvis Films FAQ: All That's Left to Know About the King of Rock 'N' Roll in Hollywood.* New York: Applause Theatre and Cinema Books, 2013.

Taylor, Tony. "Marianna Hill: The Girl Who Turned Elvis Off!" *Motion Picture Magazine*, April 1966.

Wallis, Hal. Memo to Paul Nathan. June 23, 1965. Hal Wallis Papers, Margaret Herrick Library, Academy of Motion Picture Arts and Sciences

8. Mimsy Farmer: From AIP to Italy

"14 Deb Stars 'Coming Out' on Nov. 24." *Los Angeles Times*, Nov. 11, 1962.

Adams, Marjory. "Fonda Film Dubbed 'Marshmallow 'Tobacco Road:' No 'Hateful' Films for Producer Daves." *Boston Globe*, Jun. 9, 1963.

Berry, Mark F. "The Mimsy Farmer Experience." *Video Watchdog*, No 161, Mar/Apr 2011: 20-43.

"Film, The: *Road to Salina.*" *Film Bill*, Vol. 2, Issue 3, March 1971: 5, 8, 9, 13.

Kleiner, Dick. "Movie or Television Show? '52 Miles' Not Yet Sold to Either." *Humboldt Standard*, Apr. 22, 1966: 2.

Klemesrud, Judy. "Have You Heard About the Farmer's Daughter?" *New York Times*, Aug. 10, 1969.

McCarthy, Marilou. "Teen-Age Star Bedazzled by Premiere: 'It's Work,' Says Mimsy Farmer." *Chicago Tribune*, Jun. 14, 1963.

McGee, Mark Thomas. *Katzman, Nicholson, Corman: Shaping Hollywood's Future.* Albany, GA: Bear Manor Media, 2016.

"Mimsy Farmer Leaves 'One Nut Factory for Another.'" *Variety*, Jan. 31, 1967.

Paul, Louis. *Italian Horror Film Directors.* Jefferson, NC: McFarland & Company, Inc., 2005.

Stein, Elliot. "Planetary Fantasies." *Film Comment*, Jan/Feb 1977: 53-57, 64.

Wilson, Earl. "It Happened Last Night" *New York Post*, Jul. 31, 1969.

9. A Flint Girl Named Bond ... Diane Bond

"Active Girl." *Chicago Daily Defender*, Aug. 17, 1966.

Bond, Diane. "Trapezeasy," n.d.

Mann, Dave. *Harry Alan Towers: The Transnational Career of a Cinematic Contrarian.* Jefferson, NC: McFarland and Company, 2014.

Swingin' Summer, A [pressbook]. United Screen Arts, 1965.

10. Nicoletta Machiavelli: Heroine of the Spaghetti West

Bauer, Ann. *"Nicoletta Machiavelli, Bella Donna di Seattle."* The Spaghetti Western Database, *Dec. 11, 2009. http://www.spaghetti-western.net/index.php/Nicoletta_Machiavelli,_bella_donna_di_Seattle*

Belmont, Trixie. "Ladies First: Actress Signed." *The Sun*, Jul. 19, 1966.

"Hollywood's Fastest Gun Stars in Western Movie." *Chicago Daily Defender*, Jun. 6, 1968.

Hughes, Howard. *Spaghetti Westerns*, Harpenden: Kamera Books, 2010.

Mennella, Francesco. "Italian Actress: A Famous Name." *The Sun*, Jan. 14, 1966.

Reynolds, Burt. *My Life*. New York: Hyperion, 1994,.

Streebeck, Nancy. *The Films of Burt Reynolds*. Secaucus, NJ: Citadel Press, 1982.

Weisser, Thomas. *Spaghetti Westerns—the Good, the Bad and the Violent*, Jefferson, NC: McFarland & Company, Inc., 2005.

11. Maggie Thrett and Screenwriter Stephen Yafa Remember *Three in the Attic*

McGee, Mark Thomas. *Faster and Furiouser: The Revised and Fattened Fable of American International Pictures*. Jefferson, NC: McFarland and Company, 1996.

12. Motorcycle Mama! Valerie Starrett in *Run, Angel, Run*

Margulies, Lee. "Whodunit? That's the Big Question on *General Hospital*." *Los Angeles Times*, Jan. 26, 1975.

Rowe, Pearl. "Secret Storm Over *General Hospital*." *Los Angeles Times*, Jul. 16, 1978.

Stidworthy, David. *High on the Hogs: A Biker Filmography*. Jefferson, NC: McFarland & Company, Inc., 2003.

Wooley, John and Michael H. Price. *The Big Book of Biker Flicks*. Tulsa: Hawk Publishing, 2005.

13. We'll Ask, He'll Tell: Christopher Riordan on *The Gay Deceivers* and His Teenage Movies

Interview with Michael Greer. *Gay Scene*, Dec. 1974. http://queermusicheritage.com/jun2003b.html

14. Lada Edmund, Jr. Is *Out of It*

Gelmis, Joseph. "Disenchantment Spells Fadeout for Director-as-Superstar." *Newsday*, Jun. 18, 1972.

"Go-Go Dancer to Break Out of Gyrating Cage." *The Hartford Courant*, Mar. 13, 1966.

"'Hullabaloo' Girl Has Word for Over-Agers." *The Hartford Courant*, Oct. 17, 1965.

"Lada Edmund, Jr., Comes to the Collins Drive-In." *The Cedar Rapids Gazette,* Jun. 1, 1969.

"Lotsa Advice But Not Much Aid: Williams Complete $250,000 Feature." *Variety*, Sep. 20, 1967.

"'Out of It' American Film Entry." *Los Angeles Herald Examine*, Jun. 30, 1970.

"UA Picks Up First Film By Young Duo." *Variety*, Sep. 4, 1968.

15. She'll Strap You On: Talking Edy Williams in *Beyond the Valley of the Dolls*

"Getting Intimate with Edy Williams." *Interview*, July 1973.

Haber, Joyce. "Ashley Famous May Sue Fox." *The Atlanta Constitution*, Dec. 13, 1969.

Knapp, Dan. "She Oughta Be in Pictures." *Los Angeles Times*, Sep. 14, 1969.

Martin, Betty. "Movie Call Sheet: Deb Star in Featured Role." *Los Angeles Times*, Dec. 2, 1965.

Oliver, Myrna. "Seeks New Role: Now She Wants to Shed Mate." *Los Angeles Times*, Oct. 17, 1975.

Scheuer, Philip K. "Producer to Try No-Name Actors." *Los Angeles Times*, December 14, 1965.

Thomas, Kevin. "King of the Nudies on Biggest Film Caper Yet." *Los Angeles Times*, Nov. 30, 1969

Von Hoffman, Nicholas. "Cynthia's Fate." *The Washington Post*, November 6, 1969.

INDEX

CPSIA information can be obtained
at www.ICGtesting.com
Printed in the USA
LVHW03s1348090918
589610LV00032B/2695/P